THE MA[BINOGION]
OF THE MABI[NOGION]

Elizabeth Leader.
25ᵃ Danvers St
London SW3

The Gwyddon—The Earliest Archbishop of Britain.

THE
MABIN
OF THE
MABINOGION

by

MORIEN O. MORGAN

RESEARCH INTO LOST KNOWLEDGE
ORGANIZATION

c/o Mr Robert Cowley
8 The Drive, New Southgate
London N11 2DY

Distributed by
THORSONS PUBLISHERS LIMITED
WELLINGBOROUGH, NORTHAMPTONSHIRE

First published as
The Royal Winged Son of
Stonehenge and Avebury
This Edition 1984

British Library Cataloguing in Publication Data

Morgan, Morien O.
    [The Royal winged son of stonehenge and Avebury]
    The Mabin of the Mabinogion.
    1. Mabinogion
    Rn: Owen Morgan   I. Title   II. The Mabin
    of Mabinogion
    891.6'6'31   PB2273.M33

    ISBN 0-902103-09-1

Printed and bound in Great Britain

TO THE READER.

Abraham received Three Divine Messengers under the great spreading branches of the sacred Oaks of Mamre, or, correctly, Memra, the Chaldean name of Christ, the Greek title of the Chrism associated with the Word of God. The Priest-King Melchisedek, who was not a son of Abraham, and was, therefore, a Gentile, administered to Abraham Bread and Wine ; then blessed him and received him into the sacred brotherhood of the City of Peace. Gen. xiv. 18, 19, 20. The same Ambrosia, in two kinds, is still the principal visible symbol in the Christian Church, which is "after the Order of Melchisedek." Christ is called the Shepherd—Stone of Israel. Gen. xlix. 24. It is obvious that the stone, which is a Shepherd of the nation, implies that the said stone is the national emblem of the said Shepherd. Deut. xxxii. 18. We learn that the Rock at Horeb, which yielded "Water" to the nation in the Wilderness, was the symbol of Christ-Messiah. 1 Cor. x. 2, 3, 4. The great apostle tells the Corinthians, who were familiar with the Rock emblem as an Obelisk, that the Manna and Water of the Rock were two forms of the sacred drink and "meat." Ex. xvi., 15. All ancient Greeks were perfectly familiar with the Ambrosia, for in their Vintage feast in honour of the Sun's fertilising heat, under the name Bacchus, they partook of the portion of the wine consecrated and named Ambrosia. When St. Paul states that the Rock "followed" the nation in the wilderness, he asserts, mystically, that the Divine essence— "Water"—the Divine Ambrosia—the basis of all created things, and, therefore, of the said Rock itself, had followed as a river. To this day in Wales it is said of a dried up fruit of the earth, "It is devoid of *Rhinwedd*" (*Virtue*) or Ambrosia. They therefore understood perfectly Paul's meaning. The Sunbeams were symbolised by a Stone Pillar in the solar rites of Greece, Egypt, and, indeed, in all countries. Sometimes oil, as being the basis of nourishing fluids, was used symbolically instead of Bread and Wine, as Ambrosia. The Druids called Ambrosia Rhin, or Virtue, of all nourishing essences, but instead of the juice of grapes, they used the juice of apples, as well as oil, as Ambrosia. In India Ambrosia is called Amrita, and as a fertilizer, descending through the sun, it is called in the Bible the food of angels, by the Gentiles, the food of Gods, but by the Druids was regarded as the food of Fairies. Carnal creatures take it mixed with solids and water. The "fruit" of the Tree of Knowledge of Good and Evil is alluded to by the serpent as the food of Elohim, or Gods. Gen. iii. 4.

Moses at the foot of Mount Sinai erected a circle consisting of twelve stone pillars, and an Altus in the centre, and then proceeded to hold what appears to be a National Eisteddvod, after the plan of the Kimmerians of the Euphrates Valley and of Britain and Gaul, to which we learn many of the Gimirrai had immigrated. Gen. x., Ez. xxxviii. 6., where they are called Gomerians. Jacob had slept and dreamed pleasantly among the stones of sacred Bethel, and had seen in his dream a ladder reaching from earth to heaven, and Christ leaning against it (Hebrew version), and angels passing to and fro over it. Jacob lifted up one of the stones, and made a pillar of it, and poured down it Ambrosial oil, and thereby consecrated or blessed it, as Melchisedek had blessed Abraham, his grandfather. Gen. xxviii. 19. Joshua erected a stone at Shechem, near the sanctuary, and informed the assembled nation it could both hear and speak, and the Lord Jesus likewise spoke of stones which were able "to cry out." Josh. xxiv. 27; Luke xix. 40. In verse 2 of the same chapter Joshua represents the Lord as reminding the Hebrews they originated beyond the river Euphrates, where recent discoveries prove the Gimirrai dwelt also. At Gilgal Joshua erected a circle of stones, as Moses had done under the hill of Sinai. The reader is reminded also of Elijah's circle of twelve stones on Mount Carmel, and then, states the Septuagint, " poured a sea around its outward circular trench,"* like that around Stonehenge, Avebury, and each of the ancient Mounds on Salisbury Plain.

The foregoing examples, agreeing with Druidism as a creed, induced the author to make researches with the object of discovering the common source of the two great creeds. The results are the following pages.

"Rhydd i bob meddwl ei Farn, ac i bob Barn ei Llafar."

* *Vide* Homer's Iliad xviii.

Ashgrove, Glyntaav,
    Pontypridd, Glam.

LIST OF ILLUSTRATIONS.

The Druid Fathers at their Public Prayers, led by the Archdruid. The Pristine Gorsedd in its original purity.

CONTENTS.

———◦◦◦◦◦———

xiii.

CORRECTIONS.

Page			Line		Read
8	...	...	21	...	Hippa
33	...	...	1 to 7	...	see footnote p. 36
40	...	...	10	...	of Coelus
49	...	...	22	...	Agnosto Theo
53	...	...	26	...	by Cariadwen
57	...	...	22	...	lo !
79	...	...	18	...	Agnosto Theo
83	...	...	27	...	Zacharias
99	...	...	9	...	thirteenth
110	...	...	5	...	Agnosto Theo
125	...	...	15	...	Zacharias
128	...	...	24	...	Oannes
132	...	...	12	...	body, case of the
168	...	...	15	...	doubt
191	...	...	last	...	Precession
206	...	...	6	...	Gwyn
212	...	...	8	...	were
213	...	...	30	...	Kneph
227	...	...	9	...	alternately
227	...	...	22	...	Katkins
229	...	...	9 and 11	...	Corpse. Pandora
230	...	...	5	...	(see 248) that of
241	...	.	next to last		Persians and Medes
255	...	...	26	...	Hebrews xi. 26
290	...	...	13	...	Ursa
290	...	...	32	...	King Sol
292	...	...	31	...	Christ-Elohim
290	...	...	19	...	water from the Rock
304	...	...	24	...	Taurine

The Descent into Hell ... 55, 202, 141, 228

For Cave, see Dean Stanley's "Palestine," page 179, and Virgil's Aeneis, chapter vi.

THE FACE OF CARIADWEN:
The Queen of Heaven.   "There Shines the Image of the
MASTER MIND."—Homer.

INTRODUCTION.

THE DRUIDIC COSMOGONY.

The Druids believed in the existence of an incomprehensible
First Cause. He they called Celu. The name is an active verb,
and signifies Hiding. He is the Coelus, Agnosto Theo (the Unknown
God of the Greeks). The Druids entertained the belief Celu had a
female Consort, and to her they gave the name Cariadwen (Holy
Love). They gave to her the following titles: Nydd (dd sounded
as th in then). The name signifies Turner of the Wheel: the Solar
System. That is called Rhod in Welsh, and pronounced Rode.
They believed that the earth is immovably fixed in the middle of the
universe. But observing the motion of the stars from East and
down West, they concluded that the firmament was one vast wheel
turned by the housewife of the "house not made with hands."*

*This idea gave origin to the "Praying-Wheel" of the Ancients,
and the Wheel of St. Catherine. She is Neith of Egypt with the
shuttle, and the Greek Minerva with the distaff.

In that wheel, seated in a chair, they believed the Sun made his daily round, and the Druids, under Phœnician influence, called the seat the Chair of Baal (Cadair Belin). (History of Taliesun, 19th stanza). This chair is symbolised by the chair of the National Eisteddfod of Wales.

The third title, including Cariadwen, is Ked. This signifies Guardian and Preserver of the "furniture" of the House and its riches.

The fourth is Gwrach. The original meaning of this name is a female endowed with masculine courage. It is identical with Virago in its literal sense.

Celu and Cariadwen are incomprehensible Spirits, but are the originators of crude matter in its original and formed condition compared to the embryo and "tread" in an egg.

They held matter came and comes still, in an embryotic condition, from across the Ocean from the source of all elements, in a liquid condition, and they name the said essence, feminine and passive in its nature, "Rhin y Pumwydd," or Essence of the Five Trees, an euphemistic figure for the essence as the source of the Five Senses, apart from Soul. This essence was brought they supposed every spring over the seas in a sacred Boat shaped like the Crescent Moon, and propelled by the spirit of Cariadwen. The first cargo that was brought was steamed forth into space by Cariadwen by applying intense heat to the bottom of the Divine Boat, which now became a Cauldron, in Welsh called Pair Cariadwen. The steam from the Divine embryotic essence was the first "Circle on the face of the Deep.' That afterwards the sacred Ark, which bears the characters of Cauldron and Ark, departed to "the Isles of the Blessed," for a fresh cargo of essence, and returned every springtime, and that the same steaming of the essence took place, and that in that manner the strata of the earth were piled one above the other in the course of countless myriads of ages. The Druids were scientific men, and knew that passive essence without an active essence, is inert, and therefore is stagnant. They saw that sap of vegetation was productive of fruits, and therefore it had in some way been fertilised by the active agent. Then they found, or thought they did, two agents in the operations of nature. Those are, First, the fertilising agent that converts the passive essence into vegetation and fruits. Second, that the fruits of vegetation after being taken as food yield from the blood by the chemical and scientific arrangements of the internal structure of the body, a fertilising essence. They regarded the said two as separate agents emanating from Divine feminine and masculine sources. One masculine agent is Warmth, and the other was the first to operate on the Passive essence of the Cauldron of Cariadwen. This was in accordance with Divine intelligence, for it was necessary to produce eatables beforehand for the nourishment of the creatures of flesh and blood which the fertilising essence would, in union with the passive essence, produce. The active Warmth they personified under the name Gwyion Bach. He is Bacchus of the Greeks, and the Wine he is said to be the "God" of is simply the liquid—employed in their mysteries to symbolise all fertilised saps of all fruits yielded by herbaceous productions of the earth. It appears the earth as yielder of fruits alone was personified as Crairwy, described as a maiden of great beauty. The introduction of the Sperm into the Cauldron or Ark, is described as Three Drops descending into it and mingling with the warmed essence, and as surprising Cariadwen very much. This is given to convey that there is no sexual relation existing between the source of the Three Drops and Cariadwen, Queen of Heaven. The Three Drops are charged with the divine nature and constructive skill of him whose agents they are. One drop causes the passive sap to yield Males, the second Females, and the third, Hermaphrodites. The passive sap of the earth, animated by the impregnating influence of the Sperm, is personified under the name Gwen. The name signifies Female Holiness. She is the Venus of the Greeks. The prefix Ven is from the Celtic Gwen. Indeed, until comparatively recent times, and until two V's were joined to form the letter W to represent the long O (oo), which is the sound given in Welsh to the letter W—the name Gwen was spelt Gven, and in mutations, Ven. The material earth was regarded as a vast Garden "which the Lord himself planted." The Lord here referred to is Elohim, the Word, otherwise the Mind of Celu. Divers ancient nations have given divers names to him as a personality. The Greeks called him Christos and the Three Drops, Chrisma, or Holy Oil. Fools have called this oil Ointment, and the Christos, the Anointed. The Greeks called him the Logos, or the Loud Musical Tone of Agnosto Theo, or the Unknown God. In Celtic, he is often called Y Llev-Velus, or the Sweet Loud Tone. As Mind he is also Meen, Minos, Menu, etc. But the favourite title given to him by the Druids was Hu Gadarn, or Invincible Hae, the U of the Celtic having the sound of æ.

> Hu Gadarn, Por,—hoew geidwad,
> Brenin y Gwin a'r Gwawd.
> Hu Gadarn, Lord, animated Saviour;
> King of the Wine and Praise, &c.

In this summary we have said nothing about the ideas of our Celtic ancestors respecting the Sun. The luminary being visible to the eyes of the material body, must be, they said, material itself. All material things have sprung from the same dual sources as the earth itself. Therefore, the Sun has either sprung from the Sacred Ark of Cariadwen, often called an Egg, or from the essence transmitted from the said Ark-Egg for the earth's construction. The Druids held the view the Sun had had a separate birth, independent of the earth, and symbolised the two as having emanated from two separate eggs in the Ark of Cariadwen. It will be seen in the allegory in succeeding pages, that in Druidism, the Cauldron and its essence, and the Egg from which the Sun under the title of Taliesun was "born" to Cariadwen, the sun was a later product than the Earth. Therefore, that Taliesun was held to be younger than both Crairwy and Gwyion Bach, if not also than Gwen (Venus). Moreover, the sun was supposed to be a living personage who could see and hear and enjoy the fragrance of the flowers of the garden earth, hence the Egyptians placed sweet smelling shrubs beneath the nostrils of their solar emblem (p.65). Although we find ample traces of the solar Bull, and the earth as the White or Holy Cow, in our Druidic literary fragments and in local place names in Wales, the Isle of Man (Mon-Cow), yet the weight of evidence is in favour of the conclusion that the Druids very early, at any rate before the Christian era, abandoned the solar Bullor depicting the sun as a Bull when on each March 25th the luminary rose in the Zodiacal sign of Taurus. It is exceedingly probable the abandonment of the Bull and Cow symbols of the Sun and the Earth, by the Druids, was when the Egyptians saw the necessity in consequence of the shifting of the Spring Sun from Taurus to Aries (Ram), the Druids adopted the human emblems for both, while the Egyptians continued to employ animal emblems, such as the Ram and Ewe, instead of Apis and Hathor. In the remains of Egypt, Babylon, Phœnicia, etc., we find a general inclination to adopt human emblems, instead of the old animal ones· The result is the many "Gods" and "Goddesses" as monstrosities—half men and half animals. The Greeks gave the Christ as the Father (Jupiter) a fine pair of Ram's horns.

One of the names given by the Druids to the Sun was Taliesun, a name signifying High-Iesun. In very ancient Welsh poems the name is transferred to the great Hebrew Jesus, but omitting the prefix High. Later the terminal n was omitted from the name, and in the Welsh N.T. the name is rendered Iesu. Iesun signifies glowing heat, or Fervid Blaze. As usual with the Bards, the Sun received from them many attributive titles, the best known of which is Arthur. This name signifies, like the Greek name Ge-Ergon (George), cultivator of the Garden-Earth. Taliesun is identical with Apollo, the brother of Bacchus, in the same sense as Taliesun is the brother of Gwyion Bach. In the British system Taliesun is the Sun himself, and Gwyion Bach is the Nocturnal Heat left by the Sun behind him in the atmosphere, when he sets in the evening. Gwy, the first of the compound in the name Gwy-Ion, signifies Dew, which is still called in Welsh, Gwy-Lith, or Lesson of the Dew. The terminal Ion as in Iona, signfies a Dove as the symbol of Hu Gadarn, the Word of Almghty Kelu, his mysterious Father. But in Druidism, uninfluenced by the Phœnician visitors to the West, a Wren appears to have been employed as the emblem and not the Dove. Doubtless the reason for selecting the Wren was the shape of its nest, and the fact that the nest of the Wren, by its ball-like shape, completely hides the Wren as the Orb of the sun was supposed to do for Hu Gadarn. In him is life, and the life is the Light, a phrase borrowed, states Bishop Powell, from the writings of Plato in reference to the source of Light from the Sun. It was found that the Earth's nightly exhalation ascending into the vault of the sky, absorbed the heat left there by the departed sun, and then the Dew, impregnated with the fertilising warmth, descends on the earth and fructifies all seedlings. This is the reason why Bacchus is associated with juices, the chief being wine in the East, but juice of the apple in the West, the "Garden of Hesperus," a name for the Druidic circle as the emblem of the whole earth as the Garden of Arthur (Sun). The name Bach (small), the root of the name Bacchus or Bakchos, appears to refer to the small globules of dew in which the Divine attribute of fertilising warmth comes down.--This warmed dew is, very likely, the origin of the Roman Catholic ideas about Holy Water.—Apollo is shown shooting arrows. Those arrows on the bow of the sun, signify the Sun's rays. But in Bardism the rays are called Gweres, now erroneously spelt "Gwres." In the word "Gwers" (a Lesson) we have the ancient spelling retained. Gwer is the Welsh for Oil, and it corresponds with the Greek Chrisma. The reason for calling a Lesson "Gwers," is that the mind of the pupil increases in wealth under the influence of the imparted riches of the mind of his teacher, as the riches of the earth increase and multiply under the influence of the fertilising beams of the Logos Spermaticos within the sun, and using its material substance as its vehicle of transmisson to the earth.

In the story of Jesus he assumed the character of Gwyion Bach (Bacchus) first, by converting Water into Wine at the Wedding Feast of Cana of Galilee. When afterwards he says he is the Son of the Man who is in the Heavens (Ouranos), he assumes to be the Son of Iu-Pater or Father Hu the Invincible, the personified Seminal Word in the sun in the zodiacal "House" of the Sign Lamb. The Sun as a material body was regarded as the Son of the Seminal Element in the constitution of the Word. It must be distinctly borne in mind the figure of a Ram given to the sun by mythologists refers to the sun in the sign of Aries and not to the sun's tenant called Iu-Pater. He is Seminal in his nature and soul as a Spirit, and is therefore called "Gods" and in Genesis is called Elohim or Gods.

When the Dove descended on the head of Jesus, at his new birth from the sacred Boat of the "Spirit," in imitation of the birth of the son Taliesun from the Boat itself—that on the Jordan was an imitation thereof—the Father and his Soul, or the Holy Ghost, descendded into his head, and he then became the sun himself walking Palestine. But we enter at large on the mysterious subject in the following pages.

The Mabyn and
The Rocking Stone
And their Old-World Story.

WARMTH AND LIGHT PERSONIFIED.—THEIR UNION.

GWYION BACH AND TALIESUN (LOFTY HESUS.)

The solar drama appears to have been annually performed in many localities in Wales, and
doubtless also in many other localities in Great Britain and Ireland,
until the time the Druids lost their hold of
England, Scotland, and Ireland. The Druids spoke
the Welsh language, and in that tongue are pre-
served their sacred dramas, called Mabyn Ogion, or Adherents to the
Babe Son, which dramas are too often now in fragmentary condition.
In those fragments which have come down to us, we find very clear
allusions to three noted localities in Wales, celebrated as places
where to the last days of Druidism as a religion, the said dramas
were apparently annually performed. Those localities are Pontypridd (as now named), Bala, and Borth, Cardigan Bay. In the last-
named locality that portion of the drama dealing with the descent of
the Sun into the underworld of Hud and Lledrith, which go under the
name of Annwn and Gwenydva, or Hades and Elysium, was annually
performed between that locality and Arkle, Ireland. The lunar-
crescent-coracle, called Arthur's Barge and Coroogl Gwydrin, or
the coracle of the Water Buffetings, and often called by the names
Dinas Diachor‡(Wide and High), and Duw-Lun(Lunette Goddess*)

---

‡Mic Din Bych : Not Tenby nor Dinbych, but the hymn of the
sacred conical Mound T. Gwyn ("Twyn") anywhere.
*"Teyrn Hedd, tros for a ddaw ; Duw(ies) Llun ; Gwyn eu
byd Cymry or arofyn.—"Avalanau," Merddyn, Myv. Arch. of Wales,
Vol. I, p. 150, stanza 3.

because the shape of the sacred barge resembled the crescent moon. That barge contained the image of the Sun, as old Taliesun or Arthur. But the return journey of the barge to Borth during which a new body as that of a babe was supposed to be made for him in the coracle by Cariadwen, the consort of Celu, was to be understood to signify it was done while passing through the underworld, to the South-East of the horizon.

Y Coronog Fabyn a dan hir—gell,
A caerau cedyrn y Pair yn Gandryll :
Fe gyfyd baner yn ei sefyll—
Gwae Arglwydd pen y pebyll!

(Translation.)

The Crowned Babe Son will pass through a long cave;
But the forts of the cauldron* will burst asunder;
He will uprise with a banner;
Woe to the Chief of the Tents!

Prince Aneurin, Iolo MSS, p. 266, 14.

The performance between Pontypridd and Gilfach Goch (Red Inlet), and on Cardigan Bay between Borth in the East and Ireland in the West, was precisely the same as that annually performed between Egypt and Phoenicia, across the Mediterranean, only that in the last-named performance the coracle was named Ketena, and Taliesun was called Adonis. Vide Adonia of Phoenicia But in the Egyptian and Phoenician or Palestine aspect of the Solar drama, we have set forth the supposed annual death of Adonis (Taliesun) on March 25th, and his regeneration and return on the 27th as the Crowned Babe (Mabyn) as the "Son of the Morning,' to rule the sky, and impart light to the Earth. But in the Pontypridd drama, we have set forth dramatically the first Creation of the Sun, and, in that creation, the primordeal warmth united in

*Here is implied the forts of Black Wnigs or Pluto.

him, otherwise the amalgamation of Apollo, whose light is symbolised by a bow and arrow, and Bacchus, whose fertilising warmth is symbolised by clusters of grapes adorning his brows. Greek mythology represents Apollo and Bacchus, as two brothers. Thus, while the Greeks represent them as two separate Gods, the Druids represent Apollo (Light) as having absorbed Bacchus (Gwyion Bach) or Warmth from on high, simultaneously with the advent of the Word, called Hu Gadarn (Invincible Hu or Iu)—into the Sun, which then became the channel of both Heat and Light.

The father of Gwyion Bach is called Gwr Eang, or Universal Power, while the Sun bears among many other titles the name Gwyn ap Nydd, or the Holy One, Son of the Spinner; a title of Cariadwen or Holy Love—As was natural in representing dramatically the condition of things before the Sun was first created, it is represented that universal darkness prevailed. It appears the owl, the nightingale, and night crow, were sacred to both Cariadwen and to the great goddess Minerva, because their voices are only heard in the domains of night. The Welsh name for nightingale is yr Aws, corrupted to yr Eos*. Yr Aws signifies the Beginning of Movement. This seems to allude to the Beginning of the Movement of the Wheel (Rhod) of the Solar System from, as the Ancients inferred, judging by the motion of the planets going down from East to West, and up to the East, the starting of the machinery of the Cosmos or Creation.

DRAMATIC NIGHT SCENE ON THE PONTYPRIDD COMMON IN THE OLDEN TIME.

(A Summary from the Myvyrian Archaeology of Wales.)

The Goddess Cariadwen was preparing for the coming world. She had two children, and they were named Crairwy (Sacred Egg) a damsel most fair, and a black son named Black Wings, A. Ddu or

---

*Eos is the Greek name of Aurora, or the Dawn.

the Evil Spirit. Whenever the letter A. is mentioned in Druidic mythology, a pair of wings is meant as the symbol of an active spirit. Thus A.wen, or Holy A., signifies Holy Spirit, A.dda, or Good A., signifies Good Spirit. To this day a pair of wings is referred to as A.d'en, or A daen, or opened out A.—Any number of wings are alluded to as A.d'enydd, a name for the act of spreading out wings. The name Adda, or Good Wings, a title of the Sun's rays as Wings, was borrowed by the translators of the Hebrew Bible into Druidic language, and applied to Adam, the first man created according to the Rabbins. Whereas the first masculine created being—the only begotten Son of the Creator—according to the Druids, was Hu Gadarn, whose residence was the Sun, or the one whose rays resembled wings. Black Wings or the Evil Spirit, remained, and still remains, a bodiless spirit, and the Raven, and sometimes the Black Crow of Night, were his emblems —Darkness was his home.—Strange to say, Cariadwen is called "Mam y Drwg," or the Mother of Evil, but no mention is made of the father of Black Wings.—In Genesis he is said to have first appeared in heaven as Inordinate Ambition, and after having been expelled from holy company, he next appeared in the Garden of Eden. He there, we are told, wrought so much mischief on souls and bodies that the Son of God, or the Eternal Word, had to descend to Earth in the form of one of his own creatures, to give souls a chance to correct, if they please, the evil influence of the fallen Archangel, or Black Wings.—The Hebrews claim to be descendants of Adam through the line of Seth, the second person of the Hebrew triad, Cain, Seth, and Abel. Abel, or the Father of God, for that is what the name signifies, was killed, and Cain became the father of the Antedeluvians. Cain is revived in Japheth or Japetos. But, strange to say, the name Seth is a title of the Egyptian Typhon, or Satan, Black Wings, and the correct form of the name is Sat or Set (1) the terminal "h" has no right to be there at all. The Hebrews write it St, without any vowel between the s and the t, and without the terminal "h." Seth is revived in Shem, which signifies Name.

To return to the Night Scene. Cariadwen, who had been

---

(1) Egyptian Book of the Dead, p. 10. Osiris, Horus, Typhon or Set.

busily preparing for the coming world, had her cauldron—another name of the Coracle or Barge—as a symbol in the play on Pontypridd Common—it is there still, and is called Rocking Stone, but called Kelwrn in the local place names, and the full name of the farm upon which it stands signifies the Alders Grove of the Kelwrn or Cauldron.* We are told that, in addition to the great mother Goddess Cariadwen, and the Cauldron, there were near it the following personages—Gwyion Bach (Bacchus), Mor Du (Black Sea or Night). This character is spelt by copyists Mor Da, or Good Sea, which is nonsense. It is evident that the correct form is Mor Du, and that he is Universal Night personified as the Nurse of Black Wings. The Black Sea of the Crimea, and the Red Sea of Egypt, are mythological names, derived from the same ancient personifications in the solar drama.

Another spirit called Mor Vran, or Night Crow, is also there. But he is identical with Black Wings, and is set up as the antitheses of Ion, the White Dove, symbol of Hu Gadarn, the bodiless Word as Son of God. Black Sea or Night, who is described as blind, is by Cariadwen ordered to light a fire under the cauldron, which is full of protoplasm, and it seems Gwyion Bach is there too, but no work is assigned to him to do. His wife is Crairwy. He is really the personified Divine Warmth. This new fire — strange fire — which night personified had to kindle, was not the ordinary or natural cause of heat in the cauldron; the ordinary divine warmth, the natural one, came from Gwyion Bach, the son of Him of Universal Power, the Dove of our Enclosure (Caer Ein Ion), the vault of the heavens.

Cariadwen had observed that some mysterious Three Drops had descended unknown to her into the protoplasm in the Cauldron with strange result, namely organic creatures, clothed with bodies of flesh and blood, came running out of the cauldron, from which hitherto only inanimate herbage, in endless varieties, were produced.

Cariadwen instantly thought of her Black Spirit Son, and con-

*Gwern y Kelwrn and Maen, as Coed Pen-y-Maen or Stone of Prayer.
Maen and Mynu and Dy-Muno, signify the same thing.

cluded that were she able to obtain tne Three Masculine Drops (1),
which caused the passive protoplasm to yield organic creatures as
males, females, and hermaphrodites, or Neuters, she would be able
to clothe her Black Spirit Son with a body like that of one of the said
characters, and thereby hide under it the ugliness, and therefore
the repulsiveness, of him whom, it is implied, the Goddess was
downright ashamed of to let him appear in the Coming World.

It appears implied that she, as Mam y Drwg (the Mother of the
Evil Son), was equal to the work of ordering a Strange Fire (2) to
be kindled by Night, the natural nurse of Black Wings; for
Black Wings is distinctly called Avagddu, that is to say, Black
Wings, Nursed by Night. The Cauldron (the original source
of matter) Cariadwen had designed should boil, or rather
simmer, as it appears, for a year and day.—In the Druidic mythology the "day," in the correct solar time is December 21, but in the
Egyptian, and, therefore, the Julian, Calendar, borrowed by Julius
Caesar from Egypt, is December 26, St. Stephen's Day. This is the
"day" of 40 hours during which Cariadwen ever after clothed the
Mabyn Son, or Sun, of each succeeding new year with a fresh body,
to be the habitation during the year of Hu Gadarn, or the Divine
Son of Celu (Coelus).—Therefore, it seems as if Cariardwen had a
foreknowledge of the coming Mabyn or Crowned Babe, and that she
was then more partial to her elder son, Black Wings, than to the
coming Mabyn. She thus sought to prefer the body intended for
Hu Gadarn, by the agency of some one of the Three Drops, for her
Black Spirit Son. It will be seen that Gwyion Bach, or Bacchus,
that is to say, Masculine or Fertilising Warmth, the father of all
herbacious productions, was the rival of the Strange Fire, which
Blind Night had been directed by Cariadwen to kindle. Gwyion
Bach is the cause of fermentation in Crairwy, the beautiful damsel
daughter, the incipient Earth personified—she is identical with the
infant Diana or Dieni (unborn), daughter of the Crescent-shaped
Cauldron, whose image (Llun—Luna) is the Crescent Moon, and
still the Egyptian and Turkish Empire Emblem, and the Sun as a
star is shown rising from it. It is also the breast-plate Moren worn
by the Archdruid of the Druidic Gorsedd to this day, and his head

(1) Vide Genesis ii, 17.
(2) Lev. 10, 1; Num. 3, 4; 26, 61.

as emblem is implied as rising from it. Moren means born from the sea. Gwyion Bach, as the Warmth from on High, to be applied to the seeds of the incipient Earth, was to begin to be applied to the Earth's seed on the first day of Spring, March 21, or 25 in the Julian time. As that time drew near it is represented that the Warmth called Gwyion, and the Strange Fire which Mor Du had kindled by order of the Goddess, came into friendly intercourse with each other, with the result that the Sacred Three Drops in the Cauldron, which seems to have got there by the secret action of the Seminal Word (3), leaped out of the Cauldron. and fell on Gwyion's "finger." The drops were scalding hot, and Gwyion's finger smarting, he placed his finger in his mouth. The result resembled the result of Adam and Eve swallowing the sap of the fruit of the Tree of the Knowledge of Good and Evil.—Gwyion's eyes, too, were opened, like theirs were, and he saw into futurity. What is implied is, that the Three Drops had descended, as an Emanation from the Son of God, the interpreter of the wisdom of the Creator, and, therefore, is called Menu, or the Mind of the Creator, as well as called Hu Gadarn, etc. In Druidic mythology the Sun's Divinity is called Menu, the Son of the Three Proclamations, by the Creating Word (Menu) (4).

This appears to be analagos to the said Three Drops as the concreted essence of the Voice uttered Three Times, called Triton, or Three Tones, that is to say on March 25, June 25, and September 25, as representing fruitful portions of the year. Those three chief points include four others, making a total of Seven—Septentrio—referred to in Rev. iii, as the Seven Spirits of God, and the Seven Churches, the Scriptural idea being borrowed from the seven lamps or lights on the Golden Candlesticks. Their opponents are the seven heads of the Red Dragon (Rev. 12, 3), and seven she devils in Mary Magdalene.

The term Seven Spirits of God is an old Druidic mode of describing the Sun while passing through the seven planetary spheres during the year, transmitting seven times the Wisdom or

---

(3) Logos Spermaticos. Justin Martyr's Apology, p. 68.

(4) Jesus was similarly proclaimed thrice at Bethlehem, Beth-a bara, and on Mount Tabor.

Emanations of the Creator, down to the Earth by the agency of the Sun as Seven Notes or Music of universal harmony.

Owing to the Divine influence which had accompanied the Three Drops, called in Hebrew Ains, Eons, or Eyes, as those of Water Springs, among other things which dawned on Gwyion's suddenly imparted understanding, was that he must avoid the anger of Cariadwen. Here, again, we find attributed to her a spirit consonant with the Mother of Evil.—Gwyion Bach ran away, so as to escape if possible from the avenging fury of the Goddess, the Mother of Black Wings.

We are told that at the moment of the catastrophe to the Cauldron, for it is said it burst into two halves, and being now without the fertilising Warmth, or Gwyion, from above, and also deprived of the fertilising Three Drops from Hu Gadarn, as it appears, the liquid protoplasm in the Cauldron itself became putrid and poisonous, and ran down into a neighbouring lake, and poisoned the horses of Gwydd No Garau Hir. These are the fabled horses of the Sun while he is in the 8th Sign of the Zodiac, counting from the Bull, which is Greek fable engrafted on the pure Druidic Allegory. Bryant, in his Analysis of Ancient Mythology, says the horses of the Sun in the allegory are the result of a linguistic mistake as early as the time of Homer—Hipha (Ark) being mistaken for Hippo (A Horse).

THE THREE DROPS AND GWYION BACH.*

Judging from the allegory in which are described the Cauldron the source or fountain of the Protoplasm (Annelw) by means of which element all matter was, and is, built up into solids, Gwyion Bach, or the Dew of the Little Dove—the name "Little" having reference to its Wren symbol—it appears the Druids sought to set forth, drama-

---

*This is the Holy Oil called Chrisma in Greek,. and one anointed with it was called Christos. An anointed Obelisk was a Christos, "The Rock was Christ." An anointed May Pole was also a Christos.

"In the Sun hath He set His tabernacle."—Psalm xix, 4, LXX. (Translation of the Seventy.)

The allusion in the Psalm is to Hu Gadarn (Invincible Hu) in his two-fold nature of Christos and Holy Spirit in the Sun, who is personified as Taliesun, or High Priest. Deo soli invicto mithrae.

tically, the order of the progressive manner they supposed the Sun was originally created. It is represented that the Earth and Vegetation had been already created by the influence of the fertilising Warmth descending in dew and rain from the Word of God. In the first place, in Vegetation, by the co-operation of the feminine essence or sap from below ascending from the Cauldron or the Sacred Shrine of Cariadwen; and the masculine warmth, or heat, descending from the Word of the Creator Celu (Coelus). In the second place, a new element of a material nature, described as Three Drops, descended frcm the masculine principle ot the Word into the same essence of the Cauldron, and produced a different result than organic Vegetation, namely, organic creatures of flesh and blood, with some amount of intellectual life and understanding. This is proved by the superior understanding which came to Gwyion Bach (Bacchus) the moment the Three Drops passed from his "finger" into his mouth. This indicates that Bardic philosophers set forth even the fertilising warmth, which descended from above in dew and rain, under the figure of a dramatic personality of some sort. But his transmigration, passing as life into successive animals, and finally becoming Taliesun (Sun—Son), indicates that the personality was regarded as a spirit. It is clearly taught that the Three Drops, which had descended from the Word of the Creator, were imbueu .n some degree with the nature of the Word, and that Word with the Nature of the Creator himself. A fertilised egg was regarded as the mysterious depositary of both the male and female principles of life, like that in the essence of the Cauldron; the male principle of life conveyed from the Word; and the co-operation of both of which was essential to produce an organism endowed with a degree of intellectual life in a third or the offspring of the egg. And that, in addition, heat from the female, and heat from the Word, in the Sun; that is to say, Hu Gadarn, in the Sun, was essential to give activity and to develop the Divine dual-principles in the egg, concealed in its Embryo. It appears the Druids supposed the measure of intellectual life imparted to animals, and also to man as a mere physical being, apart from soul, was that which the active seeds of male and female, in combination, imparted to their physical nature; that the united seeds possessed a degree of wisdom seemed indicated by the delicate organism produced by the combined, unconscious, action of the seeds within the egg. The fully-developed bird perforates the egg, and the babe forces the uterus, by the strength of vitality, and the force of unconscious intelligence imparted to each by the mysterious accompaniment of that which causes the physical and organic development of each. In Genesis, man's development is indicated as in two stages, but in the inverse order to the Druidic order.— In Druidism, a weak conditon of intelligence, is given to Gwyion Bach. He in the next stage imbibes the stronger emanation of the Word—seed—described as Three Drops, and he is instantly able to calculate effect from cause. He knows that Cariadwen will seek to destroy him for imbibing the Three Drops, which she had sought to enable her to make by their agency a body for her son Black Wings. Afterwards, the Holy Spirit, as Soul, is described as descending into the head of Taliesun (Jesus, Joshua) through the middle of the top of his head, "trwy fy Iad, Enaid i'm pwylliad." In Genesis 2, 7, we read first of all, the Word (Lord God) breathed into his nostrils the breath of life, and man became a living soul, but not till then. He was a living being before.

THREE APPLES.

From the earliest ages the Druids symbolised the Three Drops euphemistically by Three Golden Apples in the Sanctuary or the Garden.

These are the Three Golden apples which Venus had obtained from the Garden of Hesperus (Britain), and which she gave to Hippa Menes (1) to enable him to battle and conquer, and marry, the lovely goddess Atalanta, as the result of a race between them. There cannot be much doubt that divested of Greek embellishments, Atalanta is Britannia, as damsel Crairwy, the daughter of the sea, symbolising all the earth personified.

The Three Golden Apples, it will be seen, are associated with what the Earth and the Sun had produced, by co-operation, and in what sense will be readily understood by the readers of preceding chapters. It really signifies the Logos Sper-

---

(1) The **Mind**, or **Word**, in the Sacred Cauldron, or Thebet or Ark, named **Hipha** by the Greeks.

maticos marrying Nature, who is captivated by what the Three Apples symbolised.

Here we have the intimation that the Druids supposed the physical life of carnal beings was a lively principle within the Substance of the Drops themselves, and that by becoming blended with the feminine essence, as the tread of the male bird co-mingling in the hen with the feminine essence, afterwards formed as an egg, imparts to that substance the element of vitality imbued with intelligence. Had the Druids possessed the microscope, they would have concluded that Spermatozoon was that life, in its most elementary condition in the male fluid. That fluid was supposed to be mysteriously transmitted from the seminal Word into the Cauldron of the Mother of Nature, and co-mingling there with the other element, and the masculine heat, which was deemed to be the parent of Vegetation, passed, mingled with both, into the Vegetable productions, and produced the carnal beings; first, out of the substances of the Earth itself; and, secondly, as the result of eating what the Earth and Sun had produced, by the sexual co-operations of feminine and masculine agents. The first stage is the origin, and the second sex is the perpetuating one. The Three Drops, transmitted from the seminal principle on high in the twofold Word of the Creator, partook of the nature of their source, and, therefore, imparted a knowledge of Good and Evil to each creature which they produced. But the Soul did not enter the body until that body, as tenement, was completely finished to receive the Spiritual, or Soul, principle, from the Word as Holy Spirit. The Ancients believed the human tabernacle as a habitation for the Soul was not complete until the end of six months after generation. Remember the story of John the Baptist. This idea seems to be based on the fact that the fertilising impulse imparted to the seeds of the Earth on March 25th, does not arrive at mature result until September 25th. The Druids symbolising euphemistically the Three Drops by Three Golden Apples, and the said apples being upheld on a cross tree whose horizontal bar pointed north and south, and whose upright beam symbolised the line of the Equator, and, therefore, the middle of the garden of the Sun, the cross tree came to be designated, from the three golden apples upon it, the Tree of Knowledge, of Good, and Evil, in reference to the Divine nature of the Essence in three kinds which the apples upon it symbolised. The beehive-shaped Earth, symbolised by each tumulus, was the Garden which the Lord Himself planted. Great Britain surrounded by the sea, was the earliest symbol of that Garden, and it is called Garden of Hesperus or Hesus (Jesus), and each of the Druidic Circles and mounds likewise symbolised the garden which the Lord himself had planted. Each Circle and Mound was called T. Gwyn, or Holy T, because on the centre of its circle, or on its summit, stood aloft the "tree" with the Three Golden Apples upon it. And the whole island, as a symbol, was the Insulae Pomorum, or the Apples Island. In Genesis, Adam and Eve, with the Word's own breath, or Holy Spirit (St. John 20, 22), in them are said to be still excessively ignorant, with the eyes of their understanding not yet opened, for they were like beasts, and did not know enough to realise they were naked. But the moment the juice of the fruit of the Tree of Knowledge of Good and Evil touched their natures, it had a far superior effect upon them to that which the breath of the Word (Lord God) had had upon them. "She (Eve) took of the fruit and did eat; and she gave also to her husband (Adam) with her, and he did eat. And the eyes of them both were opened, and they knew they were naked, and they sewed fig leaves together, and made themselves aprons." St. Paul follows the same reversed order in the following verse: "The natural man receiveth not the things of the spirit of God, for they are foolishness unto him, and he cannot know them." I Cor. 2, 14. The sacrament is here the emblem of the juice. The story is a very strange one, also because implying the "Serpent" foretold them the truth, and God the reverse, as to the effect the fruit would have upon both.

The Druids' Mound, encircled by a trench of water; an island of the sea, and a stone circle, were each a symbol of the Earth as the Garden of the Sun. Adam is really the Sun, and Eve is Nature (Venus), and the early Druids in translating Genesis into Welsh, gave Adam one of the titles of the Sun, viz., Adda, or Good Wings, and Eve is Iva, or I., a symbol of the line of the Equator, or symbol of the Wand of Venus. Britain is referred to as the Garden of Hes, Tal Iesun, or Jesus, or Tall Hesus, and it is described as containing Three Apples. Glastonbury, because it had probably one of the sacred Mounds, came to be regarded as Insulae Pomorum, or Island of Apples, instead of the whole of Britain. The line of the Equator is Titania's Wand, and is personified as Venus or Gwen. Glastonbury was never an island.

In Hebrew the Three Apples, called vulgarly "Golden Balls," are called Ains, or Fountains, or "Eyes"; and to this day a spring of Water is called in Welsh the Eye of the Fountain or Water Spring.

It is represented in the allegory of the Cauldron that the organic beings which ran out of the Cauldron's essence, surprised and deeply interested Cariadwen, the great Mother Spirit, and finding they were produced by the action of the Three Drops, which had recently so mysteriously dropped into the essence of the Cauldron, she felt if she could secure for herself the said Three Drops, she would be able to clothe in a similar body her own Black Spirit Son, Black Wings, or in the Vernacular, A. Vag Ddu, or Black Wings, Nursed in a Sea of Night. It will be recollected that a pair of wings was one of the Druidic symbols of a Spirit, apart from a bodily frame, and that by Black Wings was meant the Evil Spirit. Now Gwyion Bach is the personified masculine warmth descended in dew and rain, and is the Father of Vegetation. It will be observed that the Three Drops had, as the allegory describes, been imbibed by Gwyion Bach, or Divine Masculine Warmth, and the drop being essence derived direct from the seminal element of the Word of the Creator, partook of the Divine nature of its source, and Gwyion Bach was by it materially endowed with Divine intelligence and foresight.

BACCHUS—GWYION BACH AND SATYRS.

The reader who is acquainted with Greek Mythology will recollect the allegory describing Bacchus (Gwyion Bach) coming from India, in the East, through the Red Sea, accompanied to the west by vast multitudes of Satyrs, or half animals and half human beings. By Satyrs is meant animal bodies endowed, as all creatures are, with understanding. That intelligence is regarded as the endowment of progressive, incipient souls, hence the dual character given to the allegorical Satyrs, creatures of flesh and blood. In the Greek fable, the Red Sea is the fabled River Styx (1). There Bacchus

---

(1) It bears also in Scriptures the character of Lliionwy, as the Jordan did, viz., the passage both into carnal existence, and the

and his companions, are described as coming west, and passing through the Dardanelles into Greece. From the Dardanelles they all assume the human form, and thereby attain the highest sublunary perfection. This doctrine is based on that of transmigration of souls.

In the allegory of the Exodus, the story is manipulated into a national history, and while agreeing with the Greek allegory as regards the passing the Red Sea, differ from it as regards the character of the companions of Bacchus (Moses). Substitute for the Dardanelles, the Jordan River, and Palestine is placed instead of Greece.

In the more ancient Druidic allegory, the River Gwyll Ion-Wy, the Styx of other nations, is that over which in the Underworld Bacchus—should be Taliesun, and as Jesus, it is so in the Old Testament and New—crosses as a victorious general. with newborn souls whom he is guiding and protecting in their march upwards. Moses is Bacchus or Gwyion (1). He drops the leadership, and Jesus (Joshua) takes the leadership in his stead. Moses, as well as his multitudes of souls, had to pass up through the creations of flesh and blood, to reach by evolution, the highest state in it, namely, manhood*. After spending more or less time in that state, another river, that of Lliionwy, or the River of Death as regards the dissolution of the carnal body, but River of Life as regards the state of eternal felicity of Gwynva, or Celestial Kingdom of perfected souls into which those made perfect attain on the other side. Here Jesus (or Joshua) our Taliesun, is the leader. This last invisible river, Lliionwy (Jordan) is crossed by souls only, and to symbolise the crossing over it in safety, the Welsh name for a coffin is Ark, Arch, or Boat. And to symbolise the soul has done with material sustenance, the said

passage into heaven or spiritual existence. The Jews crossed the Red Sea and the Jordan at the time of the Vernal Equinox or Spring time. They omit the intermediary stages of transmigration, but imply them by the "Wilderness."

(1) Manetho, a learned Egyptian priest who wrote 300 B.C., states the Egyptian name of Moses was Osarsiph, and that he was a priest of Heliopolis, which is the City of On referred to in Genesis 41, 45—50. Cory's An. Fragments, p. 132.

*Ephesians 2, 5.

Ark (coffin) was adorned with flowers, as in this world, harbingers from the Spirit World beyond the river, across which the departed had gone to live for ever and ever. Instead of flowers, the Jewish poetical figures describing the delights of heaven are "Milk and Honey." It appears, judging by the numerous flora found in the about fifty inland lakes of Wales, where the drama describing the river which perfected souls cross, at the dissolution of the body into the circles of the Gwynvyd or Holy World, that the water lily was the usual coffin or bier decoration at Druidic funerals. Those white water lilies must have been brought from abroad to the lakes of Wales by the Druids, and since their times they have continued to propagate themselves down through the centuries, as silent, beautiful, witnesses of the poetic souls of our ancestors, who earnestly and honestly wrestled with the mysterious ways of God in the system of the Universe.

Other nations than the Druids supposed all souls at death descended into the shades of the underworld, and that the souls of the good were there kept in captivity by Pluto, who barred the egress from Elysium or Paradise, where they were in felicitous captivity. But Lucan, the Latin poet, had learnt of the Druids the foregoing teaching of the bards about the river Lliionwy, and the Gwynva beyond it, and he writes as follows :—

THE DRUIDS.

"If dying mortals' doom they sing aright,
No ghosts descend to hell in dreadful night ;
No parting souls to grizly Pluto go,
Nor seek the silent, dreary, silent shades below ;
But forth they fly, immortal in their kind,
And other bodies in new worlds they find."

But in the allegory of the Exodus, the "Wilderness" is made to correspond with the circles of Abred, or transmigration of Druidism, the Jordan with the River Lliionwy, and Canaan with Gwynvyd or Heaven.

In the Greek allegory the space between the Red Sea and the Dardanelles, is made to correspond with Abred, or the "Wilderness,' the Dardanelles with Lliionwy, and Greece with Gwynvyd or the Heaven of Souls made perfect

THE ANCIENT TAFF FERRY.

Now, in a smaller way, the ancient Taff Ferry at Pontypridd. is made to correspond with the Red Sea ; and the Rhondda River with the river Lliionwy (Jordan) ; and the Mound of Pwll Gwyion with Gilgal. And the space from Gelli Gwyion, across the mountain to the Cave of Duw-Lais (Dyllas) (Voice of God) opposite the Holy Hill (Y Graig Wen), near Trebanawg, is made to correspond with the entrance into Gwynvyd, or Heaven. On the opposite side of the mountain the forest is called Graig Ddu (the Unholy Hill), and at Pontypridd, in close proximity to Graigwen, is Darran Ddu, and the two localities evidently refer to the respective starting places of the opposing forces in the Solar Drama. We find the same kind of dual names on the Abergwynfa side of Penpych, Rhondda Valley, viz., Gwynva and Nant-y-Gwyllion, or the Holy Place, and the Brook of the Black Ones, which is in the direction of Maesteg. Here the play was associated with Llyn Mawr, or Great Lake, on the mountains. The solar line here is East and West.

We detect the same Oriental corruption of Druidism in the rites shifted from St. David's Head, South East and South West, to Borth, Cardigan Bay, East and West, made necessary by shifting the performance of the solar allegory, dealing with the then supposed death of the old Sun's body at the end of the solar year, and his return, regenerated as a Mabyn, or Crowned Babe, at the beginning of the next year, that is to say from December 20th and 22nd, to March 20th and 22nd; or, according to the Julian and Egyptian Calendar, from December 25th and 27th, to March 25th and 27th. Thus we see the ceremonies were performed at Pontypridd in March instead of in December. No doubt, the innovation came here from Palestine with the Phoenicians. As we point out elsewhere, we find a trace of the Phoenicians here in the name of Talchan (Tylcha) or Sol Rex, near Tonyrefail.

These are indications that even the earlier Druids had adopted the same yearly Calendar as the Egyptians and Romans ; for in that case, the time would be **December 25th or Christmas Day** ; and afterwards, when the annual death of the old Sun, the sojourn of bodyless Hu Gadarn, or the Word of Coelus, as two principles,

Seminal and Spiritual, or Father and Holy Spirit, in Gwenydva. (Elysium) under the northern hemisphere in the Underwood, was the meaning of the popular custom of carrying the Wren about in an Ark during a "day" of forty hours—from sunset on December 25th until sunrise on the 27th. In that case the reappearance of the regenerated Sun, as the Mabyn Taliesun, would be celebrated in some localities at sunrise on December 27th. There is one circumstance which seems to conclusively prove that the earlier Druids had adopted the same yearly calendar as the Egyptians and Romans, namely, the custom still at St. David's Head, and in the Isle of Man, of carrying about the Wren on December 26th, or St. Stephen's Day.

The Sacred Boat of which the Rocking Stone is the representation. It is, too, the Thebet, or Ark of Noah and Moses. The Bird is the Wren of Druidism, the emblem of \|/ the Word of the Creator, fleeing into the Ark for refuge from the Typhon, the Arabic name for Deluge, meaning Satan.

THE PONTYPRIDD ROCKING STONE.

In the allegory, the Cauldron became now the source, or feminine parent, of all created things, vegetable and carnal bodies; vegetation fertilised by warmth and carnalities by propagation. Therefore, the Cauldron is supposed to be stationed beyond the system of Nature; for the Cauldron is its source. As we show, Cariadwen, or the Great Spirit Mother, is represented by a gerat sacred barge, having the essence in its hold, like the egg containing the embryo. This is followed in the structure of the Pontypridd Kelwrn, Cauldron, called "Rocking Stone," which is in two sections, a small one lying on the greater. The same idea is followed in the story of the Ark of the Covenant upheld in the Chasm of Jordan, the Chasm being the symbol of the said barge; and Miriam, the symbolical mother of the Hebrew Nation, upheld in the Chasm of the Red Sea. The Jewish nation were, in the instance of the Jordan, symbolically born from the upheld Ark, and in the instance of the Red Sea were sympoucally born from Miriam*, whose name signifies Mary (Marina) Mother, while Moses was Bacchus (Gwyion Bach), with the Wand as the symbolical Phallus of Jupiter, and Aaron was another name for Pan El,* or Peniel; Joshua and Sword, and Eliazer, the High Priest, symbolised the same characters. The Ark of the Covenant stood in the Jordan in the position occupied by Miriam in the Red Sea.

It must be borne in mind that what is dramatically set forth in the Druidic plays, were illustrative of what is supposed to have actually occurred before, and during, the progressive creation of the Earth, and afterwards the Sun and Mankind, and that the said plays were performed in many localities. Traditions respecting the old plays, and priest and priestesses dressed in dramatic characters, are the sources of our so-called folk lore, and place names such as Gelli Gwyion, etc. It is clear animals such as a stag (Caru, to Love), black boar (Twrch Trwyth) were used in the said plays. The sacred plays of the Middle Ages were their successors.

We repeat, all things below carnal natures in the system of Nature, were supposed to have sprung into existence by the influence of fertilising warmth coming in dew from the Word of God (Genesis 2, 6); and everything carnal, that is to say, of flesh and blood, by the male fertilising influence upon the essence of the Cauldron, the Thebet, or Ark of Noah. Then comes in the system of transmigration. That is to say, the introduction of Soul into carnal beings.

The first stage of carnalities enteerd by the incipient soul was into the nature of fishes. This is the lowest stage of carnalities given in Genesis 1, 26.

---

*Miriam represents Nature; the Ark of the Covenant represents Nature as the transmitter into the World of Spirits.

*Priest of Saturn who annually sacrificed the He Goat emblem of Pan God.

Now to the east from Gwyion's Lake, in the Rhondda River,
is stationed the Kelwrn, or Cauldron, on the southern end of Pontypridd Common. It is now called also, Y Maen—Coed-Pen-y-Maen
—and Maen signifies the Stone of Prayer, and a Rocking Stone.
The "rocking" is in imitation of the sacred barge, symbol of the
Spirit Mother Cariadwen's Boat on the ocean beyond the limits of
the material creation on Earth, and signifies the original source of
evolution from the water element. Thus the Lake of Gwyion was
in the Rhondda River, below the foot of a mountain, which foot is
now called Tarran-y-Res Dyn, or the Rock of the Tight Race, which
is on the farm on the west side of the river, and known as Pwll
Gwyion, corrupted to "Gwaun," but correctly, in English, the Lake
of Gwyion. It will be seen on referring to the allegory, that the
first creature of flesh into which Gwyion Bach entered, after diving
into the lake still bearing his name, was a fish. In another
allegory touching the same solar transmigration, a frog is the
figure employed. It is difficult to say whether life only is implied
or incipient soul and life together. Cariadwen assumed the disguise of an otter, and pursued the fish or frog
containing the Three Divine Drops. In Druidic Mythology, the starting point where intellectual life emerged after
passing from Gwenydva (Elysium) through Annwn (Tartarus) to the
lowest rung of animal existence, called the circles of Abred—Ab and
Rhed, or the Father of all things that run, or speed along, was
called A. Van, in the same sense as the modern A 1.—A. Van Lli
Ion Wy—as the symbolical ascent to manhood's station from the
Underworld, viz., the Annwn, Gwyll Ion-Wy (Styx), and Gwenydva
(Elysium) of the Druids. Therefore, the Rhondda River, or at any
rate the Lake of Gwyion ("Pwll Gwaun"), symbolised here for the
purpose of religious play, Avan Lliionwy, and the fish or frog into
which Gwyion first entered on his career of transmigration, his first
evolution, as inspired by the Three Drops, into carnal creations. The
hare, given as the first in some versions, is a late error of some
copyist, unless the hare, which for some unknown reason was very
sacred in the eyes of Druids, implies the start from Gwenydva
(Elysium). * Gwyion Bach ascends from the Lake still bearing his

---

*According to Greek mythology the God Pan once assumed
the form of a hare.

name, and faces West. It is startling to find that opposite his place of ascent from the Lake of Gwyion is a vast circular ancient mound, corresponding exactly with the Gilgal of Palestine to the West of the Passage of Bathabara, where the Jews crossed the Jordan from the "Wilderness." Dr. Inman has proved that Gilgal, as a name, refers to Sex, and now Joshua (Taliesun), having entered into the domain of Carnalities, entered into the domain of Sex. It will be recollected all the Jews were circumcised in Gilgal. No doubt a stone pillar, as a symbolical Phallus, stood in the middle of the Gilgal Double Stone Circle, and also on the summit of the Lake of Gwyion- Mound, Pontypridd. The local name, Rock of the Tight Race (Taran Res Dyn), fixes with certainty the very spot where the Rhondda River was annually crossed both by Gwyion and the chasing Cariadwen. For the purpose of the drama, the space from the Rocking Stone and the Taff River represented Gwenydva and Gwyllionwy (Styx); the space from the west side of the Taff to the ascent from the western side of the Rhondda or Lake of Gwyion, would represent Lliionwy. The old ferry over the Taff River, where the great one-span bridge has stood since 1756, represented the passage over Gwyll Ionwy (the bardic River Styx), and the ferry boat, the boat of Pwyll, Pen Annwn, or The Wary, the Chief of Hades. He is the Charon of Druidism. He is simply referred to as Pen, like Taliesun Pen (Head). In Virgil's Eneas, c. VI, the passage of the Styx is described.

RHUAD DWR, OR RADYR.

In the Taff Valley the name "Radyr," given to a hamlet below Pontypridd, is a corruption of Rhuad Dwr, or Water Roar, the Welsh name for waterfall. Doubtless in very remote days the water of a vast lake, extending up to Pontypridd, fell over a very high dam here, with the roar of a Niagara. In the "Cambro British Saints" we find a brief description of the bursting of the said lake we think at Radyr.

TAFF LAKE AND "RADYR" WATERFALL IN THE OLDEN TIME.

When the Cardiff East Docks were dug out, the workmen came upon vast deposits of red sand, and vast numbers of horns of cattle imbedded in it, supposed to have been carried towards the sea in the immense deposit of red sand of the red limestone of the lake, when the dam burst asunderti, and let out the vast accumulation of water extending, judging by the probable height of the dam at the time, to at least Treforest, a mile below Pontypridd. There is abundant geological evidence that the lake, whose bottom touched the inner side of the dam, and formed a great whirlpool, caused by the rush into it of the Taff River, found an outlet behind Castell Coch, and down through Machen, to the east, to the sea.

Again, when the Pontypridd, Newport, and Caerphilly (Caer Philip Basset, of the time of Henry III) Railway was being made, the old bed of the Taff River going in that direction was passed through. The deposit of the bed was 40 feet in depth. At present foundation for pillars of the viaduct of the new line across the opening opposite Castell Coch is being excavated. The whole breadth of the opening was found to be a steep slant full of sand, to a depth of 70 feet. It was the spot where the force of the flow of the river struck behind the barrier and scooped out the very rock to the said depth.

It is certain that in the remote past, the period we are dealing with, the Taff River opposite Pontypridd was, in consequence of the checking effect to its flow by the lake held back by the dam at Rhuad Dwr (Radyr), as well as the flow of the Rhondda River which joins here, was at least a hundred yards in width. When the foundation for the houses on the north-west side of Taff Street, Pontypridd, was dug, it was found to be a long sandbank of the purest quality. And when the foundation of St. Catherine's Church in the town, was dug, the soil was found to be studded with large round pebbles, bearing traces of the action of water. Doubtless the opposite side of the river reached to the foot of the rising ground of the Common, on the south end of which stands the Rocking Stone, symbol of the Ceubawl or Hollow Tree, as a Canoe, or Ark of the Sun (Cybele).

At night, during the performance of the dramatic scene at the ferry over the local Gwyllionwy (Taff—Styx) with many Druids bearing blazing torches on both sides of the Taff River, the spectacle must have been a weird one, and calculated to deeply awe the spectator. They would be dressed as Gwylliaid : hobgoblins, and Satyrs. Probably they would chant melancholy dirges representing the cries of wandering ghosts, not permitted to cross over to the Elysium, and having no mistletoe boughs to mollify the Druidic Charon. These suppositions are founded on the probability that the Egyptian corruption of Druidism, to the effect that the dead returned to the shades below, had reached Pontypridd, which by indications seems to have been the case. It will be understood that in uncorrupted Druidism, the space from the ascent from Gwyllionwy to Lliionwy, and, therefore, from the ferry of the Taff to Gwyion's Lake, would be symbolically the space traversed through the circles of Abred ("Wilderness") or the Soul passing through the circles of animals. Lliionwy River, symbolically the Lake of Gwyion, would be the position occupied by man, as free agent, after traversing all the circles of Abred, or transmigration. The Lliionwy Stream, therefore, indicated by its symbol, the Lake of Gwyion, on the Rhondda, would in the play, symbolise the "line" between the top of the circles of transmigration, occupied by man in this life, and the lowest circle of the circles of fairies (Angels) in the Kingdom of Heaven, symbolised by the country beyond, or to the west of the lake or river. But in the corrupt system of Druidism which came to be practised here, under Phoenician or Oriental leaders, the Adonia customs of Phoenicia* became mixed with the purer old system of Bardism, and the lowest circle of transmigration came to be depicted as commencing in the Lake of Gwyion, instead of at the ferry of the Taff. It is precisely the same error as representing the beginning of life after crossing the Jordan, instead of after crossing the Red Sea. By the Satyrs which followed the Greek Moses or Bacchus (Sun) from the Red Sea, we have it indicated that in that allegory the circles of transmigration commenced there and manhood's state commenced at the Dardanelles. That is uncorrupt Bardism. In consequence of placing the lowest circle of transmigration on the west side of the Gwyion Lake, we have in the play the region from there through Gelli Gwyion Valley across the brow of the mountain to Duw Lais

---

*Observed at the Vernal Equinox.

cave ("Dyllas") the route of the transmigration of Gwyion. In the said cave his metamorphosis into Taliesun took place annually, and he emerged with a loud melodious shout—cry of the birth—from the cave, in white, and his brow dazzling with a gold crown with radiating gold beams, as the Sun containing in himself symbolically, the Word, the only begotten Son of God Celu, called Hu Gadarn. He would descend from the heights to the Trebanawg hollow, representing the River of Life, Lliionwy, like the Jordan and the Dardanelles, and ascend from it on the other side, to the Graigwen or Holy Hill, to Dinas, the Mountain of Aran. This mountain was the Jerusalem, or Mount Zion, of South Wales. I Chron., 21, 18, and 2, Sam. 24, 18.

THE ORIGINAL MOLTEN SEA.

Imitated by King Solomon.—I Kings vii, 23.

Ancient Lamp found in France (Montfaucon). The Cauldron, the Three Drops as Three Lights, Gwyion Bach (Bacchus) Avagddu, and Taliesun (Apollo).

ESSENCE OF THE CAULDRON.

To symbolise the Consolidated Essence of the Cauldron, and to represent as such the fabric of the Earth, an egg was a favourite emblem. Easter egg is the old-world emblem preserved by the masses. The egg of Leda, a lady with whom Ju Pater, in the guise of a swan, had commerce, and "Leda laid an egg," as a consequence, is one of the wild rhapsodies of the Greeks, and is the same symbol The earlier Druids held the belief that the Sun had a new body each year, and that he was each year a Mabyn, or Babe Son; that his new body was a special creation, and that his body was derived from a separate substance, but of the same nature as that from which the Earth was and is derived, but represented by another egg. This is the second egg which Pliny, the younger, states was in vogue among the Druids, and that in that they differed from the Greeks. The two eggs represent, one the earth's substances, and the other the Sun's substance. They appear to indicate two eggs from the one Cauldron*. The egg representing the Earth represented feminine essence fertilised by heat; the other egg fertilised by the Seminal Word, and the Word thereby becoming the father of his own Sun's body, and all carnalities.

SEMELE.

The Druids believed the Sun's body was annually miraculously constructed out of the purest essence of plastic matter whose source was supposed to be Cariadwen. But in the East it came to be believed each succeeding Sun's body was annually created in a cave, from a mother in that cave who was a young goddess, supposed to be the mother of his substance, and that he thence was transferred into the barge of the great Mother Goddess Cariadwen (Isis I.), who, while the Babe Sun was in the boat, or shrine, on the S. E. Seas, introduced the Word of God into his head. Thus Bacchus is transferred from the body of the young

*Here the proper figure for the Cauldron is Nyth, or Nest.

Virgin Semele into an Ark; Moses transferred from Miriam to the Boat on the Nile; and Jesus, born of the Virgin Mary in the Cave of Bethlehem, and afterwards while in the Boat on the Jordan, called his Baptism, receiving the Word into his Head, in the semblance of a dove, which was also annually represented as descending from the sky on the head of young Horus (Sun) of Egypt while ascending from the crescent-shaped barge; and the Wren which annually descended on the head of Taliesun (Sun) while ascending from the boat called Corwgl Gwydrin or Ceubawl (Cybele). The birth from the boat was called regeneration. The birth of the body from this young goddess in the cave — the goddess, it will be seen, was originally an egg (Creirwy), and, prior to the adoption of an egg as a symbol, she was essence in the sacred barge—was called, the first generation of the Sun's body. The first Generation was of the Earth, earthy; the second one, that of the Lord from heaven—the Dove, or the advent of the Lord (Dove) from heaven, that is to say, the Word uniting itself with the earthy substance of the Sun's body, made luminous by his heavenly tenant, "In him was life and the life was the Light of men."[*] A reminiscent of the period when the contents of an egg was used symbolically as the emblem of the plastic substance of purest essence with which the Sun's body was supposed to be annually miraculously constructed, is the still popular saying that on new-year day (Christmas Day of the Old Calendar) daylight increases in length, the measure of the stride of a cock, emblem of the Phoenix. The male Jews kill a cock, and the Jewesses a hen, on the Day of Atonement. Tishri 10. On the morning of the Day of the Passover every cock was removed from Jerusalem. In the same sense Cariadwen as the parent of the egg of the mysteries is alluded to as a hen; sometimes as a serpent, and often as a fish. Delphus (Greek for Womb) is the Dolphin, a symbol substituted for the Barge of the new birth—second mother of Apollo (Sun), hence the fish called Dolphin. Here a great fish is used as a symbol instead of a boat, called Thebet in the Bible. A whale is called Cetus, from Ced (to preserve) one of the four titles of Cariadwen. Sometimes the second mother of the Sun is called Navis

---

[*]In the Sun he has set his tabernacle.—Psalm xix, 14.

LXX'S Translation.

(Boat), hence Nave of a Church, and the Oriental baptismal font, symbol of the Virgin Semele (Gwen, Venus) standing upon the Nave or Navis (Boat). Semele is the Greek symbol of the Mother of the Sun's body. The Church has reversed this, and made the Font to be the symbol of the spiritual birthplace. But by the rite of the Baptism of Confirmatoin, the Church represents the Spiritual birth. In Greek the Navis is called the Ketos (Whale) and Ketena, a Boat.

It may be remarked that this ancient doctrine of the Druids was the reason why Pelagius taught that baptism was unnecessary under Christianity, that the font was really a symbol of the Natural Birth, and that the Spiritual Birth was from the Navis. He consequently held that no water should be used.

THE PUPILS OF THE CAT'S EYES.

Being in shape like the open surface of the Boat as the symbol of Ced, the cat was sacred to her under the name Isis I (Cariadwen or Ced), and the sistrum is a symbol of the Uterus which was the same thing as the Virgin Isis II, Gwen or Venus. It will be seen presently where comes in Semele. The Druids carried the boat from place to place in procession, and called it Cath (Cat). It appears the native Druids were at first much opposed to the cat symbol of Ced:—

> Ys trabluddir y Gath Vraith,
> A'i hangyvieithon.
> (The spotted cat shall be disturbed,
> Together with her men of foreign language.)

—W. Archae, p. 73.

Doubtless the "men of foreign language" were the Phoenicians. But it seems even the cat came to be adopted by the Druids, for Taliesun, who should have said the sun's substance was derived from the essence in the Crescent Boat, says—speaking of the nature of the Sun—that his body was derived from the essence of the earth—another Eastern heresy of the Semele School—and the earth being symbolised by the Crom-le-ach, upheld by a tripod of stones, says:—

Bum Cath Benvrith
Ar Dri Phren.
(I have been a grey-headed cat
On a Tripod.)—Ibid, p. 44.

Here the cat is set up as the Boat, and the Crom le Ach its emblem. The Ark of the Mysteries came to be called Cath.

See p. 437 of Davis's Rites and Mythology on the cat symbol. Davies falls into the common error of supposing the moon itself was worshipped. The crescent moon was simply the Llun (Image) of the barge, as well as of the cat's eyes. We discover here a very curious fact. We find in Egyptian mythology several Druidic Welsh names, almost identical with the said names in the present vernacular.

Nydd pronounced Neth, but the dd, like th in then, is Neith in Egypt. Like the Druidic Nydd—a title of Cariadwen as the turneress of the Solar Wheel—the Egyptian Neith is shown with a spinning wheel. Tad (Father) is Thoth in Egypt. Nev (the vault of the sky) is Kneph on the Nile. It appears extremely probable that when the Egyptians adopted the pupils of the cat as a symbol of the sacred boat of Ced (Ked) otherwise Cariadwen, whom they call Isis I, they called pussy Ced, and that the name cat is a corruption. St. Catherine and her wheel, are the same symbols as Neath and her wheel. Then, when Egyptian Mythology, or Druidism corrupted, came to Britain with the Phoenicians, and the cat was introduced, the Druids did not realise at first that the cat's eyes were used as symbols of their sacred barge, and they adopted the foreign name, and called cat, Cath (the "th" as in thrush)* The earlier Druids themselves, however, never fell into this absurd error. To the end of their system, the Cauldron Boat of Cariadwen was the mother of the Sun's brilliant body, and the Almighty Celu (Coelus), was both the father and mother of the Sun's Divinity, called Hu Gadarn, Llev-Velus, the Word, the Wisdom, the Mind, Menu or Brain, of the Creator. But the Druids held that the Sun's body was annually constructed in the Cauldron of Cariadwen itself, to be a fitting tabernacle for the Son of the Creator, to adopt it as his annual habitation.

---

*Cath-Reine signifies Cat Queen.

TWO MOTHERS.

The error of Oriental religionists resulting in attributing two mothers to the Sun, namely, one for his body, and another to his Divinity, appears to be due to two causes: (1) The supposition that the Sun's body was miraculously derived each year from the essence of the Earth, instead of from the Cauldron from which the consolidated earth itself had come; (2) ending the year (the sacred one) on March 21st or 25th, instead of December 21st or 25th, and thereby confounding Venus, or Semele, with the Sacred Barge or Boat, symbolising Cariadwen (Minerva, Medusa, Crescent, Navis, Delphus, Athene, Ketena, Ced, Isis I, Cetus, all the same one. But except India, in all Eastern Countries the Sun God is said to be annually born in a cave such as that in the Holy of Holies at Jerusalem, and the other at Bethlehem. It is perfectly plain Druids believed the Sun to have a separate life, apart from God inhabiting his head. And that the natural life of the Sun had , in accordance with the supposed law of transmigration, or Metampsychosis, passed up by gradations from the lowest aquatic creature, such as fish or frog, to the highest, or Divine man. That is the meaning of the following extraordinary statement in the Poem of Varieties. (Yr Awdl Vraith) in the Myvyrian Archaeology of Wales:

> "A phum Can Mlynedd,
> Heb vawr ymgeledd,
> Bu yn gorwedd
> Cyn cael Anima."
> ("He (the Sun) was for 500 years
> Lying down (like a beast), without much comfort,
> Before he had Anima.")

Anima is here used in the sense of the Word of the Creator. It is well known at the present day that by the Phoenix the Ancients symbolised the Sun, old and young alternately.

In I Clements' Epistle, Chap. 12, 2, etc.,we read the following which is based on the Druidic lesson respecting the gradual development at the beginning of the Sun's rational life, and afterwadrs his annual life and death, and his eventual fitness to be after 500 years associated with the Word of God as the Crowned Babe (Mabyn):—"There is a certain bird called a Phoenix (Sun); of this there is never more than one at a time, and that lives 500 years. And when the time of its dissolution draws near, that it must die, it makes itself a nest of frankincense and myrrh, and other spices, into which, when its time is fulfilled, it enters and dies. But its flesh putrifying, breeds a certain worm, which, being nourished with the juice of the dead bird, brings forth feathers; and when it is grown to a perfect state, it takes up the nest in which the bones of its parent lie, and carries it from Arabia to Egypt, to a city called Heliopolis, and flying in open day in the sight of all men, lays it upon the altar of the Sun, and so returns from whence it came. The priests then search into the record of the time, and find that it returned precisely at the end of 500 years." "And the wise men followed the star to Bethlehem, and when they were come into the house (cave) they saw the young child witn Mary his mother, and fell down and worshipped him. And when they had opened their treasures, they presented unto him gifts, gold, frankincense, and myrrh.'"

"From Egypt I called my Son." It seems as if the Praesepe (Manger) was like the nest of the Phoenix, and that the frankincense and myrrh were brought "from the East," whence the old Phoenix (Sun) had come after the young Phoenix of Bethlehem, "the Sun of Righteousness." The Praesepe was, as Dean Stanley points out, at the mouth of the Cave. ("Sinai and Palestine," p. 44, footnote.) The Praesepe was mounted on a tripod astride the Cave at Delphi. But here the Virgin (Venus) represents Semele, the mother of Bacchus (Sun), and also Miriam, the foster-mother of Moses (Sun). But at his baptism by John, the Boat of Bethabara was his second mother, and it was then the Word in the semblance of a Dove, descended into his human life and body. The Cave symbolises the same parent as the Boat of Ced, Delphus, etc.; and the Virgin Mother in the Cave, symbolises either Semele or Venus (Gwen), as the mother of the Sun-God's body. It is implied in the case of Bacchus that the cave supplies the essence with which the body is constructed, and the Virgin Venus, or Semele, the organ of natural law constructing it. Thus the cave stands absurdly for both the cave and the Egg (Creirwy), the latter as the essence in a consolidated condition, and the tread as the Three Drops fertilising the egg, out of which Taliesun (Sun) is said to have been born. It is said Gwyion Bach (Bachus) was nine months in the belly of Cariadwen. This signifies that later Druids fell into the eastern error of confounding Cariadwen and the Boat with Venus or Semele and the Cave, and supposed the immaculate conception of the Sun's mother took place annually on Mar. 25th, and was born on Dec. 25th. This error came, doubtless from Egypt into Britain with the Phoenicians. The presence of the latter in the district of Pontypridd is indicated by the name Talchan, now Telcha, given to several farms at Tonyrefail (Talchan is Phoenician for the Lord Sun. Bryant's Analysis, Vol. 2, p. 470.)

It appears as if the Phoenicians had borrowed the name Tal, in the Druidic name Tal-Iesun (Sun), and used it in the sense of a proper name for the Sun, and that Tal-chan, as a name for the Sun, is Tall King (Sol Rex). That the Phoenicians joined together Phoenician and Welsh names, we have exemplified in the name of Bel-tan, or the Solar Fire, or literally, Fire of Baal. The Sacred Cave, that is to say, a cave set apart as a religious emblem, seems to have been sometimes named Argau, or Arched from Above. A mount, with an arched hollow at its foot, and called Mons Argaeus, and now, says Bryant, called Mount Argau, near Tyana and Caesarea Taurica, is shown in Bryant's New Analysis, Vol. 1, p. 215. Pausanius, states Bryant in p. 218, on the authority of Phocis, says, such a cave or cavern was sacred to Venus, and in it divine honours were given to Venus or Aphrodite." The reader will, after reading over preceding pages, understand the reason for it. The mode of worship among the Atlantians (Adlaisians) or the worshippers of the echo of the Voice of God in Nature— Llavar Duw yn llavar Anian, otherwise Bathcol—"betrays a great antiquity, as the temple seems to have been merely a vast hollow in the side of the Mountain." "Vide Dyllas." And the said hollow or cave would be symbolically on the south-eastern side of the Earth exactly below where the young Sun of the new year is seen rising at sunrise. Such were the strange notions of the Ancients. But to those who commence the year on March 25th, the Cave would be supposed to be on the east side of the Earth.

THE BIBLICAL ASPECT OF THE ALLEGORY DESCRIBING CARIADWEN AND HER CAULDRON.

GWYION BACH AND TALIESUN.

THE ALLEGORY OF THE CREATION UNRIDDLED.

(Myvyrian Archaeology of Wales, Vol. I, p. 17.)

In the East Druidism became corrupt, but its grand outlines are clear enough in the Bible. Thus in the allegory of the Exodus, Egypt and Goschen, and the Nile flowing between, are Tartarus and Elysium, with the River Styx flowing between. In Druidism those are Annwn and Gwenydva, and the River Gwyllionwy, or the Dark Waters of the Dove (Iona). The Red Sea is the Gate of Life, the Lliionwy, or the Flood of the Returning Dove. The Wilderness of Sinai of the allegory is transmigratory life with its windings to and fro. The River Jordan is the River of Life, that is to say, the line, compared to the line of the Equator between summer and winter, between this life and a future state. In a spiritual sense it is the line occupied by mankind between the brute creation and the angelic creation beyond the grave. In Welsh a coffin is called Ark (or Navis), and it symbolises the Boat of the Spirit conveying souls across to Gwynfa in the sides of the North. The Gate of disembodied Spirit Life admits to Gwynfa. The allegorical Gate of Life, admitting to natural existence or bodies, is down in the south-east, and the sun comes through it on the morning of each new Solar year. The Gate of Life is in a supernatural wall, and in allusion to it December is called in Welsh "Rhag Vur," or the Protecting Wall.* Its use is to protect, as a fence, the lives of the weakest in the Circles of Abred, from falling back to Annwn (Tartarus), for "Ni eir i Annwn ond unwaith" (there is but one visit to Annwn), and that visit was under the defending care of Hu Gadarn (Hea Invincible), on the way from Gwenydfa, the World of Origin. In the Jewish allegory, Moses is Bacchus (Sun) wielding the power* of Jupiter, or Father Iu, March 25. Miriam, or Mary Mother, is Venus, for whom, as will be shown, Semele is substituted, the personified power which clothes souls with material bodies, and the

---

*Virgil's Aeneis, B. vi, 740 and 745.

*Symbolised by the Rod.

face of the earth with verdure and floral beauties; Aaron (Aran) is the Sun in Capricornus (He Goat), on December 25th, and he is Pan, humanised from the waist upwards, and a he goat downwards. Thus we have the Sun personified by two characters, viz., Jupiter (in the "House" of the Ram Sign), on March 21st and 25th, and Pan (in the Sign of the He Goat) on December 21st and 25th, and the Anima of the Earth as Venus, wife of Jupiter, on March 25th.

It must be borne in mind that each of the two is regarded old at the end of each of the solar years, and renewed or reborn at the beginning of each of the succeeding ones. The Sun, as containing the Seminal Word, is called in reference to h.s tenant, Jupiter, a babe, and is called the Infant Jove on March 27t.1, 40 hours after the death of his predecessor. The error of calling the Sun an "Infant" on March 27th, instead of December 27th, was committed by those who invented the Zodiac, and placed the first sign (Ram) coincident with March 25th—27th. To this error we are indebted for an Infant Pan of ~ecember 25th—27th, and an Infant Jove on March 25th—27th. Pan and Jupiter are represented by John and Jesus.

In the Greek original version, Jesus states he is the Son of the Man, who is in heaven. This is rendered correctly in the Welsh version as "Mab y Dyn," not Mab Dyn or Son of Man, as in the English version. St. John 3, 13. That man is Father Iu, the Seminal principle of the Word in the Sun, whose body on March 25th is the Zodiacal Ram.

But Pan comes as Elijah, and appoints Jesus as his incarnate priesthood who from being king only becomes high priesthood as well. Following the plan, Moses was younger than Aaron. Pan El is old on December 25th, and is renewed as Infant Pan El on December 27th. As represented by Aaron, the high priest, he is old on Tishri 10th (September 21st old style), but is renewed or reborn on Tishri 14th (September 25th), and the new birth of his high priesthood is the s gnal for the revelry of the Feast of the Tabernacle to begin.

THE CRY ON THE CROSS.

Giving two separate characters to the Sun during the same year arose from the introduction of the system of personifying

34

The Infant Sun as the Infant Body of Jupiter or Jove; and the Infant
Body of Pan.   Lamb and He Goat to imply their respective Zodiacal signs.
Goddess with the Horn of Plenty, Nest of Birds to imply Springtime.

(Montfaucon).

the Egyptian Signs of the Zodiac, and it is the basis of the two years, one sacred, and the other secular. The sacred year was associated with the monarchy, and the civil or secular with the priesthood, for at the end of the sacred year, the Ram, symbol of the body of Jupiter, was slain by the Jews, and at the end of the civil one the He Goat (Pan) was slain in honour of Saturn, whom the Jews had substituted for the Creator. Jesus died as both High Priest and the King of the Jews. It was as the Hind or He Goat, he cried "Eli, Eli," on the Cross (title of Ps. 22), and the cry was to Saturn, father in Eastern mythology of Ram, Pan, the Word, and Venus. The Hebrews represent Moses, Miriam, and Aaron as being succeeded by Joshua (Jesus), the Ark of the Covenant, and Eliazer. Those names were given to the renewed Moses, Miriam, and Aaron for two purposes, viz., to manufacture a "history" for themselves, and to mystify students.

To revert to the cry of Christ on the Cross. It is open to doubt whether the words of Psalm 22 refer to Saturn at all. In the East, the old Sun of the dying year was supposed to be the father of the ensuing young Sun. Thus the old Phœnix was the father of the young Phœnix that budded, as it were, out of his ashes. The old Sun, containing Jupiter, was the father of the young body of Infant Jove, and old Pan* was the father of young Pan succeeding him, exactly as old David was the father of Jesus, called the son of David, and as young Pan (Jesus, as the young High Priesthood), and as the son of old Pan, called John the Baptist, both by John's recognition by "leaping" in old Elizabeth, a "daughter of Aaron," and by his ceremony of transferring Jesus from the Moab side of the Jordan to the Canaan side, at the spot where the Ark 'of the Covenant had given the symbolical birth to the nation into the earthly Paradise.

---

*It will be recollected that one of the titles of Pan in Hebrew was Elijah, and "Eli, Eli" etc., was understood to signify calling for Elijah. Elizeus signifies God—Ram. Jesus on the cross recited the old Psalm (22), used anciently in reference to the symbolical death and resurrection of the priesthood, on and after the Day of Atonement.

The Hebrews also gave to their nation in Palestine the position beyond the grave given by Druidism to the sanctified souls in heaven.

<hr />

CHRISTIANITY RESTORING THE OLD SYSTEM.

In the Christian system, the old Hebrew error is corrected. Jesus is both high priesthood and king, and, therefore, is both Johua and Eliaser's high priesthood personified, or in other words both Moses and Aaron,* and the Church is the Ark of the Covenant conveying the dead from a state of nature to the Realms of Spirits. The Church itself is called Navis (Boat), of which Nave is an abbreviated form. The River of Life upon which the Navis floats or rides is the Druidic River of Life, namely, the Line running east and west, and in building ancient churches those points and that line were religiously observed. As we have often stated, the northern side of the line traversed by the Sun from March 25th was compared to heaven, the abode of eternal rest, and of eternal summer bloom. To the south of that line winter and death dominated. That region was compared to the world occupied by animal lives struggling upwards to be men and women occupying the Line of Liberty, that is to say, of Free Will, at the summit of the circles of animals, and on the threshold of the lowest circles of the circles of angelic lives, up and beyond this life. In the Christian system the Church by the font adopts candidates for the realms of holiness beyond the river, and the Navis, that is the Church herself, conveys her passengers to the realms of life everlasting. The author of the Book of Revelation actually borrows from Druidic mythology to set forth the position of those outside the Church, and compares it to the Circles of Abred, or transmigration, as follows: "He that overcometh shall inherit all things, and I will be his God, and he shall be my son. But the fearful, and unbelieving, and the abominable, and murderers, and whoremongers, and scorners, and idolators, and all liars, shall have their part in the lake which burneth with fire and brimstone, which

<hr />

*That is to say, the linen tunic worn by Aaron, and the he goat he annually sacrificed, were the symbols of the high priesthood, apart from Aaron himself.

is the second death."* Rev. 21, 7, and 8. This is the antithesis of the second life. The hell of eastern and southern nations is burning hot, and the above was written by an Eastern scribe, and to intensify the idea of heat he introduces brimstone into the picture. But the hell of northern and western nations of antiquity, before the eastern and southern ideas spread into the north and west, was cold; and where nations dwelling in eastern countries would introduce brimstone as an intensitive, northern nations would introduce snow and ice as an intensitive.

According to the Druidic religion, animals were clothed by nature with fur or hair because their lives had to traverse the circles of cold Abred from the bottom, to the line of Man and Free Will. But man is left by nature naked, because he is left a free agent, either to clothe himself or go naked, and to do good or to do evil. Thus the Druids regarded the fur and hairy clothings of animals as the garments with which Nature, personified as Gwen, a name Latinised to Venus, clothes souls in a condition of profoundest humiliation and dependency, while engaged in traversing in animals the circles of transmigration. The fire, brimstone, and hell-lake of the East is an awful thing to attribute to have been provided by the Fatherhood and Motherhood of the two Eternals.

The Ancient Druids speculated as to the Fatherhood and Motherhood of Taliesun's (Sun) body, and the earth's body.

THE GENERATION OF TALIESUN'S (SUN) BODY.

In the foregoing we see that the Orientals placed the birth of Bacchus coincident with the animation of Gwyion Bach by the influence upon him of the Three Drops.

The Druid philosophers, in their profound study of the problems of the Universe, came to the conclusion that both vegetation and carnal bodies had evolved from a primordeal essence of a passive nature issuing forth from the mysterious mother of all things. In the first place, the fertilised essence had yielded vegetation, and secondly, carnal beings.†

---

*Returned to the circles of brutes.
†Coloss. i, 16.

It is clear the Druids supposed that three distinct kinds of inoculatory essences were used in the mysteries of generation from the feminine essence. It is said the Virgin Mary conceived on March 25th, and on December 25th her miraculous son was born, exactly the time of the year Jupiter begot Bacchus, or the Sun's body, by Semele, or the young sap of the Earth. The Cauldron, we were given to understand, was warmed to a certain pitch by feminine heat from Cariadwen, and a corresponding amount of masculine heat from the Word of Coelus (Celu). [P. 7 and 24]. The feminine heat is personified as Crairwy, and, as already stated, the masculine heat was personified as Gwyion Bach (Bacchus). The universal primeval darkness, light not having yet been created, is personified as Mordu or Black Sea, and apparently the sea so called derived its name from this personification, in consequence of the solar play of the Druids associated with that sea, when they dwelt from Constantinople to beyond the Caspian Sea and in the Crimea. Matter itself was personified also as Calen, and to this day a lump of unformed substance is called Calen in the Welsh language. It is said the essence of the cauldron, after losing the heat of the Three drops, became poisonous. This is the figure employed to describe the state of rottenness into which things are reduced once they are bereft of vitality, such as an egg in a state of rottenness.* The story about the horses poisoned by the rotten essence is, according to Bryant and Faber, to some extent, based upon a mistake of a word in translating from one language to another. The same error made the blunderers to represent a mare as being the Mother of the Sun, thus representing Cariadwen in that character. We distinctly see in the allegory traces of the Lesser and Greater Mysteries of the Druids, and the alleged bursting of the Cauldron is a Lesser Mystery Lesson, and the signification was the Greater Mystery.

---

*Incubating heat applied to an unfertile egg bursts the shell, and causes the liquid rottenness to spout out.

THE CAULDRON.

[Pages 5, 7, and 24].

We now return to the Cauldron and the Three Drops. Cariadwen, who is represented as very wise and scheming, hankered after the Three Drops which had come into the essence, and had produced there such curious creatures as carnal bodies, one of which bodies she thought was so desirable for her ugly spirit son Black Wings. She decided to make an experiment with a view to extract the Three Drops from the protoplasm, and to apparently use one of them in some unexplained manner to provide a flesh and blood body for Black Wings. It appears here that it is implied Cariadwen was already familiar with Ova, and that the Three Drops were to be used to fertilise an Ovum, for in the allegories she is sometimes described as a hen which laid two eggs, but they did not yield anything for the want of fertility, and it appears that an egg was regarded as a consolidated substance, which in the system of unanimated nature stood somewhere between the Vegetable and the Carnal. In the mysterious darkness of eternity, stars studded the firmament, and she is said to have been a student of the planets, and busying herself in making selections in chaos (Calen) of floral seeds suitable for the beautiful world which, by and by, was to come into existence in scientific order. When chaos is alluded to, Calen is its personification ; when essence, it is compared to an egg, and the personification is Crairwy.

It will be noticed that Cariadwen is alluded to as apt to act independently of her husband Cœlus (Celu). That evil exists is patent to all, but the Druids would not admit that Cœlus could be the Father of Evil, and to them the origin of evil was as unexplainable as it has been to everybody else. It appears as if the Druids inferred that the knowledge of the influence of the Three Drops, foreign to her own passive essence, had been acquired by Cariadwen from the very striking and mysterious results of the masculine heat (Gwyion Bach) brought about by outward application of heat to eggs. It is curious to observe that eggs, as the source of production, are in three classes of creatures : The air is represented by the eggs of birds ; earth by the eggs of serpents ; and the water by the eggs of fishes. Later discoveries have resulted in demonstrating that all animated beings start from the fertilised ova of females.

Cariadwen, in her infinite wisdom, knew that by constantly keeping the essence of the Cauldron — she is distinctly stated to be a student of chemistry—in a state of ceaseless activity or irritation by the action of heat, the three drops would remain inoperative on the essence, and that to prevent the usual result from taking place she would have to apply the heat constantly all the year round, or a year and a day. She summoned Gwyion Bach to watch the application of the heat to the Cauldron. In fact Gwyion Bach is alluded to as a personification of the transmitter of the heat from the fire, which here is the Word Coelus (Celu) under the figure of fire, the source of heat. Thus we have it they believed that the Word adopted Dew (Gwy-lith) as the vehicle in which to descend to the seeds of the earth and fertilise them. Of course we know now Dew ascends from the Earth as described in Gen. ii., 6.

Gwyion Bach attended to the fire, and while Cariadwen was absent attending to other duties, the Three Drops, scalding hot, leapt out of the Cauldron, and alighted on Gwyion Bach's finger. Hot as Gwyion Bach himself was, the three drops were still hotter, and made his finger smart so much that he thrust it into his mouth. Then a most extraordinary result followed. The miraculous drops operated on his brain in such a way as to make him know every-thing that would come to pass in the future. (Efe a wyddai bob peth a ddelai rhag llaw). This seems to be the same allegory as that in Genesis (3 c., 6, 7), in which it is implied the juice of the apple would and did make Eve and Adam wise, for its effect was that "the eyes of both of them were opened, and they knew that they were naked." But what is implied by the Druidic allegory is that the Three Drops had come miraculously from on high, from the seminal principle of the Word of God, "in the bosom of the Father," and therefore not separated yet from the Creator. And that there-fore they were emanations of Omnipotence, and partook of His divine nature, and, in some measure, of His wisdom. In the Garden of Hesperus, in Western Europe (Britain) were on a tree Three Apples.* Those were, euphemistically, the three drops of the

---

*The Wisdom, or essence of the Word, in the Sacred Cauldron, or Thebet or Ark, named Hipha by the Greeks.

allegory.* The tree is the Tree of Knowledge of Good and Evil, and stood on the middle of the Garden, as a symbol of the round and beehive-shaped earth. Therefore, on the line of the terrestrial Equator, which the upright beam of the tree symbolised. The arms of the tree pointed one north of the Equator, and the other arm south of the Equator. The first indicated the region traversed by the Sun in summer and autumn, and the latter the region of the dominion of winter, and therefore the Evil. These apples are to be seen above the doors of Jews and are called Aynes, literally eyes, or fountains, as we have already said. It is further said in classic mythology that in the Garden of Hesperus (Hesus) was a great serpent guarding the Apple Tree. She is Cariadwen under that figure, and fragmentary remains of which, over two miles long, are still to be seen near the enormous Temple of Avebury (Ab Rhi), Wilts. (Vide Dr. Stukely's work illustrated). As we have seen, the moment the Three Drops leaped out of the essence, the Cauldron burst into two halves. It is implied that the presence in it of the Divine Three Drops from on high, was what had saved it from the catastrophe earlier. The constant heat applied to it had been more than the Cauldron could endure. This appears to indicate that here, by the Cauldron, the Earth is referred to, and burnt to ashes by the heat of Jupiter, and the description agrees with that of the fate of the Greek Semele, and not with that of the Barge of Ceridwen. Thus it appears the framers of the old-world allegory had a hazy tradition also of the volcanic epoch in the history of the crust of the earth, and awful earthquakes, splitting the strata in every direction. Gwyion Bach, with a wisdom now that was his (and derived through inbibing the Three Drops descended from the Word), escaped hurriedly, knowing as the allegory states, that he had to beware of the wiles of Cariadwen. Gwyion Bach, it will be recollected, was heat from the masculine principle of the Word of the Creator, and had no mother. Cariadwen carried suspended from her waist, a Switch Rod (Rhodyl) for turning her solar spinning wheel; the revolving heavens. On her return to the Cauldron, and discovering what had occurred, she unfastened the Switch Rod, and struck Mordu (Sea of Darkness) on the head

---

*Vide pages 10 and 24 footnote.

with it, and that the blow caused one of his eyes to fall out of its socket on his cheek. Naturally enough Mordu (Morde) complained bitterly of the undeserved attack, and said he had not caused the catastrophe. Cariadwen admitted her fault, and said that Gwyion Bach had caused the mischief. She then hurried after him. Gwyion

The Head or Skull of the Bards. Golath in Syriac. The Mabyn Taliesun, and " the Crowned Babe."—(Iolo MSS.) He is called Mab Sant, or St. Son, by the ancient church in Wales.—(Montfaucon).

Bach assumed in succession many metamorphoses, and Cariadwen did likewise. Eventually Gwyion Bach descended into a grain of wheat, called Gwylad (Gwyl had), which signifies Festive Seedling. Cariadwen assumed the form of a black, high-crested hen, and swallowed the seedling. After nine months she laid an egg, and out of the egg Taliesun came forth, a radiant Mabyn, or Babe Son. It will be recollected that Gwyion Bach had swallowed the Three Drops, and thus consolidated essence in Cariadwen became fertilised by them. This part of the allegory implies the union of heat with light in the Sun, for Taliesun is the Sun personified. It will be borne in mind that the passive essence in the Cauldron—clearly here the same as Semele, or the Sap of the Earth, which was reduced to autumnal ashes by the awful heat of the Word (Jupiter) from June (Juno) to September—had come out of the spirit nature of Cariadwen herself, but now the Three Drops as fertilising essence in combination with heat, had come into contact with the passive essence in divers bodily forms of her emanations. The bursting of the Cauldron implies also the burning of Semele to ashes by the Solar heat.

We find in the allegories that Cariadwen had laid a previous egg—the earth from the Cauldron—and the Easter egg is the symbol perpetuated to the present day. In winter the egg, Earth, was called Ovum Typhonis, or Satan's Egg. What is meant is that Satan had succeeded in making the Earth inert. We repeat, the Hebrews have the Ovum Typhonis, as a roasted egg, on their tables at the Passover Supper. It is there an associate of the roasted Sun symbolised by the roasted Ram of the Passover, Nisau 14, or March 25 O.S. Under the figure of a hen, the Druids taught that substances of the earth's body and the sun's body had been yielded by the mysterious mother of all substances on the earth and in the heavens. This they gathered from the fact that all bodies are furnished by mothers, and that the fertilising principle alone, for their active construction, is supplied by fathers, and that mothers are simply the agents of the Mother of the Universe, and the fathers but the agents of the Father of all things, namely, the Word of God* (Col. i, 16.)

---

*The stem of the white water lily (Nymphaea Alba) is the Druidic symbol of the Navel of Cariadwen, connecting her with the Babe Taliesun (Sun) in her Barge.

According to the versions of Egyptian, Syrian, and Greek heresy, the Cauldron burst on September 25, and Gwyion Bach was swallowed on Lady Day, the preceding March 25th, and that Taliesun (Sun) was born from the barge (Ark) three months later, viz., on December 25th (22), when the sun appeared the first time. See Bacchus's two births, viz., three months later from the Thebet or Ark of Bulrushes, called Arech—Greek.

The two births of Moses and Jesus prove that the compilers of the Bible observed separately each of the said births. And Christians had their cave and their barge births of Jesus.

The drama of the Creation was played in all parts of Britain. At Pontypridd and the Cwyion Valley we have in the local place names still legendary traditions of it, as we show elsewhere.

DRUIDIC ANTIQUITIES OF THE RHONDDA VALLEY.

THE BABE SON AND HIS ADHERENTS.

The most notable spot in the Rhondda Valley for its past associations is between Dinas and Llwynpia, and named Coed y Mabynogion, which has been corrupted to Coed y Meibion. Coed y Mabynogion signifies, the Woods of the Adherents to the Babe Son. The name Baban, the Welsh for baby, signifies a baby of either sex, but Mabyn—the same as Mabon—implies a Baby Son. The name, Coed y Meibion, takes us back to remote times, when Druidism was the religion of the British Isles, and when the religion was illustrated by Dramatic performances in the open air, the performers being priests and priestesses dressed in characters. In ancient Welsh records the Babe Son is chiefly alluded to as the Crowned Babe. Iolo MSS, p. 265., etc.

It appears that the name Coed y Mabynogion was given to the wood that stood between where the Caer-y-Gelyn and Clydach Brooks pour their waters into the Rhondda River. Between those two brooks is another brook, named Nant Ewyn, or Foamy Brook, and judging by local traditions rife in the neighbourhood during our childhood, the centre of interest during the before mentioned performances was in the wood running on the west side of the Rhondda River, between Nant Ewyn and the Clydach Brooks. We distinctly recollect being taken by the hands between two little girls, when we ere about four years old, to see here the haunts of the fairies, called in Glamorganshire, Bendith y Mamau, or the Blessing of the Mothers; but, in all other parts of Wales, Tylwyth Teg, or the Fairy Tribe of the House—not made with hands; that is to say, the True Tabernacle.

Death had recently deprived the writer of his mother, and it is highly probable the two little maidens referred to associated the fairies with the child's lost mother. Would her blessing come from Fairyland upon the little orphan? Our route was through Amos Village, and down over the old steepwooded road on the right, and on the left lay high fields, over which runs the present road, with high hedges and woods all the way. There was then not a single habitation between Amos Village, now called Penygraig, through which Nant y Gelyn swiftly runs down to the Rhondda, and Tonypandy, a mile or more from each other. The journey was mostly through a leafy glade. One still recollects, with a creeping sensation, the conversation carried on during the journey—it was then a very long one—between the little girls, about the fairies of Cwm Nant Ewyn.

On the right of the old road, which ran lower down than the present one, in its descent to the Nant Ewyn Brook, we came to a small dingle to the south from the point where the Clydach enters the Rhondda—the Solar position of the dingle is important, as will be seen presently—and we were told it was Cwm-y-Nyddrig, or the Dingle of the Spinning Fairy. Then down the road we went to the Ewyn Brook, which then had no bridge over it. We crossed over stepping stones, and then passed up to opposite where the old Adare Inn was afterwards built in the solitudes. Here we stood, and the girls, pointing in the direction of the woods in the hollow between us and the Rhondda River, whispered, "The fairies are down there." Neither durst go nearer the woods than the road we stood on. Directly facing us on the opposite, or the north, side of the said river was a lofty, sloping mountain side, then covered with green wood to its lofty summit, and one of the girls said that long ago a serpent with wings had flown out of the woods on the hill side. Long afterwards we ascertained that the said wooded mountain side was, and is still, called y Wen Graig, or the Holy Craig, and it appears prob-able in remote days the site of religious dramatic performances by the Druids who were wont to let out of the woods of the Holy Hill the figure of a winged dragon, propelled by mechanical contrivances. Running in the hollow along the western bank of the river were visible rings or circles in the grass, which the morning dew upon them revealed.*

Those were the traces of the anc ent foundations of the venerable circular habitations of the priests of the Holy Mound. Similar ones are still seen at St. David's Head, at Efail Isaf on the Barry Railway and many other places, and on the south of Stonehenge. Sir Walter Scott, referring to these circles of green grass seen in various parts of Glamorgan, writes:

"No more the stamp of armed steed,
Shall dint Glamorgan's velvet mead,
Nor trace be there in early spring,
Save of the fairies' Emerald Ring."

-------->--------

THE HOLY MOUND OF YNIS-Y-CRUG.

On the east side of the Rhondda River, and directly opposite where the Clydach Brook joins it, was in the days of our first visit to the scene—and it stood entire till about 1862—a great oblong mound of earth completely covered with large oaks from the bottom to the summit. In the summer time the branches were so thick with leaves that the sky was hardly visible through the green canopy which they formed over the mound. The surface of the mound was carpeted with fine grass, and dotted with daisies and bluebells. During our early boyhood, we often visited the summit of this extraordinary mound, lying on the flat of the field near the river. The field itself was and is called Ynis y Crug, or the Lowland of the Mound. On the west side of the Mound, and running from

*Others are still visible at the place called Carn y Pebyll, or Cairn of the Tabernacles on the summit of the Wen Graig Mountain.

the top to the bottom, was then a recently cut dent. We enquired who had dug it, and were told that Dr. William Price, the late eccentric medico of Pontypridd and Llantrisant (died 1895), had brought men there for the purpose of digging into the Mound in search of treasures, but that soon after the men commenced digging, the sky darkened, lightnings flashed, and so awful a thunderstorm followed, that the men left the place in terror, and never attempted to dig there any more. Thus, down to our days, a vague tradition remained as to the sanctity of that Mound, erected countless ages ago in the midst of the Rhondda Valley. It is now a miserable relic of an ancient sanctuary.

> The smallest relic of a Shrine,
> Awakens in us thoughts Divine.

On the brow of the adjacent lofty wooded hill on the east side of the Mound, is a space called Cefn y Beddau, or the Ridge of Graves. Doubtless it is the ancient local cemetery of the Druids, associated with the Mound and with its public worship. A tradition existing is, that the crown of Deheubarth, or South Wales beyond Glamorgan, lies hidden somewhere to the south between Pen Rhys, or Rhys' Head, and this Mound.

Those mounds of the Druids were usually surrounded by a moat of water, and there are still to be seen, between this one and the river, traces of such a trench. Each of these mounds symbolised the whole earth, supposed then to resemble a beehive, and the trench symbolised the sea around the earth. Each of these erections bore the name Din-Rhaith, and in Ireland each is called Rath, and with each in that interesting country, is associated stories about Wraiths, Fairies, etc. It appears that those stories had their origin in traditions, arising from the dramatic personages dressed in characters, performing at the great religious gatherings of the Druids. It appears certain the English name Wraith (Ghost) is derived from the Welsh, Rhaith, which signifies in the first instance, a threshed out glade in a forest; from the custom of delivering speeches from the summit of these Mounds, a speech is called in Welsh Ar Rhaith, or on the Mound. Because laws were sanctioned, as still in the the Isle of Man, around these Mounds, law is in Welsh called Cyv-Rhaith, or In Conjunction with the Mound. A jury is called Rhaith-Wyr, or Men of the Mound. Another name given to each of these Druidic Mounds was Gwyn Gil and Cil Gwyn, or Holy Retreat, hence the mountain range between Rhondda Vach, or Lesser Rhondda, and Llanwyno Church, is Cefn Gwyn Gil, in allusion to the Holy Mound, recently carted away enclosed by the Nave of that Church. Llanwyno seems to be Llan Gwyn, or Holy High Place, with "O," sign of the active verb, added. In the Holy Land a similar place was called Gil Gal, the scene of the first Jewish circumcision, after crossing the Jordan at the close of the Exodus from Egypt into Canaan. The name perpetuated in the Bible signifies, the retreat of the Membrum Virile.

The Llanwyno Druid mound was carted away in 1894.

The name Llan Gwyno is associated with "St. Gwyno." But the "saint" seems to be a fiction, and that the name is derived from the name Gwyn-Gil. The road leading to it from the Rhondda Valley is now called Penrhiwgwynt, but really it is Pen Rhiw y Gwyn Dy, or the Top of the Road of the Holy House, meaning the road leading from Pontypridd to Llanwonno Church.

THE HOLY WELL OF DINAS.

About half a mile to the south from Ynis y Crug or Mound, is a well called Ffynon Wen, or Holy Well. It springs from Pentre Cae Cul, or Cae Main, to the west of Amos Village, now called Penygraig, and streams to Nant Caer y Gelyn, in that now populous locality. The name of the water of the well seems to imply that, as it gushed from the mountain it was employed by the Druids in the performance of their baptismal rites with birchen boughs on June 21st (25th), the date of their annual Pentecost, which they named Dydd Syl Gwyn, or Holy Sun Day. On the sloping hillside there the worshippers could obtain a fine view of the sun rising on the longest day, a most holy day in the religion of the ancient bards :—

And they with oaken wreaths appear :

. . . .

Old Corynænus compassed thrice the crew,
And dipped an olive branch in holy dew,
Which thrice he sprinkled round.

Virgil's Aeneis, B. VI .

THE SECRET OF BAPTISM REVEALED.

It now appears that the baptism of John at Bethabara, called anciently Bethania, or the House of the Boat (Stanley's Sinai and Palestine, p. 310), was symbolical of the translation from the wilderness across the Jordan into the citizenship of Canaan, as typical of heaven. The Jordan no longer opened wide to afford a passage on dry land across from the death of the Wilderness into the life of Canaan, and the ceremony had to be performed in a boat across the site where the Jordan had formerly miraculously opened to translate a whole nation over. The church is now the Ark, or boat, and is in consequence called Nave, or Navis (Boat), and the font symbolises Nature (Venus—Gwen) containing water in her pregnant matrix, which is poured out at the Spiritual birth in imitation of accouchement. Eph. ii, 19.

This baptism is now perpetuated by the act of Confirmation, called in Welsh Bedydd Esgob, at Whitsuntide, or Pentecost.

Stonehenge's lofty stones in an oblong circle are so arranged as to admit the rays of sunrise on that day of the year into the gloom of the Sanctuary. Doubtless, at the same moment the Druids and the vast congregations near this Dinas Holy Well, bowed to the rising Sun as the Mabyn, containing the Word (Hu Gadarn) of the Invisible Creator Celu, the Agnostos Theos, the Unknown God, of the Athenians in the time of St. Paul. It is interesting to note here that the Baptists of Zoar Chapel, at the foot of the hill here, always turned the stream of the Holy Well into a square pit near the building for the performance of the rite of baptism in their own peculiar way. But it does not appear the coincidence is due to anything more than an accident. By the Baptists' mode of baptism the Baptists say they commemorate the death and the resurrection of the Lord Jesus Christ. But he did not die by drowning, and he did not at his resurrection rise from the water. The Welsh for baptism is Bedyddio, which signifies Badyddu, or Boating.

Among the Rhondda brooks' bearing significant names may be mentioned Nant Wyddon, or the Brook of the Druidic High Priest (Odin). It is on the western side of the Rhondda Valley, above Pont Rhondda.

LLUN,- LUNA.

REVELATION XII, 1, 17.

THE DIVINE DELPHUS

The earlier mode of Baptism.   The Boat is the Church.   The Woman is the Font personified.   Black Wings kept back by Cariadwen.—(Staniforth).

THE HOLY MOUNT, OR THE MOUNTAIN OF ARAWN OR ARAN.

In the foregoing we have pointed out the indications as to the important place occupied by the middle Rhondda Valley in the Druidic system of religion, as carried on in South Wales, the Syllwg, rendered Silurum by the Romans nearly eighteen centuries ago. But we have still more remarkable indications of the interesting fact to lay before the reader. The locality under consideration goes under the general name Dinas, which is the Welsh equivalent for the English name City. About a mile lower in the valley than where the Nant Caer y Gelyn flows into the Rhondda river, another river, called the Lesser Rhondda, joins the greater Rhondda. The two rivers describe the two sides of a triangle, and the junction the point. This point is called Cymmer, or the meeting of the Waters.

But the locality is called also Porth. That name signifies what in English is called the Gate of a City. Therefore, the Porth, or City Gate, is so named in reference to Dinas above, in the greater Rhondda. A short distance above Porth, the valley is very narrow, but higher up, the valley makes a sweeping curve to the left, and higher still it expands somewhat to the right, so that the space here is undulating, and of considerable width. It is quite possible that Porth, or City Gate, and Dinas or City, were given respectively to the localities as suggesting the idea of a City Gate and a City beyond. But in very ancient times, Dinas signified not a city, in the modern sense of the name, but Din (Hill and Fort), and Aes (a shield). Dinas was not a name given here originally to the expanded part of the valley, but to the round hill on its southern side. Hendre was the old name of a farmhouse, afterwards called Dinas, situate on the northern side of the great circular hill or mountain encircled by hollow spaces hundreds of feet lower than the summit of the said mountain, and all around it.. On its northern side is the greater Rhondda; on its southern and western sides is the Elwy Valley; and on its eastern side is Trebanawg, or Home Among Hills. Thus, the Dinas Mountain is the original Dinas.

It is a striking fact that a rocky projection high up on its southern side is named Ystavell Aran, or the Cell of Aran. We know that Aran* is a title of the old sun of that year, December 21st (25th), and that Arthur, or the Gardener, is strictly a title of the sun in spring, when he is the Gardener of the Earth, and is, too, identical with St. George, Ge-Ergon, or the Cultivator of the Earth, like Adam and Adonis. Referring to the long night of December 20th (25th), in consequence of, as the Ancients believed, the then weakness and the consequent slowness, of the travelling sun, the Druids had a proverb, still remembered, viz., "Hir yw'r nos—aros Aran" (Long is the night—waiting for Aran). Aran signifies, like Arav, slow, as an old man's slow pace. In the east he is Pan. This Pan is the mysterious Haner Dyn (Half Man and Half Goat), of page 574, 1, Iolo MSS, and is the personified sun on December 20th (25th) in the sign of the He Goat (Capr cornus). His animal symbol in the drama is Caru (Carw) which signifies "To Love," and the original name has been corrupted in late ages to Carw, called in English, Hart (Heart), and Deer (Dear). The Wren, in the same dramatic allegory, is the living symbol, like the White Dove, a symbol of the Word of the Creator (Celu).

Celu (Coelus) like all the names of the Divine personification in Druidism, is an active verb.

----◇----

THE HIGH PRIEST AND THE HE GOAT.

The High Priest and He Goat on the Day of Atonement, were two complex characters in one, and by slaying the He Goat ritually he slew the priesthood. (St. John's Gospel, x, 18). When Jesus died he was the high priesthood and King incarnate. And Bar Abbas (likewise Son of the Father) was the symbol of the other He Goat sent to Azozel (the Devil), incorrectly translated "Scape Goat." Arthur is the Druidic Jupiter, the King whose Zodiacal sign is Ram. The body of the He Goat symbolises half of Pan; the high priest's linen garment, the human or upper, part of Pan, and Christ died as both Pan and Jupiter. All readers of the old Morganwg's priceless collection, called Iolo MSS, will recollect the following legend:

*There are many hills called Aran in the British Isles and Ireland.

ARTHUR AND HIS SOLDIERS LYING ASLEEP IN A SUBTERRANEAN SPACE IN THE DINAS MOUNTAIN.

It is said that they are lying there with a heap of gold, and a heap of silver, in the midst of them, waiting for daybreak. We have thus a hazy notion that the advent of Arthur is somehow associated with the rising of the sun. Arthur's soldiers are the personified Emanations, or Hanvods, of the sun, such as light, new souls, heat, as cause of vegetation, etc. In common with all other ancient peoples, the Druids believed there was a world of Hud and Lledrith (Fascination and apparitions) below the earth. They believed that the world was divided into two regions like the earth above, divided into southern and northern hemispheres with the line of the terrestrial equator running between the two.

The space below, corresponding with the southern hemisphere above, they called Annwn (Tartarus or Hades), and that corresponding with the northern hemisphere on the surface of the earth, they called Gwenydva (Elysium or Paradise). The subterranean equator was called Gwyllionwy, or the Dark Waters of the Dove, symbol of the Word (Logos).

In Greek mythology, this last is the River Styx, and Tartarus, and Elysium, or Hades and Paradise, the two regions, one on either side of the dark river.

THE DOCTRINE OF TRANSMIGRATION.

The Druids believed all lives in their lower stage of existence had their origin from the Mother Goddess, generated in Gwenydva, or Paradise, by the Holy Spirit in the Word, and Cariadwen (Athene), and that they were led from thence by the attractive force of the Sun's Divinity, across Gwyllionwy, or Styx, and thence through Annwn or Tartarus, and ascended with him to the upper world on the south-eastern horizon.

According to Druidism, those lives were then delivered to the circles of transmigration (Abred), or the circles of carnal beings, whose topmost rung was the station of humanity. Lives gradually attained degrees of improvement in their progressive ascent through the circles of the Animal Kingdom, till they bcame fit to be men and women. "There is but one visit to Annwn" (Ni eir ond unwaith i Annwn), and then safely with the sun from Elysium, their birthplace; and that simply in the journey through it under the leadership of \|/ in the sun.

In the system of lives, mankind was supposed to occupy a middle station between the brute and the fairy, or angelic, creations. Mankind were supposed to be free agents during their existence as human beings. That existence was supposed to be a period of probation, either qualifying for the higher stages of life beyond the grave, or to be sent back to that station among animals in Abred, to be there purified, or cleansed, from the dross or impurity of sin incurred during the human existence. Abred alone was the Hell of Druidism, and not Tartarus, Hades, or Annwn. The spiritual place above that of human existence on Earth the Druids called Gwynfa (Holy Place), and that below man was the brute place called Abred. Those two pieces were compared to the northern, or summer, side, and the southern, or winter, side, of the line of the terrestrial equator—the River of Life.

It will be remembered the old world knew nothing of the Antipodes. The Hell of the East was lost the moment America and Australia were found.

FLOWERS ON ARKS, THE WELSH FOR COFFINS.

The Druids saw that flowers and their sweet perfume were not provided to supply nourishment to build up carnal bodies, but were provided by the tender eternal Author of the Universe to gratify the sense of the beautiful in human souls. They, therefore, regarded flowers and hues of landscapes, as harbingers of a world of beauty, and eternal summer, beyond this life. The Coffin, or Ark, was the symbolical Boat which wafted the soul across to the heavenly shore of the spirit land of eternal rest and felicity. The

Ark or Coffin then was loaded with flowers, as symbolical accompaniments on the way to the world of souls. All material things were left behind in this world, and the soul was accompanied by flowers as harbingers returning home after their sojourn in another clime. Cleaning graves and decorating them at Easter time imply the same beautiful idea.

THE SUN'S SOUL DESCENDING INTO HELL.

It is believed the Sun's Soul \|/ descended every year at sunset on December 20th (25th) into Annwn or Tartarus, according to Virgil, through a cave above the south-western seas. He was supposed to cross the River Gwyllionwy, and enter Gwenydva, (Elysium or Paradise), and there to be re-clothed with a dazzling new body, and to be reborn as a babe from another cave in the south-eastern ocean on the morning of the 22nd or 27th, according to the Julian Calendar*. This is the Babe of the Mabynogion. They more generally called him, both in infancy and old age, at the end of each new year, respectively, Taliesun or Hesus, that is to say, lofty Iesun. This is the key to enable one to understand why the Infant Gods of Mythology were all said to have been born in a cave ; and the Cave of Bethlehem—not stable—strange to say, is a similar birthplace of the Saviour of the World. Egypt, the Red Sea, and Jews passing across, simply imply entering into this life, or into this world. The wilderness is this life. The Jordan and Canaan are the River of Life and heaven beyond ; and Moses and his Rod are the Sun, and the seminal element in the Word ; and the Cloud is the Holy Ghost, as the spirit element of the same Word. The Ark is Venus, the sister spouse of the Sun. Aaron is Aran, or Pan. Ystavell or Cell, of Aran is the same symbol as the cave of the Infant God, the Sun.

---

*This is the eastern view of the Sun's advent, but the Druids held that he returned, regenerated, through the same cave, into the sea, where the Holy Barge received him, and conveyed him to the South Eastern Sea, from whence he ascended on New Year's morning, a Crowned Babe, his mother being the Queen of Heaven.

ARAN'S CELL.

The projecting crag on the south side of Dinas Mountain, as already stated, bears the above name. It is near the brow of the mountain, above a farmhouse called Dinas Isaf, or Lower Dinas. The name "lower" is given to it because it is to the south of greater Dinas. It has a Rocking Stone near the crag.

Always in Welsh parlance the south is alluded to as the lower region of the earth, because the point marked in Druidism as the entrance place or cave leading into Annwn or Tartarus, is in the southern surface of the Earth. When the wind is from the south and south-west the Welsh still say, "the wind is low to-day." (Mae'r gwynt yn isel heddyw.) The same is expressed in Homer's Odyssey where the Arkite (Theban) asks Ulysses:—

"Why, mortal, wanderest thou from cheerful day,
To tread the downward, melancholy way?"
There in a lonely land and gloomy cells,
The dusky nation of Cimmeria dwells. (1).

After landing on the south-western shore of Cymri (Wales), he meets the Archon, whom Homer names the Mighty Theban, or the Arkite or Cowite. First of all the Mother of the Sun and the Earth was symbolised by a sacred boat riding on the ocean. Then the Earth came to be symbolised enthroned as a cow on the deck of the Sacred Boat. The Sun, when the Spring Sun rose in the Sign of the Bull, was sybolised as the Winged Bull, Baal, or Belin, and the Earth at the same time was symbolised by a Cow, called Baaltis. The last was represented by the Britons by the Cow, which they named Da Wen, or Holy Riches. The name which they themselves gave to Baal or Belin, was Tarw Elgan, or the Holy Bull Sun (El or Helios). Each "Rocking" Stone was a symbol of the Sacred Boat, the symbolical Mother of the Sun and the Earth. In the Bible the Boat is represented by both the opened Red Sea, and the opened Jordan. The Earth, which formerly was symbolised by the Sacred Cow, was represented in the opening of the Red Sea by Miriam, and

---

(1). Cymry, pronounced Keamre (Welsh).

in the opening of the Jordan, by the Ark of the Covenant. (2.)

It will be observed the leader, Moses, and the high priest, Aaron, accompanied Miriam, whose name signifies Mary—Mother, and that the leader, Joshua, and the high priest Eliezer, accompanied the Ark of the Covenant. Christ is both leader and high priest, and he is accompanied by the Church, his sister spouse. The Church is symbolised by the font, and from her are born the spiritual children to be fellow citizens with Christ and his bride in heaven.

Here the figures fail, for the Font is not, like Venus, an individual. The Roman Catholics have discerned this failure, and have sought to substitute the Virgin for her. But the Virgin is the mother of Jesus, and not his sister spouse.

The Jewish Rabbins say that before the Babylonian captivity, the Ark of the Covenant stood in the Temple on a stone. That Stone was originally a Rocking Stone, and is still on Mount Zion, but is now enclosed by the Mosque of Omar, which stands on the site of the Holy of Holies*. The chamber beneath the stone is the cell, of which the stone itself is an emblem, as both the birthplace and grave, and vice versa, of the Sun.

Homer reports Ulysses speaking as follows :

"When, low! the mighty Theban I behold,
To guide his steps he bore a staff of gold ;
Awful he trod; majestic was his look,
And from his holy lips these accents broke—
Why, mortal, wanderest thou from cheerful day,
To tread the downward melancholy way?"

The Odyssey, Book XI.

Each of the beehive-shaped Mounds of the Druids, as well as the circular Mountains, like that of Dinas, Rhondda, consecrated by

---

(2). Ex. 14, 21, 22 ; Ibid 15, 1, etc., 20, etc. ; Joshua 3, 14, etc. It appears implied that Miriam was carried in front of the nation into the Red Sea, in the same manner as the Ark of the Covenant was carried in front of the nation into Jordan.

*Sion, signifies a stone—Calmet.

them for the dramatic rites of their picturesque religion, symbolised the whole earth, as they supposed its shape to be. But their favourite symbols were islands, such as Barry Island, Glamorgan, whose ancient name is Bru-Aoh, or the Matrix of the Lineage, meaning the Earth, as the original mother of all Corporeal beings. In this religious rite the heretical Druids dramatically represented the south-western spot of the Mound, Mountain, or Island, as the symbolised entrance cave or passage into Annwn, and another cave, or cell, in the south-east as the outlet of the Sun from Annwn. The Hebrew tabernacle was entered from the west, or south-west, and the outlet called by Josephus "the Secret End," from the east, or south-east. It appears, therefore, the said tabernacle symbolised the same subterranean regions as did the Druidic ideas respecting the lower regions, and that the Second Veil dividing the western room of the Tabernacle from the room called The Holy of Holies, symbolised, like the Jordan dividing Canaan from Moab, and the River Nile dividing Western and Eastern Egypt, and the gulf between Tartarus and Elysium, or the "Bosom of Abraham," symbolised the river Gwyllionwy of the Druids, and the River Styx of classical mythology. It is remarkable that the summit of Mount Zion, or Moriah, was known till the time of David as the threshing floor—the Hebrew is Grn. Y Garn (Cairn, a great stone heap) is translated both Araunah, Ornan, and Aravanah (Welsh). I Chonicles, 21, 15, II Samuel, 24, 18. In our version it is called "threshing floor," and upon it the temple was afterwards built by Solomon. In Hebrew the name of the "owner" of the Grn is called Arn. It is a name much like the Druidic Aran. The temple and all its accessories have long since vanished, but the Carn (Welsh), and in English Cairn, is still there. Originally, Dean Stanley thinks, it stood seventeen feet above the level of the ground. It is sixty feet in length one way, and fifty feet in another. Below its south-east side is an excavated chamber, to which is a descent by a flight of steps. This chamber is irregular in form, and its superficial area is about 600 feet, or about 60 yards. In the centre of the rocky cave (Istavell Aran) "there is a circular slab of marble. which, being struck, makes a hollow sound, thereby showing there is a well or excavation beneath." "Stanley's Sinai and Palestine, p. 170—177." This hole is called the Well of Souls, and it was supposed the living above could speak with the souls below. Stanley believes it is the sink mentioned in the Talmud into which the blood of the sacrifices streamed. Our opinion is that the chamber itself was the antetypical stone sepulchre of the pattern of the true tabernacle, not made with hands —earth and heavens—and that on the Day of Atonement the symbolical High Priesthood was put to death by the High Priest. Under the Levitical law, the High Priest, as the Minister of the God of Israel, slew on the Day of Atonement, the priesthood, symbolised by the He Goat and the holy linen tunic which the High Priest himself wore on the occasion. (Lev. 16, 4.) Jesus being himself both the new High Priest and the High Priesthood bodily (Heb. 10, 5), assumes himself the slaying function of his antetype, and, with great subtlety, states, "Therefore doth the Father love me, because I lay down my life, that I may take it again. No one taketh it away from me, but I lay it down of myself. I have power to lay it down, but I have power to take it up again. This commandment have I received of my Father." St. John 10, 17 and 18*." The words were uttered in the precincts of the temple at Jerusalem, during th Feast of Dedication, which here seems to signify the dedication of the two He Goats for the Day of Atonement. Ibid 22. The strange observations chronicled in these chapters produced on the minds of his hearers the suspicion that he was going to immolate himself. "Then, said the Jews, will he slay himself?" St. John, 7, 22. And in the foregoing verses Jesus asserts it clearly, saying, "I lay it down of myself."

But in Hebrew the word translated "opened" signifies bored. It was the ceremony of taking possession of the body of a slave, and marking him such. Ex. 21, 6. David is alluding to his own sufferings, and that there was no vicarious substitute for him, but that he suffered in his own person. "My ears hast Thou bored," is, therefore, an idiomatic expression, and the LXX translated the expression instead of the word giving its meaning. In the same way the author of the Epistle to the Hebrews uses it in reference to the new High Priest, that he suffered himself bodily, like David did in another way.

---

*Heb. 10, 5. This verse is given here as the translation of the LXX of verse 6th, of Psalm XL. In our translation of the said verse the Words of David are rendered "My ears hast Thou opened."

THE CAVE OF ARAN—TALIESUN'S SYMBOLICAL BIRTH-PLACE.

Having in the foregoing chapter fixed, we think, unerringly the locality where the symbolical cave entrance into the emblematical Annwn (the River Gwyllionwy and Gwenydfa) stood, we proceed to discover the spot where stood the emblematical cave from which his return, rejuvenated as the Mabyn, Taliesun, was dramatically illustrated by the Druidic Priests of ancient Siluria. We crossed in our search for it, to the south-eastern side of the vast circular mound called Dinas Mountain. We found the south-eastern slope of the mountain is still named y Graig Wen, or the Holy Hillside. But after diligent search there, we failed to discover any cave in the locality. But happening to scan the brow of the mountain opposite, with our face directed towards the south-east, we were almost petrified with astonishment by observing a rocky hollow far up the mountain, and still bearing the name of "Dyllas," but correctly "Duwlais," or, the Voice of God. There is a deep hollow through which runs the ascending road, from Cymmer to Llantrisant, between Holy Hill side of Dinas Mountain, and the mountain opposite containing the Duw Lais Cave. That the High Priest who played the part of the new-born sun, as the Mabyn Taliesun, gave a loud musical shout, and that the vast throng opposite on the slope of the Holy Hill side cried, "Ein Hoes"—Our Life—corrupted to "Annos," is manifest in the fragmentary remains of Druidism presented in the Royal Records of Wales. The loud cry of the Druid Priest, who symbolised the Mabyn Sun, is called Llev—Velus. Loud, pealing, musical shout.*

<hr/>

THE NAME OF GOD.

"That is to say, God gave His name vocally and, simultaneously with that vocal utterance, all the world and their accessories leaped into existence, and life vibrated through everything. This

---

*This, as we will show presently, is associated with the drama of the night before, played at Pontypridd westwardly.

was the first melody ever heard, and the music of it penetrated to wherever God and existences are. 'And the blessed in heaven will hear it everlastingly." Bardism, Ab Ithel's Ed. p. 38.

The foregoing quotation leads us to suppose that at sunrise on the morning of each new year, when the sun, renewed like the Phoenix—the legend of the old and young Phoenix is based upon it—leaped up over the south-eastern horizon, the myriads of Druids on these mountains shouted their joy, and sang in vast bowing choirs, heartfelt welcome to the young God, in whose radiant orb as head tabernacled Hu Gadarn.

The Patriarch Job seems to be referring to the ancient custom of welcoming the rising sun of the new year as the concomitant of the dawn of the first creation, when the morning stars sang together, and all the sons of God shouted for joy. Job 38—7. By Sons of God is meant worlds, as described in the Welsh quotation.

A field on the northern side of the mountain of Dinas, and, therefore, opposite the sun at noon on the longest day, Sylgwyn, correct Pentecost time, June 21, is called Cae Gwyn or Holy Field. There, apparently, and along the adjacent slopes as far as Ffynon Wen or Holy Well, Syl Gwyn was celebrated.

ANCIENT FOOTPRINTS ON DINAS MOUNTAIN.

There are on the western side of Dinas Mountain striking indications that, in ancient days, the mountain was a place of very great importance, and a locality where vast assemblies were wont to gather together in all solemnity, to be eye witnesses of the great annual drama of the supposed Solar crucifixion at noon, in the western sky. But first of all we proceed to the principal ascending place to the summit of the Sacred Mount. On reaching the summit of the steep ascent of the road from Cymmer to Llantrisant, which runs through the ascending hollow between the eastern side of the mountain and that other mountain, with its back to the east and the western side of it, in which, near the brow, is situate the remarkable craggy dent or hollow, called "Dyllas," or Duw Lais.

(Vo'ce of God) a road branches off in a northern direction, and goes in the direction of the Rhondda Valley. It runs along the foot of Dinas Mountain, with a lofty slope wooded to the brow of the mountain. After going about a mile over almost level ground, the road makes a sudden rise describing the side of a triangle. From the opposite side there is a steep descent down the other side, both ascents describing a triangle. From the begining of the rise on one side, to the bottom of the descent opposite, is about two hundred yards. The point of the summit indicates the mountain, and the ascent into it is open, but flanked backwards on each side by a forest. The ridge, the ascent from the point, is called Gwisgan Vach, or the Place of Little Agility. The flat road on the left of the road from the eastern direction, is called Gwaun-yr-Argoed, or the Field of the Wooded Heights. That the two ascents to the point, indicating the ascent to the mountain, were originally designed to lead to the mountain, is certain, for it would have been far more easy—it has been done in recent years—to construct the road along the base of the triangular shaped ridge. Here, then, we have a high point reached by two roads coming from two opposite directions, both leading to the Mountain.

This fact, coupled with the other interesting facts we have mentioned, prove that something extraordinary was in remote ancient times associated with the summit of the Mountain itself. Another very striking reason why this spot was made the only ascent to the Mountain, was that it exactly faces the west, and, therefore, the worshippers, while ascending the Mountain went to face the eastern rising of the Sun. It was an act of impiety in Druidic times to turn one's back to the sun. Any ancient house in Wales with its front towards the west or north, and its back to the east or south, is called Ty With, or House the Wrong Way. Sometimes, as between Cardiff and Cowbridge, such a house is called Ty a'i Wedd o With, or House with its Face the Wrong Way. A house is called T in Wales, because T or the "Tau" (T—Udain) the Keltic cross, stood on the roof of each of their round dwelling-places, and the example is still followed by the churches. Each of the British and Gaulish habitations was circular, like each of their sacred Mounds. Several circles formed one house. It

seems that in allusion to this T, the ancient Britons were called
Titans, or T. Udeiniaid. The south is called De, or r ght hand
side; the notrh is called Gogledd or Sword side, and the west is
called Gorllewin, or the great region of the reflection of light.

We still adhere to the Druidic custom by entering churches
from the west towards the east, and bowing towards the east at a
certain part of the creed is the survival of bowing to the Sun.

THE SUMMIT OF THE DINAS MOUNTAIN.

It is highly probable that in ancient days this mountain was
also known by the name of Mynydd Aran. We know that the
symbolical mount, or circle enclosure, emblems of the whole earth,
circular in shape, as the Ancients supposed its shape to be, in
the East, especially in that part of Palestine called Phoenicia, bore
the name Garden of Adonis (Adonidis Hortus). Mount Zion is
referred to by King Solomon as, "A Garden barred is my Sister,"
(Heb. Version) (1). Here the barred Sistrum, the Egyptian
Symbol of Virginity of the personified Goddess, Spring
Earth, is the meaning of the expression, and employed as a figure
to describe Enclosed Mount Zion—a Virgin fortress. The Ark of
the Covenant, between Joshua and Eliezer, in the passage of
Jordan, as Miriam between Moses and Aaron in the passage of the
Red Sea, is called the Virgin of Israel. (2) Referring to the Ark
taken to captivity Jeremiah says, "Set thee up way marks; make
thee guide posts; set thine heart towards the highway, even the way
by which thou wentest; turn again, O, thou Virgin of Israel, turn
again to thy cities." (Jeremiah, c, 31, 21.) Note, not the Jewish
nation; Israel was called the Son. (Ex. 4, 22.) Then referring to
the fallen walls enclosing Mount Zion, the prophet speaking as the
God of Israel, said, "Again will I build thee, and thou shalt be built,
O, Virgin of Israel. Again shalt thou be adorned with thy tabrets,
and shalt go forth into the dances of those that make merry."
(Ibid. 4.) By the last allusions it is clear is meant the spirits of the
people, alluded to as derived from the Virgin of Israel in a merry
mood. Sometimes the enclosure of Mount Zion is called a Vineyard.

It is further said that Phoenicia, Babylon, and Egypt, had each its Virgin, i.e., Sacred Enclosure and its Ark. See Isaiah 23, 12; and Jeremiah 47, 1; and 26, 11. We make the assertion with every confidence that the Garden of Eden is the Druidic Din, or Holy Hill, the Garden of the Sun, with the definite article before the name, viz., The Din. (In Welsh "Y.") The definite article before a name with a consonant for its initial letter, has the sound of E. Thus Y Din is the Din, the name of Arthur's Hill, near Edinburgh has become corrupted to Edin (Y Din), and finally the river there has actually come to be called Eden River! Thus the article E, that is to say the Welsh Y, is joined to the Din itself. In the Gododin, a Welsh poem of the Eighth Century, it is rendered Idin, proving that even in the Eighth Century, when at the Battle of Cad Traeth, the recreant Britons of England and their Saxon allies fought against the true Britons of the North of England, the meaning of the name had been lost, and the definite article was even then joined to the name.

Another name by which the emblematical enclosure of the Druids was known, was Buarth Beirdd. Buarth is the compound of Bu (Bull), and Parth (Enclosure); and in English it is expressed by Hearth : a particular spot* In one of the earliest poems preserved in the Welsh (see the Myvyrian Archaeology, Vol. I, p. 27), we have it alluded to as follows.—Parenthetically the title in the copy is part of the first line of the poem :—

"Buarth Beirdd, hedd ein pobl oedd."

"The Taurine Enclosure of the Bards was the Sanctuary of the People."

The Bull referred to is the Tarw Elgan, or the White Sun Bull, which was contemporary with the Sacred Bull Apis, of Egypt, and Baal of Phoenicia, etc., of which the Hebrew Golden Calf at the foot of Mount Sinai was an imitation. The reason why in Britain, Egypt, etc., the sun in spring was symbolised by a Bull, and the earth by a Cow—both were white in Britain—we give in another page. It appears that the Spring Sun began to rise in the Bull

---

*It was known, also, as Caer Lavarawg, or Enclosure of Utterances ; hence, the Caer Lavarock Roll of the Round Table.

Sign about the year 4335 B.C. It continued to rise in 't till about the year 2210 B.C., when it had fallen back (retrograded) to the

*Sacred Bull Apis, of Egypt, and Dove, symbol of the Word. The Horns implying a Crescent Barge, holding the Sun. Bull-Sun enjoying the fragrance ascending from the Earth. The Winged Light at top.
—(Montfaucon

*It has escaped notice that the Golden Bull which the Jews erected at the foot of Sinai in imitation of the Egyptian Apis, is called Gods, and not God, in Ex. 32, 4, and in I Kings, 12, 28. The "Gods" are the Sun Bull Apis and the Dove; and the Dove as the living emblem of the Druidic sign $\vee$, descended on Jesus at the moment of his apotheosis. The Dove is the Amen Ra of Egypt. See St. Luke iii, 22, and Revelation iii, 22. Amen Ra says: "I am the Father of my own Sun" (Son). Bonwick's Egyptian Belief, etc., p. 122. The name Jupiter Amen is really two names, viz., a pair of wings, symbol of a spirit in the Egyptian hieroglyphics. Amen signifies Spirit Mind, and the body of the dove signifies Father Iu.

sign of the Ram. It continued to rise in the Sign of the Ram on March 25 (21) till about 155 B.C. It then retrograded to the Sign of the Two Fishes. It will do so till about A.D. 2245. This backward movement of the Sun through the Signs, as the Ancients believed, but really of the Pole, or Line of the Equator, in its relation to the Spring Sun, is called the Precession of the Equinoxes, or Equal Day and Night in length, which occurs on March 21 and September 21 every year (25th respectively in old calendars.) Thus the Sun began to rise on March 21 in the Sign of the Ram 2300 B.C.; and in the Sign of the Bull 4445 B.C. Add to the last the years 1897, and we have it that 6342 years ago the Spring Sun began to rise in the Sign of the Bull, which in Old Welsh is called Bu, but pronounced Bee. The above calculation is that made by the Astronomer Royal of England, who states that by taking different boundaries for measuring, slightly different results will follow. Plutarch states, the Cimbri, Kymry (Welsh) in their march into Italy under Brennus (Brenin—King), carried with them a bull made of brass, upon which they made their oath to carry out the Covenant. We see that the time when the White Bull (Elgan), and the White Cow (Da-Wen) were in vogue among the Britons, was not before 4355 years B.C., nor later than 2260 B.C., for at the latter date the Spring Sun had retrograded to Ram, "House" of Jupiter, which was adopted in his place. It was perfectly well known to the guides of religion among the Hebrews that, at the time of Jesus of Nazareth, the Spring Sun no longer rose in the Sign of the Ram, but in the Sign of the Two Fishes. But a difficulty was experienced by the ancient Egyptians in adopting the Ram symbol, called Jupiter Amen, instead of the Sacred Bull Apis, after the Spring Sun had retrograded from the Sign of the Bull to the Sign of the Ram. At the foot of Sinai, the Hebrews, having in the view of the Egyptians committed the horrible impiety—as we would to-day regard burning the Bible—of killing Rams on the eve of their departure from Egypt, fell back into the ancient symbolical worship of Egypt, and erected a Golden Bull, an imitation of the Egyptian Apis, discarded for the Ram by the Egyptians themselves. In the Greek New Testament Christ is called both Ram of the Passover, and the Fish (Ichthus), in the same way as the sun had been formerly called both Bull and Ram in Egypt. The miracle of the Two Fishes and the Five Loaves is a Solar one. Chr st, as the Sun's Soul on earth, operated through the Two Fishes upon the loaves which represented the earth. The sun in the heavens operates in Spring through the Zodiacal Two Fishes, and the miracle is for the purpose of showing that Christ could do precisely the same thing. It was universally believed also the sun walked the sea, and entered a sacred barge in the evening.

"Io! Io! Pan! Pan!

Oh, Pan! thou Ocean Wanderer!"

Sophocles (Ajax), 694-7ᴜᴜ.

To indicate his identity with the sun, when Jesus' eyes lost the light of life, the sun also lost his light.

It has often dawned on the minds of thinkers that the bread and fish, which Christ on the seashore invited his disciples to eat, partook of the same sacramental character as the bread and wine of the Eucharist. The Church members still at the spring season of Lent, or Easter, eat fish as a religious act. Thus we see it clearly established that if the sacrament is the real flesh and blood of Christ, it is also the flesh of a fish. It would be absurd to associate blood with a fish. The Egyptian worshippers of Typhon (Satan) ate symbolically the flesh of Osiris, and the worshippers of Osiris ate symbolically the flesh of a Black Boar (Twrch Trwyth) as the symbol of Pluto or Satan. Eating the Boar's head at Christmas is a survival of this custom.

In the year A.D. 2245 the Spring Sun will have retrograded into the Sign of the Waterer, when, if the former example will be followed, the Christian world will partake of a Waterman, as a Sacrament. It is evident that most of the animal symbols in the religious systems of the Ancients were based on the Zodiacal Signs, especially the Bull, Ram, Cow (Virgo), and the He Goat. The Bull became Baal; the Ram, Sign of the House of Jupiter; and the He Goat, Pan—half man and half Billy Goat. The Bull, the Ram, and Fishes successively became signs of the Spring Sun. The He Goat was the Sun Sign of the Winter Solstice, on Dec. 21st, but in the Egyptian and Roman Calendar, December 25th. The Sun in the Zodiacal Sign of the He Goat being at the end of the Solar Year, was always represented as aged Pan, and young again, as Pan, the Sun of the new year. It seems the object of the Ancients in adopting animal symbols, instead of human ones as Signs of the Zodiac, was to guard against idolatry, as had been the object previously in representing the Sun as on seven golden candlesticks, and afterwards as seven personages, as the annual stations of the sun while passing up and down through the seven planetary spheres along the ecliptic during his annual journeys up and down. But even during the very remote epoch, when the Bull was the Spring Zodiacal Sign, we find the Bull under the names Baal, Belus, Belin, assuming in ancient figures and statues, especially at Babylon and Nineveh the form of a winged Bull with a human face; and the earth as his consort was symbolised under the form of a cow, with a feminine face, under the names Beltis, Astaroth, Easter, Europa, Isis ii. and in Britain as Da Wen, Mon-Wen, etc.

The Ram came to be, instead of the Bull, the Sign of the "House" of Jupiter, or Iu Father, and was symbolised as a powerful man wearing ram's horns. The He Goat became Pan, with the lower half like that part of a He Goat, and the upper part like an old man—a complex emblem.

BULL ENCLOSURE OF THE BARDS.

It will be seen by the foregoing that it is very long since the sacred circle, described by the rotundity of Dinas Mountain, was the principal Buarth Beirdd of Ancient Siluria, which is the Latin name of Syllwg, which name signifies Multiplicity of Green Prospects, Latinised by the Roman historian Tacitus, in the first century of the Christian era. As we have already intimated, each of these bardic holy mounts, mounds, or mountains, being emblematical of the whole earth beehive-shaped, as the Druids believed, bore many names. Among others it was called Mount of the Congregation; Mount of the Asembly of Gods (Priests); the Holy Hill, Mount of the Tau, that is to say, of the Cross. The T, or T. Gwyn (T'wyn) was an hieroglyphical figure on each mound in each sacred circle, and on every habitation of the Britons, as Arwyddion, or Signs on Staves (Bokes) of Wood on the Garden of Arthur, or the Sun. Arddir, the "th" here should have the sound of "th" in "then," means Gardener, and in this respect, as already intimated, he is identical with the Phoenician Adonis, and the Greek Ge-Orgon corrupted and canonised, as St. George. His foe and active opponent is the Dragon, or the Destroying Spirit, whose emblems are Winter and Night. This Red Dragon is Satan. whose other emblems in Druidism are a Crow and a Raven, the national emblems of the Anglo Saxons. As the emblem of the protoplasm of the earth in a state of fermentation in spring under the rays and fertilising influence of Jupiter in the Sun, the mount was the Garden of the Sun, as his consort. Dinas Mountain, like each smaller one devoted to the purpose of Divine worship, must have borne each of the said names in very remote times in the annals of South Wales. Judging by the name given to the West by the Greeks and others, the sea-girt Britannia was regarded as one vast circular temple, like the Island of Delos, as emblem of the whole earth; for it is called the Garden of Hesper. The Hes in that name is an abbreviation of Tal-Iesun. This name in native British must have been Gardd Taliesun, or the Garden of Tall Hesus, tall here being used to imply high in the heavens. Dinas Mountain, in common with all other circular Temples within Britain, must have borne the same name, viz., Brydwen, or the Holy Featured One (fem). The Lotos, stem and flowers, standing on its single stem, as a reversed cone tapering from the outward broad circle part to the stem, was another symbol of the earth. The top of the cone of the lotos plant resembles in shape the nozzle of a watering pot and the holes in it were emblems of the grave holes dotting the surface of the earth. In summer each of those holes holds out a flower. In winter the flower is no longer there, and the hole is sealed up by nature, and beneath the seal is a seedling. In spring the rays of the sun causes the seedling to burst open its grave, and it shoots out into the water to find a home, to there grow and flourish, and multiply. This lotos and its seedlings bursting forth were adopted by the Ancients as emblems of the resurrection of the dead, and of new worlds as islands, as being offshoots of the old one. In Britain the white water lily was the chief emblem serving the same purpose as the lotos did in the East.* Most of those lakes where the Druids performed the drama of the death and the resurrection of the sun, still, especially in Wales, grow those water lilies brought there by Druids. But the "flowering Sunday" custom of South Wales and Monmouthshire is the principal popular survival of the said drama. The custom is a floral sermon. Ignorant bigots set their faces against the beautiful custom, and also the custom of adorning the Welsh Arch (Ark, Coffin) because they suppose the custom is of Papal origin.

It is said by the Greeks that the Garden of Hes or Taliesun had in its centre an apple tree, and for that reson the Garden in Western Europe is called an Orchard: Corwyn, Blaen ʌval (the holy wide circle of the Apple height).

THE DESCENT INTO HELL. CROSSING THE STYGIAN RIVER AND ENTERING PARADISE.

In Druidism it is supposed all souls have had their generation and birth from Cariadwen and the Holy Spirit, called Holy Wings (A-Wen) in Gwenydva (Elysium), and that to come from thence to this world they must cross Gwyllionwy (River Styx), and traverse Annwn (Hades), and ascend in the train of the Sun, on his return, regenerated as regards his body, and, therefore, the Divine Mabyn, or Mab, Babe, on the morning of the solar new year. Inside the Sun is the Ancient of Days, Hu Gadarn (Word of the Creator), and the Sun's body is his and Cariadwen's offspring. The Ancient of Days is the Son of the Creator Celu alone, who is both his father and mother himself. Virgil describes the two regions of the underworld as follows : —

---

* The stem was the Navel Symbol.

THE BRITISH PRE-CHRISTIAN CROSS.

Crucifixion of Pan El each December 25th (21st) in the heavens. Black Wings, Pluto, or Saturn with spear. Observe general darkness. Pan's bleeding body falling into the S.W. Seas. The escaping Word from Pan's mouth fleeing to the safety of the Coracle of Cariadwen. Two Shields.

See Revelation xi, 8. (Revised Edition).

Night rushes down, and headlong drives the day;
'Tis here, in different paths, the way divides;
The right to Pluto's Golden Palace guides;
The left to that unhappy region tends,
Which to the depth of Tartarus descends—
The seat of Night profound and punished fiends.

Aenid, b. vi, s 725.

The descent is where the sun descends on the shortest day of winter, and the Left and Right of his l ne of descent are Tartarus (Annwn) and Gwenydfa, Elysium, respectively, with the River Gwyllionwy (Styx) flowing between. Charon's ferry, Ark, or Boat, is on the Styx River, flowing through the gulf between the two regions. In Welsh, Charon is named Pwyll, Pen Annwn. In Druidism, souls do not return at the dissolution of their bodies either to Tartarus or Elysium, but e ther go to Heaven, or return to the animal circles of transmigration. And in the Oriental mythology. souls of the dead do not go to h aven, but into the "shades" below the earth, and to symbolise the "Night profound" into which souls go, we have been induced to wear black clothes as mourning for them. But the Orientals believed the souls of good people passed through Tartarus to Elysium safely if they in life had slain as sacrifice to Satan the sacred animals, symbols of the Creator's attributes through the Sun, and, therefore, objectionable to Pluto, Satan, Saturn, or Typhon, each a name of the Devil, the Black Wings of Druidism.

After describing the cave entrance into the two Underworlds, Virgil states :—
"Deep was the cave, and downward as it went,
From the wide mouth, a rocky, rough descent—"
The horrors of Tartarus are described and the sacrifice to Pluto of sacred symbolical animals, is described :
"From hence the Grecian bards their legends take,
And give the name Avernus (1) to the lake,
Four sable bullocks, in the yoke untaught,
For sacrifice the pious hero brought.

---

(1) The Uffern of the Bible.

The priestess pours the wine between their horns, (2)
Then cuts the curling hair, that first oblation burns,
Invoking Hecate hither to repair—
A powerful name in hell and upper air.
The sacred priests with ready knives bereave
The beasts of life, and in full bowls receive
The streaming blood; a Lamb to Hell and Night,
The sable wool without a streak of white,
A barren heifer, Proserpine (3) to thee.
Aeneas offers; and by Fate's decree,
With holocausts he Pluto's altars fills,
Seven brawny bulls (4) with his own hands he kills.

Aenid vi, s. 350.

It is needless to remind the reader the Bull and the Lamb were in succession symbols of the Spring Sun in theSigns of the Bull and Ram respectively, and that the curling locks of the bull's head were symbols of the Sun's rays, and were symbolically burnt by burning the curls.* Pouring wine on the head is in derision of the life-giving essence which the Sun's rays produces as juices of fruits, on earth. The wine poured on the head symbolised the same idea as the blood flowing from the wounds produced by the Crown of Thorns. The "seven brawny bulls" represent the sun during the year passing through the Seven Planetary Spheres. Rev, iii, I, IV, 6; I, 20. In the story of the death of Jesus he is said to have descended through Hell to Elysium, and there preached to the captives the prisoners of Pluto. "Because Christ also suffered for sins once, the righteous for the unrighteous, that he might bring us to God; being put to death in the flesh, but quickened in the spirit; in (as) which (Spirit) also he went and preached unto the Spirits"—

---

(2) The Wine symbolises the fertility which the Bull in the Sign of Taurus imparts to the earth.

(3) Pluto's wife.

(4) Symbols of the Sun passing through the seven planetary spheres.

*This rite is still observed by the Jews.

Spirit to Spirits—"in prison, which aforetime were disobedient. For to this end was the Gospel preached even to the dead." I. Peter iii, 18, IV, 6.

St. Paul goes farther than St. Peter, and describes what the Spirit of Jesus accomplished in his victorious march from Elysium, or Paradise, otherwise "the bosom of Abraham," in the Underworld. St. Paul quotes Ps. 68, 18, in Ephesians iv, 8. The whole passage is as follows: "Why look ye askance, ye high mountains, at the mountain which God hath desired for his abode?" Mount Zion is meant. "Yea, the Lord will dwell in it for ever. The chariots of God are twenty thousand, even thousands upon thousands. The Lord is among them, as in Sinai in the Sanctuary."

In the said Psalm the Psalmist is addressing the Word as the Shechinah or cloud as follows:—

"Thou hast ascended on high;
Thou hast led captivity captive;—(from Egypt)
Thou hast received gifts among men,
Yea, among the rebellious also,
That the Lord might dwell with them."—(the Hebrews).

That the Psalmist is alluding to the Shechinah is clear by the words, "The Lord is among them as in Sinai in the Sanctuary." It is the "implanted," or fertilised "Word" referred to by St. James, and also the renovating spiritual power of the Holy Spirit, as consisting of the Father and Spirit in the Word, as the fertilising active matter. In verse 4, he alludes to the Word as "One body and one spirit," and he alludes to the Father or the Seminal element of the Word, as "over all, through all, and in all." But the Spirit is the gift of the Logos Spiritos himself; and the apostle says, "Unto each of us was the grace (of the Holy Spirit) given according to the measure of the gift of Christ as a bounty." St. Paul makes here a clear distinction between the man Jesus and The Christ, for the latter was a title of the Fatherhood in the dual constitution of the Word. It is intimated that the Christ had authority over the Holy Spirit, and could send him (1) as a gift to his disciples.

----

(1). St. John 15, 16.

Then we come to St. Paul's use of the words of the Psalm:—
Whereof he saith:

"When he ascended on high,
He led captivity captive,
And gave gifts unto men."

Observe in the Psalm the Words are, "Thou hast received gifts among men." Ps. 68, 18. But St. Paul refers to him who "had received gifts among men," as him who had now given gifts unto men. The Psalmist refers to what can be called storing the gifts in the Spirit in the Word, and the Father in the Word in Jesus, giving the gifts of the Holy Spirit in quantity "according to measure," to men. Eph. 4, 11. Then the apostle goes on to trace the movements of the Word, and states, "Now this, He ascended, what is it but that he also descended into the Lower Parts of the Earth?" The Shechinah, as the Word, had descended among men, but the Word, after the sacrifice of the body of Jesus, also descended through Hades and Devils, to the captives in Paradise or Elysium. He afterwards ascended "far above all the heavens," and on the Day of Pentecost sent down his gift as tongues of fire on the heads of the disciples, and the gift came with the sound of rushing wings, and the result was the "perfecting of the saints."—v. 12. It was supposed by the Druids that in the visit of the twofold Word into Gwenydva on each December 25th, and remaining there until sunrise on the 27th, the Holy Spirit, symbolised by the wings of the White Dave (Ion), while the body did the Fatherhood of that Word, the Holy Spirit begot souls by his contact with the great Mother Spirit, called Cariadwen or Holy Love (fem); but immediately the Sun's, or Son's body, was ready to receive the Two fold Word into it, the said Father having begotten his body from the feminine protoplasm in the Sacred Barge, the complete Word entered the Sun's corpus, and the return to the "upper air" followed. It would appear from the fact the Holy Spirit is in Welsh called A-Wen Hevin, or the Holy Wings of June, or Juno (Dove), that the Druids supposed the gifts of the Holy Spirit in the Sun were contributed at Whitsuntide, or June 25th, which is the date of some of the recipients being made apostles, others prophets, others evangelists, others pastors, and others mere teachers. Eph. 4, 11. Those gifts, before being given them, were and are measured by the Christ, and the Holy Spirit imparted and imparts them on the day of the Druidic Pentecost, viz., Whitsuntide (June 25th), by the direction of Christ as the essence of Fatherhood in the dual nature of the Word. (Justin Martyr's Apology, p. 68.) The "Gifts" are the joint productions of the Holy Spirit Car:adwen, represented by the Navis—Church, in the lower parts of the Earth. And that in the ascent therefrom, while the Sun's material body was charged with the material essence for the fruition of material substances in Earth, the Holy Spirit in the Sun was charged as A-Wen, with a wealth of Spiritual Gifts to be given unto men, and that the divers gifts produced various results. Such is the teaching based on the Druidic speculation respecting the descent of the Sun into the lower parts of the earth, and his doings there.

The emblems of the Two-fold Word were the Burning Bush and the Rod of Moses, the Shechinah or Cloud over the Seat of Reconciliation, called erroneously Mercy Seat, and the Horn of the Heraldic Unicorn, whose wings symbolise the Shechinah. Ps. 92, 10; 22, 21. Isaiah refers to the Jewish people as the sons of the Shechinah's Horn, as Unicorns—"And the unicorns shall come down with them"—the sons of the Cherubs, or Two Winged Bulls on the Ark of the Covenant. Isaiah employs for the Jews the figure of Bullocks accompanying the sons of the two-winged bulls. Is. 34, 7. The Psalmist is alluding to the captivity of the Israelites in Egypt, and the Word delivering them, and leading them by way of Sinai to the heights of Mount Zion. St. Paul alludes to the Word as being in Jesus, and he descended to the "lower parts of the Earth," figured by the Psalmist as Egypt and Goschen, with the Nile (Styx) flowing between; and as the Word descended from the heights of Midian to deliver Pharaoh's captives, so the Spirit of Jesus descended to deliver from prison the captives of Pluto. Jesus himself taught this in his first sermon at Nazareth, and quoted the Song of Isaiah on the subject of the captivity of the Jews in Babylon—here the figure is Babylon instead of Egypt—and their prospective deliverance, and Jesus applies the song as prophetic, respecting the descent of the spirit, the Word, into Hell, to deliver the souls from the captivity of

Pluto in the Underworld, and that part of it called Elysium. Is. 61, 1-11. Luke 4, 18. Luke refers to the old ceremony of representing the regenerated Mabyn or Babe Sun (Son) rising from the sacred Crescent-shaped Barge, which, according to St. Peter, was the same as Noah's Ark, and he was right.* It was the same, too, as the Ark of Bulrushes, in which Moses's apotheosis to be a leader took place. It appears that all the members of the Solar Church underwent the same boating ceremony as the regenerated Mabyn, or Babe Sun, was supposed to undergo. St. Paul takes us to another ceremony, namely, boating by deputy, as representing each soul whose body had not during life undergone the apotheostical act. I. Cor. 15, 29.

There is in Virgil's poem already quoted what appears to be an echo of the theory of the Druids that the Sun, under the name Taliesun, descended as a disembodied spirit, the Spirit being named Hu Gadarn, at sunset into the underworld, and crossing the River Gwyllionwy, or the Dark Waters of the Dove, entered Gwenydva (Elysium), and brought thence new souls. These are the words Virgil reports Charon, the ferryman, saying to Aeneas and the Sibyl:—

Know, this the realm of night, the Stygian shore,
My boat conveys no living bodies o'er;
Nor was I pleased Great Theseus once to bear,
Who forced a passage with his pointed spear.

Aenid v., s. 530.

The "pointed spear" is the same Druidic emblem as the arrow which Abaris, the Druid, exhibited to Pythagoras at the Olympic games; the sacred sign which, on the forehead of Cain, protected him. It is now called the Broad Arrow, and is /|\ or \|/, the hieroglyphic denoting the Word whose living emblems are the Dove in the East, and Wren (Driw) in Britain. Driwydd the Welsh for Druid, signifies Wrenite. The other symbols of the Word are the Fleur-de-Lys, Trefoil, Shamrock, and the Three Plumes, or the Diadem of Wales.

---

* I. Peter iii, 20 and 21.

78

THE ANCIENT ASTRONOMICAL DIVISIONS.

THEIR PERSONIFICATIONS.

In ancient astronomy we have three primary divisions of the heavens. (1) The map of the heavens was divided into seven lines, stretching across the heavens from east to west. The top line is that traversed by the sun on June 25. The middle line is that traversed by the sun on March 25th, and the bottom line that traversed by the sun on December 25th. (2) The seven days of the week are based upon those seven lines, which are called the Seven Planetary Spheres. In olden time the Solar Decani year commenced on March 25th, and ended on December 25th. December, as its Latin name signifies, was the tenth (Decem) month. During each of those ten months the sun was supposed to traverse each of those seven lines seven times, and in the year of ten months the journeys amounted to seventy in number. The ten months consisting of seventy journeys, were called Decani, amounting to Septuaginta, or Seventy. The name Decani signifies Annual Ten, and the Septuaginta denotes seventy journeys of the sun accross the sky during the ten months, or from March 25th to December 25th. From December 27th to March 25th, when the sacred year commenced, the sun was regarded as an Infant King, or Crowned Babe, called Mabyn Taliesun by the Druids.

"When he (Moses) ordered twelve loaves to be set on the table, he denoted the year as distinguised into so many months.

By branching out the Candlestick into seventy parts, he secretly intimated the Decani, or the seventy divisions of the planets. As to the seven lamps on the Candlestick, they referred to the planets, of which that is the number."—Josephus' Antiquities, b. iii, c. viii, s. 7.

Thus for the purposes of religion, based on the solar phenomena, each ten solar months was divided into seven parts, and each part was often called a "week." (1). (3) The twelve Signs of the Zodiac

---

(1) Dan 9, 24. Ex. 1-5. Numbers 11, 16, 24, 25. Genesis 4, 24. In that part of Genesis the seven days of the week are added to the seventy. Ezek. 8, 11, 12. It will be thus seen here that a priest sometimes represented the Sun on each of the seventy lines. The Senhedrim consistd of seventy members.

are the twelve signs upon which the twelve months of the year are based. In both the seven planetary spheres traversed yearly ten times by the Sun, and the twelve Zodiacal Signs traversed by the Sun during the Zodiacal Year, were three principal stations, viz., March 25th, June 25th, and December 25th. In each station the Sun was personified. In the seven planetary spheres the Sun was Cynun, or the Principal, on June 25th; Mercury on March 25th, and Ner, or the Strong, on December 25th. But generally the three, as one Sun, went under the comprehensive titles, Taliesun, Arthur, Tegid, Morgan, Merddyn, etc. In the Zodiacal three stations corresponding with the above planetary three, the personified Sun went under the title name, Nevydd (Celestial), Nav. (Father), and Neiv—Ion, or Boat and Dove, the Dove being \\|/ named Hu Gadarn, or Hu the Invincible, the Word or Name of the Creator, Celu (Coelus), but the Word of Saturn in Judaism.

The Boat is the Holy Barge (1) or Coroogl Gwydrin of the Spirit Mother Cariadwen, mother of all things, while Celu Coelus—the Agnostos Theos of the Greeks—was the father of all things, including the two-fold Hu Gadarn himself. In Rev. xii, 1, the Virgin is described standing on the moon (crescent) : "and, she being with child, cried, travailing in birth, and pained to be delivered." (50.) The moon is the emblem of the Thebet, the Sacred Barge or Ark. It will be remembered we say throughout this work that the Crescent Moon was regarded as the emblem of the Sacred Ark or Boat of the Spirit Mother of the Goddess Venus, for whom Semele, the mother of Bacchus (Sun) was substituted. Thus the Crescent Moon was the emblem of the Mother of Venus or Semele (sap of the Earth), and she herself, or sometimes the one and sometimes the other, was in the East represented as the Mother of the Babe Sun God. See Dean Stanley's "Memorials of Canterbury," p. 230, and Note "G." p. 291 ; Ed. 1895. Dean Stanley, in page 230, states that in the museum at Munich the Martyrdom of St. Stephen is associated with the Crescent. St. Stephen's Day is December 26, and it is the day still observed in the Isle of Man for carrying the Wren. At St. David's, Wales, the Wren, on the same day of the year was carried in an Ark the emblem of the crescent-shaped Ark of Cariadwen (Iris I) with the escaped Word \\/ in it. The rev. Dean points out also that in Canterbury Cathedral the Zodiac is associated with the spot under the Crescent. St. Thomas, the Apostle, is associated with the same season, and no doubt he was placed in the station of old given to Tammuz in the older signs of mythology. It appears that the Goddess was regarded as the Mother also of the Anima of Nature personified as Cra rwy ,Dien Diana, Venus, or Gwen, as an infant, and is also called Duwies Vach, or Little Goddess. The above triads in one way or another are found in all religions, including both that of the Old and New Testaments. But in Genesis the Triad is adroitly made to include the sun in those of the seven planetary spheres and those of the Zodiac. Cain is the head of the seven, and is identical with the Druidic Cynun, or the Sun, on June 25th. Seth corrretly Set, is the head of the Zodiacal list. Including the three sons of Noah (Ninth), we have the Zodiacal twelve s gns personified in the line of Seth.

ABEL.

In Abel we have a perplexing curiosity, and to unriddle the enigma we must go to Egyptian Mythology. The name Abel or Ab—El, signifies Father of God. This God is the Sun. In the Eastern systems of religions, based on the Solar phenomena, we repeat, the Old Sun of one year, both in the Planetary and the Zodiacal systems, is the Father of the Babe Son, or Mabyn, of the next year. This goes on perpetually; one sun's body growing old, and the next a Babe Son, since the first Sun (Son) was created. It signifies a struggle perpetually carried on between the Lord of Night and the Lord of Light, and Satan annually destroying the body of the Sun in his annual old age. But always failing to touch Hu Gadarn (Invincible Hu), the Word of Coelus.

was supposed to be slain in the air by the Lord of Night, but his

At the close of each Solar Year, which the system of Egypt placed on December 25th, the Sun's body, being then old and weak,

Divinity, that is to say, Hu Gadarn, the Word of Celu, as ⤋ always escaped into the Boat of the Mother of the Sun's body, and she always sent him up clothed in a radiant new body, to the chagrin of the Lord of Night (Pluto). We repeat, Ab—El is the name of the Old Sun of December 25, as the Father of the Young Sun of December 27th, or 40 hours later. Adam is the Sun of a still previous year, regarded as old, and the father of the young Mabyn of the next, and Eve is either Venus or Semele, mother of the young Bacchus, here under the name Cain—why placed the first of three sons we explain elsewhere. Cain is evidently the Welsh Cynun, or the First One, a title of the Sun on June 21st or 25th, in the seven planetary personifications, prior to the invention of the twelve signs of the Zodiac by the Egyptians.—Herodotus' Euterpe, s. iv.

The Sun's Divine tenant is called "Invincible," because the Lord of Night is never able to slay Him, who is the Name and Word of the Creator, and is as immortal as Himself. The Word is represented on every March 25th, hurling the Lord of Night back by striking him on his head. But the Lord of Day is wounded in the heel of his body which is the vehicle in which the Word journeys round the earth. Gen. 3, 15. Isaiah, alluding to the same annual attacks, says he was bruised for our iniquities, and that it pleased the Lord to bruise him. Is. 53, 4, 10. But in Chapter 60, Isaiah says, "Arise, and shine (Heb. grow light) for thy light is come. Nations walk in thy light, and kings to the shining of thy rays (v. 3)." It is generally supposed the words "Arise, grow light, for thy light is come," is addressed to the Jewish nation. But it appears the words are addressed to the Sun, and that he who has come into it is the Word of the Creator or His Name whose light was supposed to come to him from the Creator. (St. John I, 4) The point here is that the prophet is alluding to the Sun's personality as the bruised One, and to the Word in Him as the source of light, as existing apart from the Sun's individuality as a corporeal personage "In Him (Sun) is Life, and the Life (Logos) is the Light," and not the Sun himself.

DIVINE RIVALRIES.

In Is. 14, 12, we have the prophet clearly alluding to a supposed rivalry as existing between the personified Sun and the Word inhabiting the Sun. In that chapter the Prophet addresses the Sun as an individual, and says scornfully to the luminary as Lucifer (Giver of Light), Son of the Morning, and to his fall, of course, at sunset on Dec. 25th, into the South Western Seas. But, alluding to the invincibility of the Word, which escaped out of the Sun's wreck, the prophet says, "The abundance of the sea shall be turned unto Thee: the wealth of the nations shall come unto Thee. In my wrath I (Saturn) smote thee (the Sun), but in my favour have I had mercy on Thee." (C. 60). It is noteworthy that Isaiah locates the Word on Mount Zion, and that all the gifts of nations to the Word would be brought there for him. This sentiment is eminently Jewish.—The two-fold name was the Shechinah and the Horn of the Unicorn which had taken the place of the Rod of God in it in the Holy of Holies. But the perpetual slaughter of Bulls, Rams, and Goats on the altar, was the sacrifice of the Zodiacal emblems of the Sun's personality in the Signs Taurus, Aries, and Capricornus. It was the slaughter of Lucifer, the Son of the Morning, by his symbols, in Egypt as Apis, Lamb, and Pan. He was thus "bruised" under his several symbols.

It appears that in ancient days many nations worshipped the Sun, personified as a God, and Isaiah, in common with other Hebrews, infers those nations were ignorant of the existence of the Word of the Creator within the orb. But the Prophet seems to allude to some Isles of the Sea, and to Spain (Tarshish), that knew the Word—His Name—within the Sun, and he represents the Word Himself, saying, "Who are these that fly as a cloud (Shechinah) (not clouds), and as doves to their windows?" They are the children of the Dove, \|/ or the Word. The Word goes on to say, "Surely the Isles shall wait for Me, and the ships of Tarshish, first to bring thy Sons like a cloud of Doves from far."

Delizech is of opinion that the figures "as a cloud," and "as doves to their windows," allude to the appearance of the ships of Tarshish. Does not the expression, "The Isles shall wait for me"† signify "serve me," in the same sense as the ships of Tarshish "first shall do so to bring the Sons of the Word coming from far" to the Holy Name in the Holy of Holies? Surely he does not imply that the Isles will come like ships and like a cloud of flying doves, to Jerusalem and its windows. Ships don't fly to windows.

In the Welsh translation, the words are rendered, "the Isles will 'look' for Me, and chiefly the ships of Tarshish." So the Isles and the Ships are said to be doing the same thing, which it is clear by the context is, "Will serve Me," but the ships by bringing passengers to Zion, and the Isles by serving the Word where they are. Is. 60, 9. The British Isles are clearly meant. The expression, "the Isles wait for me, "cannot possibly signify that they will follow the ships of Tarshish (the cloud of doves), as St. Jerome infers. Here Isaiah makes the profoundly interesting acknowledgement that the Isles were as sacred as Mount Zion, because the Isles worshipped the Word.

TWO INCARNATIONS: A GREAT MYSTERY INTERPRETED.

JUPITER AND JESUS; PAN AND JOHN THE BAPTIST.

John the Baptist was begotten on Tishri 14th, or September 25th. This is proved by St. Luke's statement that Elizabeth was gone six months with child on Nisan 14th (March 25th). On the next Thammuz 14th, June 25th, John the Baptist was born.

On Nisan 14th (March 25th), when the child in Elizabeth was six months old, the Virgin Mary, at the instigation of the angel Gabriel, which name signifies the Voice of God the King,, arrived at the home of Elizabeth and Zachariah, both of whom were Cohens or descendants of the family of the high priest Aaron.

Jesus as a man was begotten by the Holy Spirit on March 25, the Virgin Mary being the mother. This is an intimation that the

Word, in his two-fold nature, begot both the carnal body of Jesus, and his soul, the first by Iu Pater, the Chrisma of Christ, or Father Iu, and the second by the Holy Spirit, or Awen.

Thus Jesus' body was the humanised Zodiacal sign of the Sun on March 25th, that is to say, Aries or the Lamb of El, or Elias (St. John I, 29). On Thebet 14th, or December 25th, or nine months from Nisau 14th (March 25), Jesus was born; or six months after John the Baptist. In Greek and Welsh Jesus is called the Son of the Man, and Jupiter was by the Greeks depicted as a Man with Ram's two horns, one on each side of his temples. St. John's Gospel, 3, 13.

According to the old and incorrect astronomy of Egypt and the Roman Empire, adopted for the latter by Julius Cæsar, B.C., at the instigation of Sosigenes of Alexandria, daylight began to decrease on June 25th, or Thammuz 14th, and to increase on December 25th, or Thebet 14th. The writer of St. John's Gospel, referring to the birth of John the Baptist on June 25th, when daylight begins to decrease, and the birth of Jesus on December 25th, when daylight begins to increase, puts the following words into the mouth of the said John in reference to himself and Jesus: "He must increase and I decrease." (St. John's Gospel, iii, 30.) Tammuz is the personified Sun in Syria as old on June 25th, and he was represented as crucified on the cross described on June 25th by the line of the Tropic of the Crab crossing the line of the Meridian. This is alluded to by Ezekiel v,ii, 14, "Then he brought me to the door of the Gate of the Lord's house, which was toward the north; and behold, and there sat women, weeping for Tammuz." The death of old Tammuz (Sun) was succeeded by the birth of a young Tammuz, and the birth of John the Baptist is made to correspond with that birth. The anniversary of the birth of Jesus would be on December 25th, and he would attain the 30th year of his age on that date. At the same time John the Baptist would be thirty years and six months old, being thirty on the previous June 25th.

No Cohen, or a descendant of Aaron, could be elected high priest under thirty years of age, but was eligible at any age after his thirtieth. The high priesthood of the Jews represented the God Pan, and the He Goat and the Holy White Kirtle (Lev. xvi, 4) were the two symbols of Pan as He Goat and a Holy God. Jacob received his appointment as adopted son of Pan, at Pan-El, in the Woods as a place rendered by translators both "Penuel" and "Peniel" in the English translation. Gen. 32, 24 to 31. Observe, he is represented as a Man, who roamed the wilds at night, and feared the light of day.

It will be observed that the junction of the He Goat part of Pan with the human part of the figure is awkward, and that in consequence Pan was supposed to be always halting in his pedal movements, and inclined to assume the stooping attitude natural to the goat.

Thus, the God Pan inflicted his own infirmity of the "thigh" upon Jacob And as he (Jacob, to whom "the Man" gave the Phoenician name of Kronos, namely Israel) passed over Peniel, the Sun rose upon him, and he halted upon his thigh."

Now Jesus was the son of the masculine emanation of the two-fold Word. John the Baptist was Pan himself become incarnate to annoint and proclaim Jesus high priesthood instead of the He Goat and Kirtle, but Pan made use of the Cohen family, to whom Elizabeth and Zacharias belonged, as the instruments of his own incarnation (St. Luke I, 1-8.) Zachariah was of the Eighth course of the Cohens, or descendants of Aaron, and his course was called Abijah, or My Father is IA, without the O. I Chronicles, 24, 10. (Luke I, 5.) Thus Zacharias transmitted the essence of him called Abijah, and he was but the passive agent, being old like Abraham, for the incarnation of Pan himself as the eighth, Joshua is the Ninth, which name signifies, "The Saviour." Thus the representative line of priests was to stop in the Eighth, and the personified sun himself was to appear on earth, and is actually named in the old list Jeshua, Joshua, or Jesus, as the Ninth. The Ninth is the Zodiacal sign of the He goat on Dec. 25th. This is the reason why Jesus received that name. Pan-El met Jesus at the time of life when, according to the law, he could be elected High Priest, and by conveying him by boat from "beyond Jordan," that is to say from the Moab side to the Canaan side of the Jordan, ordained him to be for ever his High Priest, instead of any one of the Cohen family. The place was called

Bethania, i.e., Booth of the Boat, down to the time of Origen, named in the Greek, N-T- Vide John's Gospel I, 28. Jesus was King by birth.

Thus Jesus was the Son of the Word as Father Iu, as regards his body, and the Son of the Holy Spirit as regards his soul, and the High Priest** by the election of Pan himself as John, otherwise a Boat called Dolphin, whose emblem was a Rocking-Stone, as rocking on the sea, river, or lake, for the emblem was shown on all waters where Ceridwen was represented, and whose emblem was everywhere where the solar drama was performed.* Thus Jesus was King as the descendant of the Royal Judah, whose station as the Zodiacal Sun in the Lamb Sign of Jupiter, is indicated by being placed due east. (Numbers, 2, 3.) As High Priest, his second birth or apotheosis, is indicated by being "born again" from the Boat on December 25th; the same day of the year as his natural birth, or first birth, took place † When his apotheosis as High Priest and King took place, the Word himself, in his two-fold natures, descended into his head in the semblance of a dove. As explained elsewhere, Jesus, like Bacchus (Sun), was two mothered, viz., Mary, as Semele, the mother of his body, and Jupiter as his father; the Arech, Ark, or Boat, that of his high priesthood. He was two mothered like Moses, as king, whose foster mother, was Miriam, and his mother as High Priest, was the Ark of Bulrushes (Thebet), and the daughter of Pharaoh is associated with it as the genius of the Thebet or Ark in the flags of the Nile, instead of representing by it, as the Druids did, the great Mother Spirit as Cybele, otherwise Isis I, and known by other names as Queen of Heaven, a Spirit.

---

*And the Rocking Stone on mountains was the emblem of the Boat (Thebet) on the Sea. The Church as Nave is its present emblem.

**In each instance, it is to be understood Jesus was not High Priest, but the High Priesthood incarnate, for it was the duty of the High Priest to slay the High Priesthood.

†Moses as King, and Elijah, or Eli IAO (My God IAO), or John the Baptist, as Pan and Dove, met Jesus on the Mount of Transfiguration. Jesus had two birth: The first as King, born of the Virgin Mary; and the second as the High Priesthood from the Dolphin—Boat of Oannes, or Man and Fish called "Spirit," because the

The war correspondent of the London "Daily Chronicle," whose letter from Egypt appeared in that journal on February 14th, 1898, stumbled, apparently unconsciously, upon the import of the Crescent Moon in the religious systems of Egypt and Britain, namely, that it was the image of the mystic boat of the Spiritual Mother of the Sun, known by many titles, into which she received him in the evening, and from which he ascended as a star in the morning. This is what the said observer wrote:

WADY HALFA, January 25th, 1898.

"General Gatacre and the senior officers embarked on Saturday at Assouan at sunset, the beginning of Ramadan, the great fast of Islam, corresponding to our Lent; and the tiny crescent of the new moon was seen in the south-western sky riding among the flecking clouds like a silver boat in a green sea by raised reefs of golden sand."

Ark of Bulrushes (Thebet) from the River Nile.—Calmet.

The description of the personal appearance of John the Baptist is intended to identify him with Pan. Like Pan and Jacob, he was peculiar about his loins, and his wild habits made it necessary to wear a cloak like a camel's hide. And he "cried in the Wilderness," like Pan was said to do, and his cries in the woods near the temple of Delphi so terrified the Gauls, or Britons, that they bolted in terror. Hence our word, "Panic." His food was wild beans of the desert, called Locusts, Caro—beans—and honey. Mat. 3, 4. Mark I, 6.

Boat represented the spirit Mother : "So also Christ glorified not himself to be made an High Priest; but he that said unto Him, 'Thou art my son, to-day have I begotten thee.'"—Heb. 5,5. : Mat. 3, 17;

Pan El.— Genesis 32, 22–32. His visage was so marred more than
any man, and his form more than the Sons of Men. . . He hath
no form nor comeliness; and when we see him there is no beauty
that we should desire him.—Isaiah 52, 14 ; 53, 2.—Montfaucon.

Mat. 19, 28; John 8, 54. It is the Christ, and not Jesus, who says
this in the last verse. David, in Ps. 2, 7, alludes to the Horn which
made him King only. The Divine Christ conveyed the Chrisma
into the Womb of Mary (Semele), and Jesus was the result. The
"glorification" (Paean) of Jesus Christ as the new High Priest took
place on the Mount of Transfiguration. Mat. 17, 2; Mark 9, 2.
Moses and Pan (Elijah) assisted at the consecration. The time
between his apotheosis, by being "born again" of the Queen of
Heaven, and his consecration is to be regarded as a period of probation as to fitness for the office. He was then divinely invested with
the sacerdotal White Robe of Druidism, the Order of which Melchise-
dech was Priest and King.

JOHN
THE BAPTIST.
DESCENDANT
OF
AARON.

"For this is he that was spoken of by the prophet Isaiah, saying,
The voice of one crying in the wilderness, Prepare ye the ways of
the Lord, make his paths straight. And the same John had his
raiment of camel's hair, and a skin girdle about his loins; and
his meat was locust beans and wild honey.—St. Mathew iii, 3 & 4
He was the reincarnation of Elijah the Thishbite.—Malachi iv,
5; Mat. xi, 14; Mat. xvii, 3. In the last named verse, we see
John, as Elijah on the Mount of Transfiguration with Moses.
Aaron was the instrument of Saturn and was represented by
Caiaphas the high priest. As Supernatural Messenger of the
Angel of the Covenant, the God Pan "crying in the Wilderness,"
became man by a Divine incarnation, and he was, therefore,
"much more than a prophet."—Luke vii, 21 ; Mal. iii, 1 Luke 1.

It will be borne in mind that all "Gods," or Goodes, of the nations of antiquity, were personifications of the Aeons, or attributes of the Word, manifested through the Sun's corporeal body passing through each sign or mark of the Zodiac, and before the invention of the Zodiac, through the seven planetary spheres whose signs are the names of the planets, during the year, beginning with the sphere of the Sun on June 25th, the longest day, and ending with the station of the Sun in the sphere of the planet Saturn on December 25th. The middle sphere, that of Mercury, March 25th, is sacred to both the sun and the earth, personified as Venus. Hence in Welsh Friday is called Gwen-Ner, Venus and Nereus or Strength. As explained elsewhere, Venus or Gwen, Holiness in Welsh, is the sister of the Sun; and the Greeks, and probably the Egyptians, invented another feminine character called Semele, to occupy the station of Venus, as the annual mother of the Sun's body under the name Bacchus. This became necessary owing to the departure of the nations from the primitive teaching that the Sun's annual new body was Divinely contributed from the protoplasm in the Ark, Thebet, of the Great Mother, between sunset of December 25th, the date the old Sun's body was supposed to die under the murderous hands of Black Wings (Pluto), and the Sun's reappearance on the morning of the 27th as a Crowned Babe (Mabyn), constructed by the Great Mother out of the protoplasm in the said Ark, by the co-operation of the fertilising influence of the seminal principle of the Word, called Pater Iu, or Jupiter, which had, as was supposed, escaped from the wreck of the old Sun into the Ark, or Thebet, at sunset on Dec. 25th. In Greek mythology it is Semele's ovum, "seed of the woman," which is fertilised by Jupiter, called also the Holy Ghost by St. Mathew i, 18, and by St. Luke i, 35, on March 25th, as explained elsewhere. Here Semele is described as the Mother of the Sun's body, instead of the Druidic Cariadwen, or Holy Love, by the agency of the Sacred Barge, whose image was the moon six days old, and ten days old in Egypt, etc. In the system of holy days of the Roman Empire, borrowed chiefly from Egypt through Greece and Phoenicia, we find the dates of the said holy days indicating still the dislocation of the Druidic system caused by the introduction of Semele into it. Thinkers have always been puzzled as to Matthew's and Luke's reason for stating that the Holy Ghost, and not the father, was the parent of Jesus. The reason is that the Dove, or the Word, was the emblem of both Holy Ghost, and the Father. The Dove emblem was called also Alawn, or Full A (Wings). Sometimes the sun of March 25th is called Mercury and sometimes the Ram of the Zodias*.

On March 25th the Roman Empire observed the Hilaria, in honour of the Mother of the Sun (Bacchus), that is to say, when Semele annually conceived by the act of Pater Iu—Vernal Equinox. Aug. 21 a holy day was observed in honour of the Great Mysteries. On September 25th a holy day was observed in honour of Venus and Saturn, who is placed in the room of Nereus of the Druids— Autumnal Equinox. We see here a very striking feature, viz., old Saturn associated with young Venus, like old Joseph associated with young Mary. In the first place, Venus is transferred to September 25th from March 25th, to make room for Semele in the last mentioned date; and Saturn is transferred from December 25th to September 25th, to make room for Pluto on December 25th; the Roman triad being Neptune, June 25th; Jupiter, March 25th; and Pluto, December 25th. The Jews place Saturn as both the Creator and Destroyer on September 21st—25th, or Tishri 10th and 14th, and represent Saturn under the names Israel, Aran, or Aaron, and and slaying Pan (Goat), his son. Aran is a Druidic title of the Sun on December 25th, who is the Phœnician Kronos (Time) as shown in Cory's Ancient Fragments, p. 21.

September 27th was observed in honour of Venus as a mother. Here it appears Venus as a mother fills the character of Ceres, as the mother of the fruits of the earth. December 25th, 26th, and 27th, three days in honour of Phœbus (Sun), and on the morning of

---

*This is the reason why sometimes Venus is said to be the wife of Mercury, with a full scrotum, and sometimes the wife of the Ram of Jupiter.—"The Bride of the Lamb."

the 27th the Dolphin—Delphus—Womb of the Mother of the Babe Sun—rises in the morning. It will be recollected a Dolphin was an Oriental symbol of the crescent-shaped Boat of the Druids. It will be seen that these days in the Christian system are transferred to March 25th, 26th, and 27th, or Nisan 14th, 15th, 16th lunar, and the sepulchre of Christ, with a Great Stone over it, is the emblem of the Dolphin Mother of Phoebus. Originally, the emblem was a Rocking Stone, called Cybele by the Greeks, and wife of Saturn. Here the old Savage is placed as the Almighty.

The Babe Son. Dolphin substituted for Thebet or Ark—Mother of the said Babe. Pine Tree whose cones symbolised Male testes. A Phoenician form of the Druidic name Coracle.—Montfaucon.

The Mother of the Sun being a Spirit was supposed to use a material Boat for her purpose. But some nations substituted for the boat as an emblem, the Symbol of a whale or Dolphin.

THE INEFFABLE NAME.

"My Name is in Him."—Ex. 23, 21.

In the solitary woods which still abound in the North, the primitive Scandinavian bent ın prayer, fixed his thoughts upon the abstracted essence of Divinity his creed taught him to adore. In these forests, "He seemed to reign in silence, and to make himself felt by the respect which He inspired. To attribute a form to the Deity would have been profanity among the Scandinavians, and in this point they much resembled the Persians and Ninevites and Jews. . . They represent him as a Winged Being in a Circle.— "Ancient Cities of the World," p. 367, by Routledge and Sons, Ludgate Hill. "I have hallowed this house which thou (Solomon) hast built, to put My Name there forever, and Mine eyes and My Heart shall be there perpetually." I. Kings, 9, 3.

This is the Name which the Jews throughout the world still believe and say the Lord Jesus purloined away in his thigh from the Temple, and by it performed miracles, but the evangelist say that it descended on the head of Jesus at his Baptism, or his rising from the Boat of Pan-John. It was long believed the infant Bacchus was carried away in the Yarech (thigh) of Jupiter. It is now known the Greek word is Arech (Ark). Jesus* received it as a \|/ Name in the Delphus, Ark of John, symbolising the Womb (Delphos) of the Queen of Heaven.

It appears that the sign within the Solar Circle is the Sacred Dove as the symbol of the Ineffable Name, or Word, of the Creator. It is still most sacred among at least half of mankind. It is called Tri Sul—a Welsh name—throughout India, and is inscribed with chalk on the forehead, the middle line being red, "And they shall see His face, and his NAME shall be in their foreheads." Rev. 22, 4. In the Diadem of Wales it is the plumes of three feathers, and the words Ich Dien are Eich Dyn, or your Virile Power. As the Government mark of Great Britain it is called the Broad Arrow. It is, including the sun's circle, represented by the head and face of the Prince of Wales, IAO, hieroglyphically rendered. Cynun is a title of the Sun on

---

*As the incarnate Sun.

each June 25th, and we say Cain is the sun bearing this title. When Cain was born, Eve (Venus) his mother, is represented as saying, "I uave had a man who is the IAO," meaning the sun with the Winged Word or Name in his head. Kanitti ish ith IAO—Genesis 6, 1. The correct translation is, "I have gotten a Man who is IAO." The sign is called Nod Cyvrin, or Secret Mark, in the Welsh language. Cain is represented as having had placed upon him a Mark of such great sanctity that no one would dare touch him. He thus bore the sacred mark of the British Government. Cain is said to have gone to the Land of Nod, or the Holy Mark. Cain is described as the first of three; and so is Japheth, the father of Gomer, of the Isles of the Gentiles. — Genesis x., 5. As we explain elsewhere in this work, the O is the sign of the Sun itself hieroglyphically. The I and the A are the sign $\vee$, a symbol set forth in Egypt by the Dove under a pair of wings astride the back of the Solar Bull (Taurus) Apis (65). In all the old Welsh inscriptions on carved stones, as the monumental stone on Margam Mountain, Glam., the A is always rendered upside down. It appears that the horizontal stroke was used to distinguish it from V.

Again, the head of Jesus was the same as O, and the Dove was the $\vee$ The Jews use the letter Shin on the Phylactery on the forehead to symbolise it. The head of each Jew is still the symbol of the Sun, with the Druidic symbol of the ineffable sign, $\vee$, upon the forehead as the intellectual part. It will thus be seen what was the nature of the sacred mark on Cain as his defender or protector. It is highly interesting to find the Welsh Nod (mark) associated with Cain, and it proves conclusively that the writer of Genesis was familiar with the language of the British Druids. In Welsh Nod still signifies a sign. Nodi is the Welsh verb to sign consent or assent as to Nod in English.

We read as follows of the Sun : "The First Begotten, the Giant, was the first who made a sign to be an emblem of the first vocalization that was ever heard, namely, the Voice of God—that is to say, Duw (Coelus), pronounced His name $\vee$ and simultaneously with the music (of the Name) all the worlds and those things relating to them, and the Universe, leaped together with a tremendously loud pealing, joyous vociferation. And the song was the earliest ever heard, and its musical sound permeated to everywhere where Duw and his existences are," etc. " Baadism," p. 38. The Words in Job 38, 4, are, it appears, based on the above sublime conception of the unfolding by the Almighty, by the agency of His Word, of the Beauties of Creation, and the beaming forth of the light of the Sun, the first time through the primeval darkness.

IAO is then the Monogram imitated by IHS, and signifying the Word and the Sun. It is, too, the Shemitic Awful Name of God, rendered "Jehovàh" in our translation, both English and Welsh. This, we repeat, is the name which the Jews universally believe and declare Jesus of Nazareth purloined from the temple of Jerusalem, and that he carried it away concealed in his thigh, and that it was by the instrumentality of this miraculous Name, he performed miracles. It is, too, the Arrow which Abaris, we believe, of Bath, exhibited at the Olympic games to Pythagoras.

In the foregoing pages we have solved the IAO mystery, which has puzzled the profoundest scholars of many countries, from the earliest ages of authentic history. We have shown that I and A are the dispersed symbols of \|/ (Dove), and that the O is one Sun symbol containing it.

It is impossible to overestimate the importance of the facts revealed in the foregoing lines. The so-called "cloven tongues" which are alluded to in the singular number, was the V or Holy Wings, the A-Wen, or Holy Pair of Wings, the Druidic symbol cf the Holy Spirit as the Wings of \|/ As the middle stroke "the Rock," an emblem of the Phallus, representing the body of the Dove, implied by the Stone Column, was the Christ himself as the symbol of the seminal principle, or Father, in the compound emblem.— I. Cor. 10, 4. Acts 2.

On the Day of Pentecost, Peter represented this "Rock," or Stone Pillar, which, as the symbol of the seminal principle of the two-fold Word, was the same emblem as the Rod of God in the hand of Moses, while the rushing wings from on high implied the Holy Spirit, and identical with the fire of the Burning Bush, and afterwards implied by the Shechinah as the Wings of the Unicorn. Ps. 92, 10, 14, 15.

The Pentecost of the Bible is the Sulgwyn, Whit-Sunday, or White Sun Day of the English. It was always observed on June 25th or 21st, by the Druids. But the Jews were guided in its observance by the stations of the moon, and therefore irregularly.

BISHOP COLENSO ON THE NAME IAO (JEHOVAH).

In the following quotations we have a concise scholarly summary of the views of the ancient scholars on the subject of the monogram IAO. This will appear as if the Druids of Britain either during their earlier sojourn in the East, strictly preserved the secret among their own order, or that the secret had gone to Phoenicia, Egypt, Persia, and other Oriental countries, from Britain in an imperfect form. It will be seen in the following references to "four" forms in the various representations of the Holy Name. Those "four" are the three strokes and one circle. This proves that the Orientals only possessed a superficial knowledge of the outward form, and did not possess a correct knowledge of its esoteric meaning. But it seems that the compilers of the New Testament narrative describing the descent of the \|/ on, and into, the O (Head) of Jesus, were in full possession of the profound secret as to the meaning of the Monogram IAO.

THE GREAT HIEROGLYPHICS.

After the descent of \|/ into his head, Jesus having become also Christ, repeatedly said when he himself was speaking, it was not his individual self that spoke, but the Father in him, and it is said he returned to his own country in the power of the Spirit. The Father and the Spirit were the \|/ which had descended into the O (Jesus's head) as the Head of the Sun of Righteousness, or Shemesh, with healing in his wings or rays. The wings symbolised the A Wen, or Holy Spirit.

(Translated and abridged by Bishop Colenzo, from Movers's 'Phonizie," chap. xix, p. 539-558).

(1). The mysterious Being to whom we have already referred at different times, states his lordship, belongs to the Phoenician Religion; and His Name is indicated as Phoenician by the Ancients themselves, in the passage quoted below from Johannes Lydus and Cederenus.

(2) We shall first, however, lay at the base of our enquiry the important extract from Macrobius' "Saturn," I, 18, which we here produce in the proper connection. Orpheus manifestly declares the Sun to be Dionysos in the following verse:—

"One Zeus, one Aides, one Helios, one Dionysos."

"The authority of this verse rests upon an oracle of the Clarian Apollo, in which is another name also of the Sun, who in those same sacred lines is called IAO. For the Clarian Apollo having been consulted as to which of the Gods was to be considered to be the one who is called IAO, pronounced thus:

It is right that those knowing should hide the ineffable orgies, for in a little deceit there is prudence and an adroit mind. Explain that IAO is the most High God of all—in winter Aides—"Hades, Saturn, Typhon, Pluto, Dis, Mars, Siva, Ahriman, Black Wings (A Ddu)—and Zeus (Jupiter), in commencing spring (March 25th), "and Helios in summer" (June 25th), and at the end of autumn (September 25th) "tender IAO." Here the material Sun's three personifications, viz., on March 25th, June 25th, and December 25th, are mistaken for IAO.

It may be interpolated further that the priest who spoke as the Clarian Apollo, is incorrect in the last, and is guilty of the same error as the Hebrews, indicated by ending the Civil year the Period the Annual Atonement ended, namely directly before the commencement of the Feast of Tabernacles, namely, at Sunset on Tishri 13, counting night before the day, as the beginning of the 14th, which is September 25th old style*.

In correct Druidism, the Vernal Equinox, sacred to Zeus, was called Hu Dad Eilir (Jupiter), or Father Hu, the Renovator, and the Autumnal Equinox—March 25th and September 25th respectively — to Ceres, who is Virgo in her character of Mother Earth, and called Tynghedwen, or Holy Fortune. Observe the Sun on March 25th is in the First Point of the Ram (Aries), and on September 25th in the sign Virgo, and both due east, hence the east point is called in Welsh Dwyrain, or Two Parents. In Druidism the sun in winter is Hero (Gwron), and, as Arthur, he fights Aides, the evil spirit (Black Wings), whose symbols are the Red Dragon (Rev. xii, 3), Black Wings, Saturn, etc. The error sprang in Egypt, where to Typhon was given the third position in the Triad, Abel the third in the Jewish Triad signifies Ab and El, or old sun of the previous year, the Father of Helios as a Mabyn or Babe Sun, on December 27th, or the next, that is to say, the third which is the Sun as Old at the end of the Solar year, is the Father of the young sun of the next. But the Jews, while still adhering to the name of Father of El as to the third, represent him as killed by Helios (Cain, Osiris), and immediately proceed to represent Adam (Ad Hama), the old sun of a still earlier year, as the Father of Set, which is rendered Seth in our translation.

Set, as explained elsewhere, is an Egyptian title of Typhon,

*Practically the Civil Year commences on Tishri 1st, but the shape of the moon ten days old signalled the actual ecclesiastical beginning of the civil year.

Satan, or Black Wings. Then the Jews represent Seth or Typhon (Arabic for Deluge, and called Boar, Bore, in Phoenician), as being the ancestor of their Holy Nation, and Saturn is placed as the Most High God, and the Father of IAO. (The Word and Sun, or \|/ and O); and that he was constantly craving for the blood of Helios as Ram, Jupiter's Sign, and Pan (He Goat), the Sun signs on March 25th and December 25th respectively; but in the Jewish system, the latter on September 21 (Tishri 10th, Lunar Year). The interval betwen the tenth evening and the fourteenth evening, when the Feast of Tabernacles commenced, is unaccounted for. Probably the Saturn High Priest (Israel), carrying upon his shoulders the high priesthood representing the God Pan, lodged during the interval in the symbolical grave below the stone of the foundation, below the floor of the Holy of Holies. Modern Jews cannot account for the cessation of ceremony between the evening of the 10th and the evening of the 14th each before the day.

It appears the High Priest, personally, was the Minister of Saturn, and the He Goat and the White Linen Kirtle which the High Priest donned for the occasion, symbolised the impersonal High Priesthood, representing the God Pan—Half Man and Half He Goat. Observe the adroit way the names Israel and Pan El are handled in Genesis 32, 24, to 32, Jesus' body represented the high priesthood, and he left the white linen stained with his blood behind him in his grave, as a symbol discarded, and left behind on earth, and his own radiant glorified body was the high priesthood itself.. 1 Leviticus xvi.

In another Egyptian Triad we find Osiris, Horus, and Isis ii (Venus as Ceres), and the Church symbolised the three as Joseph, the Infant Jesus with the sacred Dove over his head, and the Virgin Mary. The God Pan in an Egyptian illustration is shown stretching forth a wreath to Isis II.

EGYPT'S HOLY FAMILY.

We now proceed with Bishop Colenso's quotation: "The meaning of the Oracle, the interpretation of the Deity, and the Name according to which IAO signifies Father Bacchus" (Gwyion Bach), "and the Sun" (Taliesun), "has been worked out by Cornelius Labeo, in a book entitled, 'Concerning the Oracle of the Clarian Apollo.'" We must here interpolate that Cornelius Labeo also is in error. By Bacchus and Apollo are meant the O, symbol of the sun's material frame, and I.V., the first the Father, and the last rendered A, or Wings, is the Word as the Father and the Holy Spirit in the Sun, under all its various titles. Gwyion Bach is heat alone; Taliesun absorbed it, and both Light and Heat became united as one in the Sun's luminous body.

(3) We again return to the quotation: "Jamlichus, in his work "De Mysteriis," speaks repeatedly of such mysterious (Egyptian or Chaldean) divine names. In reply to Porphyry he remarks that they were not names without meaning, the signification of some, he

says, (vii, 4), had been imparted by the Gods themselves, as in fact the Egyptian Deity, Thoth" (Tad), "had, according to Plutarch, composed a book about them; that others were too holy for their meaning to be made known. Those, however, which could be understood by men gave explanation about the might and order in rank of the Gods, and through them, the soul was led up to the Deity. Jamlichus adds yet further, that there was another mysterious reason why the secret names of the Gods were Assyrian, Chaldean, or Egyptian. The Assyrians and Egyptians were holy nations, and their language was a holy language—the language of the Gods; and it is fitting that men should also address the Gods in a language known to them." The Pentateuch by Bishop Colenso, Vol. V, ps. 305, 306, 307. Appendix 3, Book of Genesis.

Then we have the following further on in the same Appendix 3 : "Next we see from the Oracle of Apollo, IAO was the Most High God of all, and was in reality the Sun-Deity, in a four-fold signification." We know, on the contrary, he was the Word in the Sun, as Two Wings, one body, and the Circle O. Further, he is said to be Adonis, and "Adonis was actually named in Byblus and in Lebanon (Phoenicia and Country of Palestine)," the Most High God, exactly as here IAO is styled in the oracle." Last of all we quote the following as confirmation of all we have said.

"Then Sanchoniathon (Phoenician Historian), names the God who in Byblus was called the Most Great of the Gods, Agrueros, whose symbol he says,"was carried about upon a wagon drawn by oxen, and in his usual manner he ascribes to him the invention of four courts to houses,or the use of caves." This is exactly the same ceremony as the Druidic one of drawing a shrine containing the Sacred Beaver (1) (Avanc) in it to land from the sea, or lake, as Sun emblem. And the other ceremony of carrying an Ark with a Wren in it on a bier on St. Stephen's Day, December 26th, both at St. David's Head and in the Isle of Man. In Byblus and Egypt it is clear

---

(1). Because amphibious as the Sun was supposed to be, we have the Beaver, Wren, and Dove successively symbols of the Sun's Divinity.

the inhabitants mistook the Word and the Circle for the Most High
Himself. And the three personifications of the sun himself as three
other gods. The Shrine, or Ark, in each instance, was the symbol
of the Sacred Boat (the Church) of the Goddess Cariadwen, Mother
of the Sun, and the protectress of the Word after his escape on the
destruction of the Old Sun's body at sunset on every December
25th, but on Tishri 10th, Day of Atonement, or September 21st,
among modern Jews.

THE HIEROGLYPHICS OF THE INEFFABLE NAME.

THE SACRED SYMBOL \|/ AND O.

SIGNS AND ALPHABETICAL MODES IN REPRODUCING IT.

We find the honest and truthful Ancient Bards of Wales, after
losing the real meaning of the Sacred Sign of the Holy Name, or
Word, of the Creator, Celu, still clinging to certain letters in combination, as containing some Ecclesiastical secret of great sanctity.
This is said in the following curious lines—

"To Pan-ion (we sing) a canonical song, as it is called;
Clearly we see he is on our side;
We have him, O.I. and W. He is OIW always to every soul."—
The Monk Bard, John, of Kent Church. 1380 to 1420.

The most familiar name of God in the Welsh language is Duw,
the English sound being given to the U, and the Wl (oo) is now silent.
We were at first inclined to believe the initial O, in O.I.W.,
was the error of some transcriber, but we find the O. is a letter used
mystically by several other Ancient Bards, and that to them the
OIW was another mystical cognomen consisting of three hieroglyphics. Both Taliesun ab Iolo, and Ab Ithel, in recent times, have

avoided giving in their translations of the above extraordinary
verse the name Pan Ion, which signifies the Sun on December 25th
(21) in the Sign of the He Goat, and Iona, the Sacred Dove. We
have the same form of hieroglyphical compound name in "Yr Awdl
Vrauth," as follows :

> Him Pan Ion made,
> In the Land of Ebron Vale ;
> With his two blessed hands,
> In the fair form of Adda.

This should be A.Ddov, or Peaceful, the A being a pair of wings,
symbols of the Holy Spirit, or Psyche.   This Addov, all recent Welsh
writers translate Adam in the Welsh translation.

Like all other former writers, Nash, in his "Taliesin," has stupid-
ly supposed the "Adda" (A.Ddov) of the Welsh mystical poems, is
the scriptural Adam.   It does not appear to have occurred to their
minds, that the Welsh "Adda," or correctly, A-Ddov, differed entirely from the Scriptural Adam, a man, as seems likely enough ;
unless Adam is really the Persian Ad Hama, or the Lord Sun,
Dominus Sol, who has been since adopted by the Hebrews as
the first man.   It never occurred to them that the initial A is really
the hieroglyphic denoting the wings of the Sacred Dove, as the
spread-out rays of the Sun as Chemosh with healing in his wings.

It appears that the name Eb-bron is the Scriptural Hebron and that
Eb-bron, or the young of the Breast, is the original form of the name.
But former writers had not the advantage of particulars about
Colonel Conder's discoveries of hundreds of Druidic remains, such as
Cromleachs, Maenhirs, and Dolmaens, in Palestine, and especially on
the East of the Jordan near the Dead Sea.   But the story of Abra-
ham and the three Adonai in the Sacred Oak Grove of Mamre, or
Mem Ra (the Word of Ra or Rhi), near the Ancient City of Eb-bron,
ought to have suggested to them Druidic associations.

The following prove conclusively that the Ancient Bards looked
upon OIO, DIV, and OIW, as different names of God from Duw—

OIO Dduw; o Waedd Hu Gorn:
Pa beth yw y cyfryw Gorn?
OIO God, of the blast of the Hu Horn.
What is that horn?
O.I. and W. and a Lamb. (2).

Many other instances could be adduced, to prove that the old Bards deemed the Bardic name in question differed from Duw, the present Christian form of a name of God used in the Welsh Churches. But the last illustration seems to indicate that they associate OIW with Jupiter Amen, whose symbol was the Sun in Aries (Ram), March 25th, and that Duw came to be regarded by the Christian Druids as Coelus (Celu) himself. This seems to prove the Druids did not, until the Romans came to Britain, commit to writing their religious tenets.

The hieroglyphic \|/ was at first rendered by letters as follows :—OAI, OIV, and now OIW. It is well known that W is a later letter, and that it is made up of two V's. Formerly V had the sounds of both long O and U, and that, at present, W. has the sound of the English oo. We can see that the original form of the symbol, adopted in the transition from the mere Sign Symbol to the Alphabetical, was OIV. The I and the V, are dispersed, the middle vertical bar being used as I. This bar signifies the body of the sacred dove or Wren which, as substance, was the Bardic symbol of the Seminal Element in the Word of Coelus (Celu). The V sign is the two wings of the Sacred Dove, and the pair was the Symbol of the Holy Spirit of the same Word, or Name, or the Tender, Sweet, Melodious Voice of the Creator. In the earliest hieroglyphic emblems, the combined \|/ and O were in a circle.

That O is the emblem of the Sun itself with the Word as Father and the Holy Spirit, in the Circle of the Sun.

---

(2) Bardism, pages 20 and 21.

The Ram is the Sign of the Sun in the Zodiacal Sign of the Ram on March 25th with DIW (Father, Holy Spirit, and Sun) hieroglyphically rendered together, only that the W has been evolved out of the long o or the oo.

But let not the reader suppose the Father in the Sun is the Most High, nor that the Holy Spirit in the Sun is the Most High. They are the Seminal principle—the Logos Spermaticos—in the Word symbolised by the letter I; and the wings are the emblem of the other principle, namely the Spiritual one, in the two-fold composition of the Word in the Sun. In the East the alphabetical form the hold of a ship ; and the Piilar of Poaz, the Membrum Virile.— now clear that the name Iu Pater (Jupiter) is a title of the Seminal Word exercising, as Father, his fertilising influence through Aries (Ram), in March and April, beginning on Lady Day. (1). We know that it is mystically taught that the Sun is the Son of the Seminal Word, and that Jupiter (Iu Father) is represented calling to the Sun (Bacchus) in battle, "IVO." (2).

We are now met with the difficulty as to how the Druids came to transpose the symbol O from the last to the first initial position? It seems that at the beginning they, coming from the East, wrote like the Phoenicians, Hebrews, Egyptians, etc., did, from right to left, and that they wrote the O first as they had formerly done in writing OAI beginning with the I; the present D, instead of O came probably from the example of the Romans in writing Deus and Dios. This confusion is made evident enough in p. 67 of "Bardism," where it is stated it was written OIO in the time of Taliesun, a term signifying the Druidic period. In fact, the figure O placed first and last here is the emblem of the Sun's Orb, and was the emblem of the head (Pen-y-Beirdd) of the Chief Druid, who, as the incarnate Sun or Hesus, bore likewise the name Taliesun's Head. In the foregoing we find the O lingering in its original position, after the same emblem had been transposed to the first position of the new mode of writing from left to right. In the same page of Bardism, we are told OIU was a later form than OIO, and it is clear the OIV, OIW, DIW, and DUW, mark the gradual progress or stages of the error from OAI, the original departure

---

(1). Jesus was begotten by the Christos on Lady Day, March 25th, and born nine months later, on December 25th.

(2). Bell's Pantheon 'Bacchus."

from the sign of ⑂ and O, or IVO, or OVI, in the East. The A was anciently in the form V, and the cross bar to distinguish it as A.

The Phoenicians had it in the form of OAI, and the Hebrews followed their example.

CHRISTENING, AND GODFATHER AND GODESSMOTHER.

In the Church of England at the present day Christening is used as a term for Baptism. But to Christen signifies in the first place to anoint, and in the second place to make into a Christian, or a follower of Christus, or the Anointed One. At the christening of a babe two sets of parents are represented, namely, the natural parents of the baby, and the Godfather and Godmother.

The so-called "God Mother" should be Goddess Mother. The Sun was supposed to be two-fathered and two-mothered. His body was supposed to be annually begotten by Jupiter, or Christos, or Father Iu, on the body of Nature, personified as Semele. Like Adam, he is, therefore, "of the Earth earthy." The Word was both Father and Holy Spirit, or Eros and Psyche, and in the descent of the two-fold Word, escaping from the wrecked body of the old sun of the year before, into the miraculous barge of the great Goddess Mother; Jupiter, otherwise Eros, otherwise Cupid, otherwise Christos, begot there from the primtiive protoplasm a new body for himself and the Holy Spirit, and the body was called the Babe Son, and the Holy Spirit at the same time begot souls from the feminine spirit of the great Goddess Mother, whose material emblem was the sacred barge whose emblem was the crescent moon ten days old in the East, and six days old among the Druids of Britain and France. In the history of Bacchus (Sun) after an interval of three months, his second birth takes place, from the Arech, Ark, or Barge, called Dolphin, hence John is Oannes, or Man and Fish. In the case of Jesus, thirty years elapsed between his birth from the Virgin and his birth from the Dolphin Barge of

John, as explained elsewhere. The interval of thirty years was in order to reach the time of life when he could by the law be invested with the high priesthood, according to the law of Moses.

The disciples of the Sun underwent rites of initiation. In the first place, the birth of the sun's body from Semele was ritually observed, and in the second place his birth from the Barge or Arech, Ark, called Navis, or Boat, hence the Nave of the Church. The matrix of Semele is called Fons (Fountain of Water), and the personality is the Goddess Mother, called "God Mother," emblem of her of which the Font is the matrix. The God Father is the emblem of Father Christos, the father of the sun's body. The babe is born again "from the water of the Fons," and is received by the priest as the spiritual Accoucheur. The babe is now consecrated with holy unction, as a royal child of the church, as well as the child of its natural parents. He is brought up in the nursery of the church, under the tutelage of his God Father, and his Goddess Mother who represents the font, his second mother. At the age of fourteen the child is no longer subject to the tutelage of the nursery of the Church, and he is now asked by the bishop, whom the God Father had also represented throughout, whether it is his wish to be enrolled among the citizens of heaven, and a fellow citizen with Christ? On answering in the affirmative, he is received into membership of the fraternity, and after certain rites have been performed by the bishop, he is enrolled among the saints. And he then takes his place in the Nave, Navis, or Sacred Ark, which conveys its passengers to the Land of the Blessed beyond the grave. A coffin is called Ark, or Navis, in Welsh, and signifies symbolically precisely the same thing as the body of the church. The journey of life is often called in Welsh "Mordaith bywyd," or the Voyage of Life. The coffin is decked with flowers as a ship, bound, symbolically, for a country of eternal summer bloom. The word Baptism is from a Syriac word denoting colouring, as making white or holy, hence the custom of dressing a babe in white at his christening.

THE HARP AS EMBLEM.

The harp symbol of the Druids, as the Symbolical Planetary Spheres instrument of the Sun, playing on seven strings, emblems of the lines of the Seven Spheres of the Seven Planets, his own voice being the great Octave, seems to me intended as follows:

The top beam is the symbol of the line of the Meridian, the vertical front pole, the line of the Tropic of the Crab, and the ascending bar in front of the player, the Eastern Side of the Din or Mount of the Assembly of the Druidic priests, singing or echoing praises in unison with the Music of the Word of God through the Sun*.

To this day, the harp is in Welsh called Ty Lun (Telyn), or the emblem of the House "not made with hands."

OLD SUN AND YOUNG SUN.

It appears the doctrine that the old sun of one year is the father of the young sun of the next—to us so exceedingly strange in the light of our present knowledge—is based on the doctrine that the Sun in the Sign of the Ram on March 25th, is the vehicle of Jupiter, or Father Iu, the seminal principle's "house," to employ an astrological term, and that then the Sun's tenant fertilises the ovum in young Semele, who thereby becomes the young mother of Bacchus, or the Sun's corporeal body, and that the Word, as Father and Holy Spirit, the two-fold Word, being the emanation of the Creator, enters the said body, and continues to occupy the Sun's body through all his stages until his violent death every year on the afternoon of December 25th.   Isaiah 14, 12.

*How beautiful on the Mountains (Mounds) are the feet of Him that bringeth glad tidings, that publisheth Peace (Heddwch).—Isaiah 52, 7.

At the time the old Sun perished and fell into the sea the said new body was already prepared in the Arech or Ark of the Mother Goddess, to again accommodate the escaped two-fold Word from the ruins of the old Sun, which had just perished like an old Phoenix. Many figures for the old Sun and the succeeding young Sun were employed. Forty hours, the Druids supposed, was the interval between the old and the new sun. And forty hours was the time between the death of the body of Jesus on March 25th, and his resurrection in a glorified body, or March 25th or Nisan 14th and 15th respectively. St. Augustine of Hippo states Jesus (i.e., Son of The Christ), was crucified on the anniversary of his incarnation, that is to say, on Lady Day, from which to December 25th, are nine months. The supernatural darkness recorded as having lasted from 12 o'clock till 3 o'clock (3.55) corresponds, we say, with the time of sunset on each December 25th, and the darkness implies the Sun's body being unable owing to his wounds and sufferings to emit the "light" of the "life" within him. St. John's Gospel I, 4. Thus Jesus and the Sun are represented as identical. But the sun does not set till 6.19 on March 25th. Thus we see that the time of sunset at the winter Solstice, and not the Vernal Equinox, was observed in the death of Jesus with the Christ within him since his apotheosis. Hebrews 5, 5. As pointed out elsewhere the Sun does not appear at all to those within the Arctic Circle on December 26th, which corresponds as to day of the month with Nisan 15th, or March 26th, when the body of the Sun of Righteousness lay in his stone grave, the symbol of the Ark of the Great Mother of all things, the consort of the Father of the Word, and whose Ark, Barge, Thebet, was the cave under the Rocking Stone, and the "Rock" of the Holy of Holies, and person ned Cybele, Ceubawl, or Canoe, of Druidism.

The Sun in the Ninth Sign of the Zodiac (December 25th) went by divers names. In Druidism he is Ara (Slow). At some period this name had the letter n (Aran) added to it, and in Hebrew it became Aroon, hence in our translation it became Aaron. In Druidism the sun of December 25th became also Gwydd Naw, or No, or the Ninth Presence; hence Noah. He became also Dwfn Wawl Moel Mud, Sombre Light Bald and Dumb. He is further called Pen or Pan (Chief), and he was called also Arthur and Taliesun in all periods of the year. His symbol was Caru (to love), corrupted to Carw : a stag or hind. In the Jewish system he is subordinate to Saturn, Set, or Typhon, who is mistaken for the Creator, the Coelus of the Druids, and Agnostos Theos of the Greeks. As the God of the Seventh Day of the week he is Saturn.

ROD OF GOD AS STONE PILLAR AND STAFF.

"And the Lord visited Sarah, as he had said, and the Lord did unto Sarah as he had spoken, and Sarah conceived and bare Abraham a son in his old age." Gen. 21—1. Then the generating power of the Lord which "did unto Sarah," and which caused her to conceive, is symbolised by a "Rock," that is to say, an Egyptian obelisk, alluded to as Petra, or Peter, in Deu. 32, 18, and in Isaiah 51, 1 and 2. The words "increased him," refer to Isaac, the son of him who visited Sarah and begot a son to Abraham "in his old age."

The same idea is found in Isaiah, where the Children of Israel are referred to as the offspring of the "horn" of the Unicorn*. Is. 34, 7. The "bullocks and the bulls" in the same passage, are poetical allusions to the cherubs, one on each side of the lid of the Ark of the Covenant. In Numbers 20, 8, we find Moses holding conversation with the Stone Pillar, as he had done before with the Voice of the Burning Bush. What the Rock said is given in Verse 12. The two-fold nature of the Word, as Rod and Shechinah, appears to be implied by striking the Stone Pillar twice.—Verse 11. In Deuteronomy 32, 30, 31, it is admitted the Nations had the "Rock," and their Rock had sold them. "For their Rock is not as our Rock, even our enemies judge." It is throughout, the Seminal element of

---

*Or of Shechinah. Both Moses and Isaiah describe the Jewish nation as the children of the Stone Pillar, which represented The Christ, or The Messiah.—Dieut. 32, 18 ; Isaiah li—1-2.

the Word, symbolised also by the Rod in the hand of Moses, alluded to under the figures Rock, Staff, Horn, Dove, etc. "My Rock— God," in Psalm 18, 2.

The same symbol of miraculous power is alluded to by Jacob, Gen. 32, 10; by the Prophet Elisha, 2 Kings, 4, 29; by David in Ps. 23, 4; I. Samuel, 2, 1 and 2. Hannah's song is a Phallic one, and it implies Samuel was a Divine child, lke Isaac. See also angel and staff, Judges 6, 21.

It will be understood the staff, or Pillar, symbolised all' the physical attributes of the Word, to create and to destroy. And Moses said, " . . . to-morrow I will stand on top of the hill with the Rod of God in mine hand." So Joshua (or Jesus) did as Moses had said unto him, and fought with Amalek. And Moses, Aaron, and Hur went up to the top of the hill. And it came to pass when Moses held up his hand" (with the Rod of God in it) "that Israel prevailed; and when he let down his hand, Amalek prevailed. But Moses's hands were heavy, and they took a stone and put it under him, and he sat thereon, and Aaron and Hur stayed up his hands.* The one on one side, and the other on the other side, and his hands were steady until the going down of the sun. And Joshua discomfited Amalek." Ex. 17, 9-13. Here Moses is represented seated on a Cromlech, the symbol held up by a tripod. His own arms, and the Rod of God described as a dove descending. It was anciently believed that the Word of the Creator adopted the Rod or Wand, or Staff in the hand of his representative in the Sanctuary on Earth, and transferred his might into it; in the same manner he did so with the Shepherd Rod of Moses in the midst of the sheep of Jethro. The magician's wand in modern times is a survival of the same thing. Observe Ps. 23, 4, where the Divine Rod and Staff are mentioned. The staff was in David's hand slaying Goliath. The LXX render it: "My Rod and Thy Staff," instead of "Thy Rod and Thy Staff." The Rod of Moses is called the Rod of God after the Divine wisdom entered it as a serpent..

---

*The "Stone" was intended, it appears, to imply a sacred Cromleaoh was used.

Be it observed, there are two rocks alluded to in the Bible, viz., the Rock Grn, or Cairn, in Zion called the Lapis Foundations or Stone of the Foundation, with the hollow sepulchre beneath it, as the hold of a ship; and the Pillar of Boaz, the Membrum Virile—Inman, Vol. I, p. 373, 154. Pillar Jackin is the same. I. Kings 7, 21; Ruth 3, All this chapter is based on the allegory of the Lingam and Yoni. Ruth seems to be Rhea, and Naomi to be the sacred shrine (Thebet), personified like Cybele, and called Naomi, which is in Hebrew Nym, or Fish and Water. The name of the letters in the spelling is Nun Ayin and Mem, Nain Mem.* Thus we find Rhea, or Ruth, is Semele, or Venus, the Dieni (Diana), and Gwen of the Druids. Nym, or Fish and Water, is the Sacred Barge (Thebet), and alluded to as "Water and the Spirit," the Spirit being the invisible consort of the Most High. She is represented by the Boat of the Mysteries, and referred to in the words "Except a man be born of Water and the Spirit, he cannot enter the Kingdom of God. That which is born of the flesh is flesh." That was his own birth from the Virgin Mary. That which is born of the Spirit is Spirit. That was his own second birth from the Thebet or Dolphin Boat of John. It is perfectly plain the spirit here is feminine. St. John 3, 5, and 6. Bacchus and Moses had precisely the same kinds of two mothers and two births. The name Elimelech, who was the husband of Naomi, signifies My Lord King. Here Saturn is alluded to. Boaz, or the Membrum Virile, is Pater-Petros, the emblem of Jupiter as the Seminal Element of the Word. Moses' uplifted arms on the occasion symbolised the same thing as the wings of the Unicorn, namely the Holy Spirit, and the rod the Horn thereof.

---

*Nun, a Fish; Nain is Welsh for grandmother.

THE ROD, CHRISMA, AND CHRIST.

Since writing the whole of this work, and while it was in the hands of the printer, we came across the following extraordinary confirmation of our assertion that the Rod of Moses, and the Stone Pillars of Horeb and Bethel, were symbols of the seminal principle in the two-fold nature of the Word, which, as Jesus Christ, was made flesh.

"Moses was sent with a Rod to deliver the people; and having it in his hands, he at their head divided the sea; and by it he saw water gush out of the Rock; and it was a Rod of Wood that he cast into the water of Marah, which was bitter, and made it sweet."

"Jacob put Rods into the watering troughs, and succeeded in causing the flock of his uncle to conceive, so that he should obtain their young."

"The same Jacob boasts that he passed over the River with his staff. He said that he saw a ladder, and the Scripture declares that God rested on it; and we have proved from the Scripture that he was not the Almighty."

"And when he (Jacob) poured oil on the Stone (Pillar) in the same place, he received a testimony from the God who was seen of him, that he had anointed the Pillar to the God who was seen of him. That Christ is symbolically called a Stone (Pillar) in many passages of Scripture, I have also shown, and also that every Chrism (Chrisma), whether of the oil of balsam, or of any other unguent which is compounded of ointment, is typical of Him. . . . . . All Kings and annointed persons, derive from Him their appelations of Kings and Anointed."—Justin Martyr's works, A.D. 132, p. 181. Oxford Edition, 1861.

In the instance of Elisha, otherwise Elizeus, or the Lamb of God Zeus, the Rod of the prophet in the hand of his minister, Gehazi, was not enough to raise the dead child, but Elizeus himself had to prostrate himself over the child, and place his mouth upon the child's mouth, and his eyes upon his eyes. Why was the Staff, or Rod, ineffectual? Because since the cloak of Elijah had fallen from the Divine Chariot on the head of Elizeus (or the Lamb of God Zeus) as an object in the similitude of a Dove — as it afterwards did on the head of Jesus, the Lamb of God which taketh away the sins of the world—the Virtue of the Seminal Word—the Chrisma— and the Holy Spirit, were in Elizeus's own carnal body, and not in the Sacred Rod, or Staff, as they were also afterwards in the body of Jesus himself, enabling him also to perform miracles.

Justin Martyr is right; the Word was not the Father Almighty, but the creating principle in the two-fold Word was the Father of Creation, while the Almighty himself was the Father of the two-fold Word. Jesus, after his apotheosis at the Jordan, had in him the Word, as Father and Holy Spirit.* In other words, the two-fold Word seen by Moses as the dazzling fire in the Bush at Horeb, and the Rod converted into a serpent, appeared descending on the head of Jesus as a pair of wings and the Dove's body—the two joined in unity. Jesus himself states in reply to Philip..."He that hath seen Me hath seen the Father"; and, "I am in the Father, and the Father in Me." Then he, speaking as the two-fold Word in his human nature, refers to the Father of the Word, says, as the Word, "I go unto the Father, for my Father is greater than I." Then of the Holy Spirit Jesus says, "He proceedeth from the Father," with heal- ing in his wings. The Fatherhood in the two-fold nature of the Word, is symbolised by the Chrisma of the Christ. He also tells the disciples that the Holy Spirit, as well as the Father, dwells with them. St. John's Gospel, 10 and 17.

In Druidism the Chrisma, or Holy Oil, and personified as Hu Dad Eilir, or Jupiter, is referred to as Three Drops (p. 8), and the Holy Ghost as Awen, or Holy Wings. On March 25th both are in dual unity, and are called Alawn, or Wings, or the full bird as an hieroglyphic. Proceeding from the Father the Awen operates on White, or Holy, Sun Day, the Druidic Pentecost, June 25th, the period the sun is in his full effulgence. This is the reason why the Holy Spirit was named by the Druids Awen Hefin, or Wings of the June Month.

---

*By his Second birth, now from the Boat of the Queen of Heaven.

CWRT AND DIRMYG, LLWYNPIA.

—

Cwrt is the original form of the English name Court. In Welsh it is a compound of two words, namely, Cwr— a corner, nook, a circle, a surrounded limit; and T (T-Udain). Dirmyg is a compound of three words, namely, Di (Dis) a negative prefix; 'r (the) and Myg, incense. Mygu is the verb to incense or to perfume. Myg is used in Welsh to signify, to honour or glorify. Dirmyg, or Dirmygu, signifies, to Dishonour or to Despise.

On the West side of the Rhondda, and direct west from the Holy Mound of Ynisycrug, at the foot of the Wen Graig, to the East of Pandy, are two localities called respectively, The Cwrt (Court), and Dirmyg, the Thistle Hotel, now occupying sites of ancient cottages which, till recently, stood here, and bearing the strange name of Y Dirmyg, or The Dishonour. It appears, we think conclusive, that in remote times the Druidic religious and civil observances were associated with the Mound on the Eastern side of the Rhondda River, and called The Court, while the sentences of the Court were carried out on the spot called The Dishonour, or Y Dismyg.

We seem to discern through the grey mist of centuries, two separate and distinct localities here in Mid-Rhondda, devoted to public affairs. The Mound and its several accessories in the Valley, were used for district religious affairs, and the Government; while the vast round mountain, called Dinas, was the centre of national religious gatherings, called Cymanvas.

The Court Leet of the Manor of Glyn Rhondda is still annually held in this locality by the representatives of Lord Bute, to whom belong the ancient dues of the Lord Paramount of the Lordship of Glamorgan, which lordship was won by Lord Robert Fitzhamon about the year 1093, A.D. Cwrt Lith (Court Leet) appears to be the old Welsh name for a Court of Speech, Record, and testimony by witnesses, hence, in the laws of King Hywel Dda, we have the expression, "Tyngu trwy lith neb un," or "Swear by the speech of none." Tocsyn is the Welsh for a sign or a written summons.

Tocsyn is from Toc, which literally signifies immediately.* Thus, establishing the several manorial Courts Leet within the Lordship of Glamorgan, the Norman Lord Paramount simply took over the existing courts of the Welsh king. Literally, Tocsyn is Toc (at once), and syn (beware you do not disobey). At present the Court Leet for Glyn Rhondda is held in the Pandy Inn, or the Inn of the Fulling House, which stood opposite the Factory below. The name Pandy is a modern one. The original name of the locality was Y Cwrt, or The Court. Here the May Pole was ra sed annually within living memory. Here, till recent years, stood the pound of the manor. All these are relics of the time when the court exercised civil and ecclesiastical jurisdiction, and no doubt the Dirmyg was the scene where many painful sentences were carried out by the officers of the Court Leet, or Cwrt y Llith. The Speech House in the Forest of Dean is a name of the same import as the Welsh one.

THE PRE-CHRISTIAN CROSSES.

On the brow of Dinas Mountain, facing the west, is a lofty mass of projecting rocks called Tarran Wylo'r Marw or the Crags of the Weeping Place for the Dead. That spot faces Gilfach Goch or the small Red Ravine, and the last locality is a couple of miles away, as the crow flies, beyond a mountain ridge called Pen Rhiwfer. All writers on Welsh mythology have ignored the fact that a lofty crag, or crags projecting from the brow of a mountain, is or are, called Tarran in Welsh. Thunder is also called "taran," and writers in consequence have inferred mistakenly that the name Taran always refers to thunder.

---

*It is not, as is supposed, from the French toquer (to touch), and Sein, seint (a bell). The French name Cadres is cad (war) and res (line of battle), and is a purely Welsh compound name.

Maen Tarran is translated Thunder Stone, when it really refers to a sacred stone on a crag or craig. Maen, although signifying carreg (a stone), implies a stone set apart as a religious emblem, and Maen Tarran signifies a huge rock or stone associated with religion. Pen (summit) is often associated with Tarran. It has escaped observation that the Ancients set forth dramatically in each of their sanctuaries what they supposed was taking place in the sky. This is remarkably illustrated in the crucifixion of Jesus of Nazareth. This tragedy is described as taking place at the hour of noon on March 25th, or in the Hebrew Calendar, Nisan 14th. At 12 o'clock on March 25th, the sun was and is exactly on the centre of the dome of the heavens, where the lines of the four Cardinal points cross each other. This is the shape of the cross of the Eastern Church called the Greek Cross to this day. This appears to be the Labarum, which was the standard borne before the Emperor Constantine in the third century, the period of his "conversion" to Christianity, in commemoration of his vision of a flaming cross in the sky with the inscription, "In hoc signo Vincis." In this statement we have an admission by the early fathers of the church that the cross of Calvary had a corresponding cross in the heavens. No doubt the Emperor Constantine saw, what he alleged to have seen, with the eyes of faith alone, and that the "Vision" was pointed out to him by some Christian astronomer.

Now, the cross of the Western Christian Church differs in shape from the Eastern cross. The cross beam of the western one is near the top of the upright beam. Here we find two Christian crosses, each differing in shape from the other. What is the reason for the difference in shape betwen the two? The Western cross, like the Eastern one, is a solar cross. The upright beam of the former is the emblem of the line of the meridian, north-south, and the cross beam near the top is the emblem of the line of the Tropic of the He Goat, the God Pan, which the sun travels over from the south-east to the south-west, on December 25th, O.S. At 12 o'clock noon on December 25th, the sun in the Zodiacal sign of the He Goat, is on the line of the Meridian, where the line of the tropic aforesaid touches it. Outside the south door of each of the Western Churches was a miniature conical-shaped Calvary of stones, surmounted by a cross, corresponding in shape with the said cross in the heavens. Jesus was crucified on March 25th, as the sun in the Sign of the Ram (Aries). The Hind of the Morning Dawn, that is to say, the God Pan, whose substitute in Druidism as Aran*, was the stag, Caru ("carw" is a wrong spelling), Deer, and called Haner Dyn, or Half Man, the other half being a he-goat or his substitute. As we point out elsewhere, Psalm 22 describes this last crucifix'on, but the description in the account of the crucifixion of Jesus on March 25th, is made to apply to both sufferings. In the Psalm the Hind (Stag) is represented crying, "My God, my God, why hast Thou forsaken me?" "And they pierced my hands and my feet," and referring to his bleeding towards the south into the sea called, for that reason, the Red Sea, the Hind cried dolefully, "I am poured out like water," etc.

Those two "trees" or crosses symbolise the Tree of Knowledge, of Good, and Evil, and mistakenly the Tree of Life. On Jesus' right hand was the north or the summer side of the terrestrial Equator, on which his cross stood with his back due east, and his face due west. On his right, therefore, was the "Knowledge of Good," and there hanged the Penitent Thief, named Dimas on his left, his south side, was the winter side of the Equator, or the "Knowledge of Evil," and there hanged Gestas, or the Impenitent Thief. Gospel of Nicodemus, 7, 10, 11. The Tree of Life was on the south-east of the Garden of Adonis, and each sacred mountain, or round hill, including Mount Zion, set apart as an emblem of the shape of the whole earth, as its shape was then supposed to be, was emblematical of that Garden of the Sun, who is named Arthur, Tegid, Taliesun, Adonis and at the winter solstice, or December 25th, Aran or Aaron. This "tree" was called the Tree of Life because in the first place, it was the emblem on the emblematical mount, of the cross in the heavens, where the sun's body and its life were supposed to be annually separated from each other on every Dec. 25. In the second place, that life (Hu Gadarn) returned from the south-east as a Mabyn, clothed in dazzling raiment of light, and, as the Son of Christ, crowned as

---

*Aran is still the Hebrew name for a Wild Goat.

Monarch of the Earth and Heaven—the Son of God. He thus "lived for ever" by having his body "renewed" perpetually. The blasphemous mistake of the Jews was representing the Creator as Saturn, otherwise Pluto, Typhon, whose emblems were the Boar (Twrch, Trwyth), in Britain and Phoenicia, and the Crocodile in Egypt, as the father of Hu Gadarn, or the Eternal Son, under the name of Jupiter, or Father Iu, and to be always thirsting for the blood of the Sun's body, whose tenants were Father Iu, and the Holy Spirit (soul) or the seminal principle and soul in the two-fold nature of the Word of the Creator were in him.

THE HOLY MOUNT OF WALES.

As we state elsewhere, there are indications that the Phoenician form of the Solar Allegory had been adopted at Pontypridd and Dinas Mountain by the Druids of that part of Wales at some very remote period. The summit of Dinas Mountain as the emblem of the whole earth was emblematically "Pen y Byd," or the Summit of the Earth. On the summit of a mountain called Rhiw y Garn, or the Path of the Cairn, is an immense cairn of stones. It is east of Dinas Mountain. To the west, across the Elwy Valley, on the summit of a hill called Pen Rhiw Fer, or the Summit of the Short Path, is a vast mound called Y Ddisgwylfa, or the Look Out. This is directly in line with Gilfach Goch, or the Little Red Retreat. The Look Out appears to be the station where the Druidic Phoenician Priest would stand on the morning of each fatal March 25th, to signal to the myriads stationed on Dinas Mountain the advent of the Sun over the Eglwys Ilan Mountain due east, to meet his murderous foe in the air. That foe was called Red Dragon (Rev. 12, 3), A Ddu (Black Wings), Boar, etc. It was always a day of wailing and weeping. At the hour of 12 noon, the Sun received the mortal stab, and now as, mortally wounded as was supposed, Taliesun struggled towards the west, bleeding—his blood "poured out like water," and Gilfaoh Goch was used dramatically as the track of the sanguinary fluid.

While this was taking place the vast multitude crowded to the western edge of the mountain, and there poured forth groans and tears in pious sympathy with the supposed sufferer. Ezekiel, in viii, 14, describes a similar scene he witnessed on Mount Zion, but on the longest day, June 25th. There are three periods, each differing from the other, among different nations, namely, December 25th, March 25th, and June 25th. The latter date was the time the Egyptian Osiris, Sun, was annually crucified by Typhon, his brother; and as Tammuz in Syria; on March 25 as Adonis in Phoenicia, and December 25th as Aran by the earlier Druids of the Caspian Sea region and Britain. This is what Ezekiel saw: "Then He brought me to the door of the gate of the Lord's House which was towards the north (June 25th), and behold there sat women weeping for Tammuz." The same reason of displeasure at this prompted Isaiah when addressing the sun as follows: "How art thou fallen from heaven,* O Lucifer" (Giver of Light) "Son of the morning." 14, 12. "And it pleased the Lord to bruise him." 53, 10. The whole of this chapter refers to the supposed sufferings of the Sun's body at the hands of the God, whom the Hebrew nation worshipped in conjunction with the Word, Hu Gadarn, in the Sun. Each of their sacrifices was the Egyptian living symbol of the Sun's physical body, apart from Jupiter Amen inhabiting the luminary. There is one thing on Dinas Mountain which indicates that it was sacred to religion before the introduction there of the Phoenician Solar time, namely, the existence there of a Rocking Stone, symbol of the Ceubawl (Cybele) as the oarless boat of the great goddess. This boat was the symbolical refuge of Hu Gadarn on the sea, and it is on the southern end of the mountain, and is called Ystafell Aran, or Aaron, or Aran's Chamber.

In the Phoenician system the Rocking Boat would be stationed between the east and west sides of the mountain. The meaning of

*Heavens, or sky.

the three hours of darkness when Jesus suffered, from twelve to three o'clock on March 25th, is that the sun suffered simultaneously with him. The Druids on Dinas Mountain wept along the edge of the crags at the same period, but they wept for the Sun only. In Egypt the seminal element of the two-fold Word of the Creator was symbolised by the genitals of Osiris, which it is fabled were thrown into the sea by Typhon or Saturn. This is the same idea as throwing the sword of Arthur, with its hilt ornamented with precious "stones" (testes) into the lake. It is, too, the same as the Wren, or Dove, in a Thebet or Ark of Bulrushes, on the Nile, which further is the same as Typhon shutting the body of Osiris in a box on the Nile, which Isis I (Cariadwen) discvered on the shores of Palestine. That is Plutarch's version of the allegory. He is mistaken—the box is the Thebet of the Goddess, like the barge in which Arthur sailed to the realms of the blessed. Here Arthur's, like Osiris's, physical body is introduced instead of the Word, Hu Gadarn, rescued by the Divine barge of Cariadwen. By Hu Gadarn is meant the two-fold Word, whose emblem was the Wren or the Dove—a pair of Wings and a Body. It seems that in every instance the Sun's bodyless Divinity was represented as absent during forty hours, the number of hours the Word was absent in Paradise from his body, which lay (Eastern version) during that time in the emblematical hold of the Thebet, otherwise Ceubawl (Canoe), otherwise corruptly Cybele, wife of Saturn—instead of the Creator—on the hill of Zion, emblematically a garden, is a chamber under a vast stone. All nations had this old allegory in some form or another, but at Jerusalem the Solar allegory culminated into realities, and became the origin of the Christian religion.

NIOBE, THE FONT OF THE CHURCH.

In the allegory of Jupiter, Semele, and the Babe Son Bacchus, we have that the Sun's body was created by the act of the seminal principle in the two-fold Word, the protoplasm in the barge, or Arech (Ark) of the Mother of the Sun (Bacchus). The barge, instead of bearing the names Arech, Hipha, Thebet, Cybele (Ceubawl), etc., is here called Latona, or the Crescent Moon. Of course the Ark or Llong Voel, is oarless, and a shrine on the sea, of which the Crescent Moon was the image—Llun—Luna—is meant. The different names in different languages referred to the, same object. Now we have in the history of Niobe, mother of Argus by Father Iu or Jupiter, Semele under the name Niobe, daughter of Phoroneus, and she is said by Homer to be the first mortal with whom Jupiter fell in love. It is stated that Argos was the father of Argus of the hundred eyes. Argos is another title of the sacred barge, Latona, etc. And when it is said that Argos was the father of Argus, what is meant is Jupiter, or Father Iu, as the husband of the mother of the Sun, whom the Argo represented to human eyes, she herself, as a spirit, being invisible. There is a story in Plato's Phaedo of the sacred ship Argo journeying between Athens and the sacred Island Delos, the birthplace of Apollo and Diana, Sun and Earth personified, and whose mother was Latona, or the Crescent Moon-shaped Sacred Ship. Argo is the Welsh Argau, or Enclosed. Leda, which is another name of Latona, is said to be the mother of the ship Argos, hence Virgil states of Dido, lovely Phoenician daughter of Latona:—

"A robe of tissue, stiff with golden wire,
An upper vest, once Helen's rich attire,
From Argos by the famed adulteress brought,
With golden flowers winding foliage wrought,
Her mother Leda's present when she came
To ruin Troy, and set the world on flame."

Thus to Jupiter (Argos) is mystically given the name of the Ark which he frequented in his escapes from Typhon, his half-brother.

The Greeks and the Romans seem to have supposed that each name of the sacred ship indicated a distinct sacred ship differing from the others bearing other names, and thus Virgil describes the Argon or Argos, which had brought Dido to Troy, as the daughter of Leda, a personification of the sacred ship, and then represents Latona as the mother of Dido, the Tyrian Venus, of whom he writes : —

"When in the dance the graceful goddess leads
The choir of nymphs, and overtops their heads ;
Known by her quiver, and her lofty mien,
She walks majestic, and she looks their Queen ;
Latona sees her shine above the rest,
And feeds with secret joy her silent breast."

The Druidic origin of the sacred ship is indicated by the statement that the Argo was constructed of the sacred oaks of the forest of Dodona, and it is further stated that the wood was vocal*. Homer referring to the Strait Scylla and Charybdis and the sacred ship, writes : —

"Scarce the famed Argo pass'd these raging floods,
The sacred Argo fill'd with demi gods !—
E'en she had sunk, but Jove's imperial bride,
Wing'd her fleet sail, and push'd her o'er the tide."

The Odyssey, B xii.

In the foregoing we distinctly see the identity of the Bride of Jove, or Jupiter, with the sacred ship. There is no doubt that by the Golden Fleece was meant the emblem of the sun's rays when the sun is in the Sign of the Ram. In Egypt the Ram, as the Sign of Jupiter Amen, or Father Iu—the Mind of the Creator, was carried about on a boat on men's shoulders in processions†. This reminds us of the carrying about in Wales of the sacred Boat called Cath (Cat).

The Ancient Jews before Jesus Christ, observed the mystery of the Trinity in the name Jehovah, for though the name consists of four letters in number, whence it was called Quadriliterum, yet

---

*Instinct with the Spirit of the Queen of Heaven like the Stone at Shechem. Joshua 24, 27.

†Payne Knight's symbolised language. Sec. 220.

there were but three sorts of letters in the Name: Iod signifieth the Father, who was the beginning of all things; Van is a conjunction —copoulative, and denoted the third person in the Trinity. The letter He signifieth the Son of God. Moses and Aaron, F. Fagus in Ex 23, p. 166, Ed. 1678. The Van is the Druidic V, the hieroglyphic emblem denoting a pair of wings, signifying the Holy Spirit; the Iod, the hieroglyphic denoting the Father whose emblem was the body of the Dove or Wren between the wings. The Hebrew letter called He consists of two uprights, and a horizontal bar lying across; somewhat like a cromleach, only that the latter has three uprights underneath the horizontal boulder or slab. As we show in the text, the O is the symbol of the Sun. Thus we see the Jews, though wrong as to the shape of the Van and He letters, as hieroglyphics of the original signs, still retained the mystic significations of both letters as emblems. The foregoing facts prove the signs did not originate among the Jews themselves. The three props under the Cromleach are the symbol of the reverberation called Adlais 'Echo), corrupted to Atlas, as the voice of the Word "upholding all things." Heb. I, 3.

Pelagius, or Morien in Welsh, held, in the beginning of the fifth century, that each soul was a distinct creation by the Holy Spirit, and not inherited from Adam. Therefore, that at its birth each soul was holy. Thus he denied the existence of original sin in the soul, and held that every child at its birth, owing to the holiness of its infant soul, was born fit for heaven, and, therefore, was a member of the Kingdom of Heaven, which was established on earth simultaneously with the resurrection of the Lord Jesus from the Navis, of which the hollow of his stone sepulchre was the emblem. Each child is born from the Fons of his natural mother. The Fons (Font) of the Navis, or Nave, otherwise the church as a structure, with its water, is for the purpose of symbolical "new birth," a symbol borrowed from the Fons (Womb) of each physical mother, to imply the "new birth" of the infant soul. Pelagius denied the birth of a "new" soul, other than that born in the infant babe from its natural mother.

Thus, he said, infant introduction into the church by the Fons, or Font rite, was idle and puerile.

Jesus said, "Suffer little children, and forbid them not, to come unto me: for of such is the Kingdom of Heaven," meaning the Church as a Navis, the visible symbol of the spirit mother Cariadwen, or Holy Love, in a feminine sense. How beautiful is the following, "And he laid His hands on them and departed thence." Mat. 19; 13, 14, 15. Repentance is before conversion. Conversion signifies turning back to the former holy condition of the infant soul, and the words "born again" of St. John iii, signifiy re-acceptance, to his first allegiance, of her former soul child by the Church.

Jesus himself had two generations. The first that of his body and natural life in the Virgin Mary. The second that of his soul during the visit of Mary to Elizabeth and Zachariah*. The first was the result of the act of the seminal Word as Eros, that is to say, Jupiter, "the Man who is in the heavens." The second by the act of the Holy Spirit as Psyche. Jesus underwent two so-called Baptisms. The first, his exaltation as High Priest by the ceremony associated with the Boat of John at the ferry or Bethabara, called also Beth Ania, or the House of the Boat. His second Baptism was his death, burial, and resurrection. But there was no water in his grave. "Can ye drink of the cup that I drink of? And be baptised with the Baptism that I am baptised with?" Mark 10, 39. It is worthy of attention that this baptism is the one perpetuated in the

---

*Be it particularly observed that, in Luke i, 35, the figure employed describing the act of begetting Jesus' soul and body, is a Dove "over-shadowing" a hen. The agent is the Power of the Highest, and not the Highest Himself. Mark 9, 1; Luke 5, 17; Jeremiah 10, 12; Colossians 1, 15; Acts 10, 30; Romans i, 20, and ix, 21; Luke i, 17, and iv, 14. In the last verse the Power of the Dove, and not His own is alluded to. The same bird-figure is employed by Moses as Elohim over-shadowing an egg; translated "moved" (brooding) over chaos, compared to an egg. Genesis i, 2. Thus it is taught the Amen, the beginning of the creation of God, was the Father of Jesus. Rev. 3, 14.

early Church. "That so many of us as were baptised unto Jesus Christ were baptised unto his death. Therefore we are buried with him by baptism unto death, that like as he was raised by the glory of the Father, even so we also do walk in the newness of life. For if we have been planted together in the likenss of his death we shall be also in the likeness of his resurrection." He did not die in water, nor was he buried in it, therefore his resurrection was not from water. Most people confound the sepulchre of Jesus with the Boat of John. What was the ceremony of initiation into the Christian mysteries among the early Christians we know not. Doubtless it consisted of descending into a vault, or crypt, and then ascending therefrom. Christmas boxes are emblems of the Sepulchre of the Sun's Divinity, and doubtless the Christians had a similar emblem of some sort. I. Peter 2, 20, 21.

To make it clear, it may be mentioned that the miraculous Boat, the Dolphin and the Rocking Stone were one idea represented by three emblems.

THE MABYN AND MOSES IN EGYPT.

(From a Sculpture on the Temple of Sais, Memphis, Egypt, mentioned by Herodotus. See Illustration.)

The Babe in the Ark of Bulrushes is the Sun-God Horus or Mabyn. The Old Man, passing away, is his father, Osiris, the Old Sun of the previous year.

The Falcon is the symbol of the sun's Divine tenant called Amen-RA in Egypt, and in the Bible Amen. In Druidism he is called Hu Gadarn, and is symbolised by the Wren and also by the Beaver. In the East he is symbolised also by the Dove on the back of the sun-bull, Apis (Elgan) as a written sign in Britain and India.

The Dolphin is from the Greek Delphos, a womb, a symbol

From a Sculpture on the Temple of Sais, Memphis, Egypt mentioned by Herodotus.

of the womb of the Queen of Heaven. The sun's body was held to be a substance and therefore derived from the earth's substance. After being prepared somewhere in the bowels of the earth—it was supposed in a cave—the solar Babe was supposed to be transferred to the Delphos (Boat) of the Queen of Heaven, and that there Amen-Ra entered him, and instantly his head became the transmitter of radiating light and heat from his divine tenant. This union of the divine and the earthy was called his apotheosis or deification. In Egypt and Babylon the simple Delphos-Boat or womb-boat or ark —which is called Thebet—gave way to the symbol of a great Fish, to which was given the name Delphos or Womb; and thus the Dolphin—the fish is purely imaginary—became the emblem of the womb of the Queen of Heaven. Jonah, or correctly, Iona, signifies Dove, and Iona in a great fish is an Egyptian solar legend made the basis of a romantic Jewish fable. Those who compiled the scriptural narrative describing the interment, the sojourn of Jesus in the stone-tomb part of a whole day, a whole day, and then the beginning of another day, and called it "the sign of the Prophet Iona," were masters of the inner mysteries of the religion of Egypt. It must be remembered that the Rocking Stone was the inland symbol of both the Delphos-Boat and of the later Delphos symbol. Or, in other words, of the Sacred Boat and of the Fish. In the Christian system both symbols are employed, namely, at the apotheosis of Jesus from the Dolphin-Boat of John—he is called Oanes, or Man and Fish—and his interment in, and his resurrection from, a stone sepulchre. This dual nature of the same symbol is the reason why the "baptism" of Jesus and his interment and resurrection are often confounded with each other.

The Seahorse, another fabulous animal, is the symbol of Typhon, or the Devil (the Black Wings, A-Ddu, of Druidism), threatening the solar Babe, but both the agent of the Queen of Heaven and Amen Ra (the Falcon) are on guard between Typhon and his intended prey, namely, the Solar Babe on the basket. In other parts of ancient Egypt the Crocodile was the favourite symbol of Typhon. Typhon, or Set, is the God of the Shepherd Kings.

The Lake is the symbol in the Sais illustration of the Western

Ocean. In Egypt the Red sea was the annual scene of the fabulous encounter, hence called "red." The expression in the Book of Revelations, c. xi, 8, revised version, has reference to the annual crucifixion of Osiris by Typhon in the air, and symbolically in as many localities on earth as the worshippers fixed upon to perform the rites of their rel gion. We may preface the Book of Revelation by the important statement that each scene of religious rites and ceremonies was symbolical of the whole earth, therefore, the symbol is called a "city" and the whole earth bears the same name. For instance, the Bible calls the whole earth the True Tabernacle: and in the Epistle to the Hebrews, Jerusalem is called the "pattern" thereof.

We now come to the quotation: "And their dead bod es will lie in the open square of the Great City, which is spiritually called Sodom and Egypt, where their Lord was Crucified." Near the foot of Mount Pisgah, on the Eastern side of the Jordan, Col. Conder discovered as follows: Nahaliel or the Valley of God, is the gorge of Callirhoe, above which on the north, stands both Meini Hir and Cromlechs. The ridge south of Wady Jedeid is now called El Maslubiyeh, or "The Crucified One." Heth and Moab, p. 141.

Here Col. Conder goes on to say, is a group of more than a hundred rude stone monuments. The "groups" are evidently of the same nature as the Cytiau or Celtic round cots found on the mountains of Wales such as on Blaen-Rhondda mountains and in Meirionethshire, where the ancient Druids were wont to assemble on great occasions to perform religious observances. It is a very notable circumstance that Col. Conder like everyone else has no other than Welsh names to describe the "rude stone monuments" in question. Egypt is to the South of the Moab ridge of the Crucified One. It is also near Beth-Peor or the Grave of Horus the infant name of the Egyptian Osiris, a locality where Moses disappeared so mysteriously. No man knew where was the grave of Moses, but we learn that he was interred somewhere near the spot where the solar drama of Egypt was annually performed, including the dramatic interment of the old sun of each recurring year. In contemplating that annual Crucifixion of Osiris (Sun), we must do as the Egyptians and the

I

Druids themselves did, namely, look up towards the sky. The Moab ridge of the Crucifixion faces south, and is under what can be described as the pole of the meridian. In the southern sky above Egypt is the line of the Tropic of the He Goat (the God Pan). That line is the horizontal beam of the Cross. Thus Sodom and Egypt were associated with "their" crucified Lord.

"They have at Sais," states Herodotus, "the tomb of a certain personage (Osiris) whom I do not think myself permitted to specify. It is beyond the Temple of Minerva," named both Isis I and Neith— the Nydd or turner of the wheel of the solar system, in Druidism— "and is continued the whole length of the building.—Around this (Tomb) are many large stone columns near which is a Lake whose banks are lined with stones: it is of a circular form. Upon this lake are represented by night the incidents which happened to him whom I dare not name.—The Egyptians call them their mysteries." —Herodotus Euterpe, clxx.

The name Moses is an Egyptian one and is a title of the Babe Sun Horus, and signifying "Drawn out of the Water." In the solar ceremonies on the Lake at Sais alluded to by Herodotus, the drawing the Babe Horus from the lake simultaneously with the rising of the sun from the south-eastern Ocean on new-year's morning, was undoubtedly annually observed with national rejoicings like those anciently annually taking place in Britain, and continued till early in this century under the name "Mab Sant."

MOSES AND JOSHUA. OSIRIS AND HORUS.

REMARKABLE COINCIDENCES.

It will be recollected that the Sun at the beginning of each year was called Horus by the Egyptians. That, he in the course of the same year, came to be called Osiris. That was the Sun's name at the time of his annual death, as Egyptians as well as the Druids supposed, as the result of Osiris's supposed conflict with Set, otherwise Typhon, the Black Wings (Addu of the Druids). But the Divinity in the wrecked Sun always escaped into the Divine Boat (Thebet) of Isis I, Queen of Heaven, where a new body was quickly constructed miraculously for his reception as the result of the contact of the Divine masculine essence in the escaped one coming in contact with the Divine feminine essence in the Boat of Isis I, who, being a spirit, was herself invisible to mortals. That escaped one was called by the Egyptians, Amen Ra, and by the Druids, Hu Gadarn. We believe the name Amen Ra is Celtic: that A is a sign implying wings, and, therefore, the symbol of the Holy Spirit; and Men, in the Celtic Menydd (Brains), and in the Greek, Meen, from which the English Mind is derived. In Celtic, Rhi is a title of the Almighty, and it is the root of the word Rhinwedd (Virtue). Therefore that A-Men Ra signifies the Mind and the Spirit of the Almighty, and therefore that A-Men Ra of Egypt is the Word of God. In Rev. 3, 14, we read: "And unto the minister of the Church of the Ladodiceans write these things, saith the Amen — the beginning of God's creation" (Greek). In the illustration the Word—Amen Ra—symbolised by the bird, is, so far, a separate identity and the babe Horus is in a condition of inertness. But the moment the Word—Amen—passes into his head he will "live" as the Druids say of A-Dda or Good Wings, meaning Winged Amen, will animate him. In the hymn to Amen Ra it is said, "Thou art the One God who came into being at the beginning of time." Papyrus, 9901 B.M. Then alluding to the Boat of Isis I, which conveys Horus with Amen in his orb (head), the same says: "The Boat of the Rising Sun hath a fair wind, and the heart of him that is in its Shrine rejoiceth, O, thou mighty youth, thou Everlasting Son, self begotten, who didst give birth to thyself."

Here is clearly taught the scriptural doctrine that the Word of the Creator came from the bosom of the Father, which, so to speak, was its birth-place. The Mabyn (Babe-Sun) is called the Son of the Boat. We have seen that another symbol of the miraculous Boat of the Queen of Heaven was the Dolphin.—See illustration.

Joshua's first name was Hosea. (Numbers, 13, 8, 17.)

Now comes the very curious coincidences: Joshua receives that name instead of Hosea, and it is stated in the translation of the LXX that he was the son of Nave (a boat) and in the Authorised Version that he was the son of Nun (a fish). We have seen that the Boat and Fish, or Nave and Nun, were two symbols of the same thing. Moses disappearing is modelled on the Egyptian story of the disappearance of Osiris at the Ridge of the Crucified One at the end of the sacred year. Joshua, coming instead of Moses, is Horus, coming instead of old Osiris, and the Nave-Nun is symbolised by the opening passage in the Jordan with the Ark of the Covenant, apparently held up there level with the deck of the usual Boat, or symbolised the body, as in the case of the soul, and a mummy case, or coffin, is always in Egypt like the human figure, and a coffin is still called Ark or Arech by the Druids of Wales. We now see the Angel and Sword who met Joshua after his new birth from the Nave-Nun of the Jordan, was Amen Ra who was now transferring himself into Joshua or Jesus as an angel. But in the instance of Jesus of Nazareth, he did so as a Dove, as he was landed on the western bank of Jordan from the Nun-Nave, or Boat-Dolphin, of John the Baptist, at the very spot of the Jordan where Joshua and the nation are said to have crossed so many ages before.

THE PONTYPRIDD MOUNT OF BURNT OFFERINGS.

INTERESTING DRUIDIC RELIC ON FOREST HILL.

TRACES OF TWO SECTS OF WORSHIPPERS.

On the summit of the adjoining hill, almost due south-west from Glyntav Church, a mile below Pontypridd, is an enormous conical mound of earth which, in the course of many centuries, has somewhat spread out by its own weight. It is at present clothed with verdure. The prospect from its summit is very fine, commanding a magnificent view of lofty mountains, verdant vales and wooded dells. To the south from its summit a view is obtained, through an opening of the venerable town of Llantrisant and Rhiw-y-Saeson, or the Path of the Saxons, of the Eastern undulating portion of the celebrated Vale of Glamorgan. The hill itself is much higher than the level of the said opening. North-west from the lofty height of the mound is the gro^{v}e of Gwyion, and the ridge of mountains running to the Cave of the Voice of God (Duw Lais) to e west.

The local place names near this mound on Forest Hill enable us to arrive at certain knowledge as to the nature of the ancient associations of the mound. A little below it is a small brook which the parish road crosses. This crossing is named Rhyd-y-Llech, or in English, the Passage of the Cromlech. The said Llech, which, observe, is a name in the singular number, must, according to the custom of the Druids, have been fixed on a tripod on the top of the green mound we are dealing with. We know that the Druids were wont to face the East when engaged in prayer on the summit of those structures of the early world, and they were also used as pulpits from which they preached to the thousands assembled on and around the sides of the circular Mount of the Congregation, when the sun was in "the side of the north." Isaiah 14, 13. But there are still more remarkable place names associated with this mound. The farm upon which it stands is named Berth-Llwyd—Ar y Berth, or on the hedge or a heap of twigs or pile of wood, is the origin of the word Aberth, and signifying a sacrifice, and it is the only name in the language of the Druids by which a sacrifice is known in Welsh. The adjective, llwyd, qualifying a Berth, or Aberth, is the ancient Welsh for holy or holiness. The Virgin Mary is still called in Welsh Mari Lwyd, and therefore, the name of the farm signifies Holy Sacrifice, and unquestionably refers to the great sacrificies that were, in pre-Christian times, offered on the top of this great mound, which has the horizon like a vast rim of a wheel in view of the spectator standing on its summit.

It is highly significant that no Cromleach was ever seen in any part of the world bearing a trace of fire upon any one of its three upright props, nor on the horizontal boulder upheld by them. Therefore, we conclude no burnt offerings were ever associated with any Cromlech. The fact that we have here two separate names of objects connected with the mound, point to two modes of worship as having, one after the other, been associated with this mound. It seems as if the original Cromlech sect of Druids were ousted from here, and that a sect of the burnt sacrifice fraternity gained the mound, and destroyed the Cromlech. This being so, one would naturally explore the neighbourhood for another Holy Mound, erected afterwards by the ejected original sect.

Down the hill and about a mile to the south-east from this mound, is, sure enough, another mound. It is in a field at the foot of the hill between the road leading to the parish church of Llantwit Vardre, and the straight road leading to Llantrisant. The name of the neighbourhood of this mound is Twyn Teg, or the Fair Mound*. A small water course crosses the road leading to the parish church, and the small ford—the road now is bridged over it—is called Rhyd Cae'r Din, or the Ford of the Mound Field.

Judging roughly, this mound is sixty or seventy yards in circumference, and the original great deep trench containing water, still encircles its outward base. A brook runs beyond its western side, and it bears the Druidic name, Nant Aran, or Aran's Brook, a name corrupted, as at Llan Aran, to Arian, the Welsh name for silver. Near here, too, is a farm called Duffryn Duwlais ("Dowlais"), or the Vale of the Voice of God. On a field between this and Garth Mountain, and on a farm called Ty'r Ysgol (English, School House), are circular traces of the foundations of habitations called Pebyll, Tents or Tabernacles. Thus we find the two localities had their respective separate tabernacles, and which indicates the two sects, one of the Druids, and the other of foreign influence, kept aloof from each other. As we point out elsewhere there is an abundance of evidence that the Phoenicians came to exercise great influence in this part of Glamorgan, as well as in the Valley of the Sacred Dee,

---

*It may signify the Mound of Fair Play in allusion to the violence of the usurpers of the other and older mound.

as the names there of Bala or Baal, and Llan Der Baal (Llandderval) signify.

Reverting to the great mound on the summit of the hill, the locality is indicated by several other place names in addition to those already mentioned. The entire plateau of the mound referred to as The Field above the Wood, in the name of Pen-y-Coed-Cae. As the name of a local farm we have Field of God in the name of Pen Coed Cae Duw, corrupted to Coed-cae Du, or Black, which is nonsense. As the station of Tudain, or the Wailing Tau, or the Druidic Cross, an adjoining farm is named Ty'r Arglwydd, or the T of the Lord—the T being a hieroglyphic signifying the line of the meridian, and the horizontal stroke across it, that being the line of the tropic of the He Goat, as Pan El, or Half Man and Half Goat, and named Caru (Stag), and also Aran in Druidic language, and Hind in the Bible. See title of Psalm 22.—The Druids, as stated elsewhere, had one of these T's on the centre of the raised roof of each of their round houses, which were circular, hence Cronglwyd, and for that reason each Briton's house is called T, and the people Titans.

When we take into account all the other place names associated with the Berth Lwyd Mound, it is highly significant to find, to the South of it, and only a few hundred yards away and close to the dingle called the Tents, a spot and mansion called Ty Mab Elis, or the House of Ellis's Son. No one now has the slightest idea as to who this Ellis and his son were. It seems pretty certain the locality marking the ancient site, close to the tents for the minor priests, is the site of the habitation where the High Priest—the Archon—of the said mound dwelt. Like the name Beltân, the name is a mixture of Welsh and Phoenician. Ty Mab (House of the Son) is Welsh, but Elis is the Phoenician Ilos, a title of the sun, and often rendered Elias in all Shemitic dialects. The lofty height of the mountain on the opposite side of the Taff Valley, and due north from the Berth Lwyd Mound, is called Pen Heol Haul Le, or the Summit of the Road of the Solar Place. Upon or about the terrestrial line due north, are three small grey stones, cairns, called in Welsh Cernydd Llwyd, or Holy Cairns. They were opened a few years ago by a vicar of Llanfabon, and a potter's urn, containing human remains, was found in the centre of each cairn. Before reaching the said cairns from Pontypridd, one passes the remains of a small earthen mound. The locality seems to have been used in the olden time as the centre of Whitsuntide festivities, always held on June 25th. A fine spring of water near the spot would on those occasions supply holy water for the lustration of the assembled worshippers on the mounain of Ilan. We now come to a still more interesting circumstance, because connecting this mound with the Oriental ideas of the Christian religion. Standing on the top of the Craig Aberth Llwyd, compass in hand, one finds that the equinoxial line crossing the mound passes exactly through the western end, and therefore over the altar due east of Eglwys Ilan Church, situate in a singular deep hollow or dent on the high hill between Mynydd Mayo and the Mountain of Ilan, on the opposite side of the Taff Valley. Therefore, the orientation of the mound is through the centre of the deep chasm in the line of the mountains opposite.

In pre-Christian times there was probably a sacred mark of some sort where Eglwys Ilan now stands, to indicate for the high priest and people stationed on the Craig Aberth Llwyd the very spot on the horizon where the sun would rise on March 25, called Lady Day, and the first day of Spring.* And the Lady in the Phoenican system of religion was Baaltis, Astarte, Ashtaroth, from March 25, which the Saxon Eastre or Easter is derived. In Greece the same Goddess is Venus, and in Druidism Gwen. Dr. Lempriere states that at Hierapolis in Syria was a famous temple to Astarte, served by 300 priests, who were always employed in offering sacrifices. Strange that in the spring time any worshippers should suppose the blood of carnalites was demanded by the Creator. The fact is, they had set up Typhon, otherwise Saturn or Pluto, as the Almighty. In the new system of Chrisianity each church had its perpetual sacrifice instead of the annual emblem of the sun, the priest now, as Newman states, "Offers the eternal sacrifice."

---

*Down to 100 years ago this Church was in the midst of an ancient Grove, which was sacriligiously destroyed by a curate named Jacob.

On the spot where in the olden time the eyes of the Archon and the mighty throng on the Craig Aberth Llwyd, gazed across the valley, the Christian Church reared another altar, and offered a new sacrifice, and the Craig Aberth Llwyd became green, dotted with daises, and the mountain larks sang in the air over it, undisturbed by the smoke of burnt offerings.

THE TWO LAMBS.

It has frequently been observed that a Garden was the place of the fall of mankind, as represented by the first Adam, and that a garden was the place of the resurrection of the second Adam, and with him and through him, of the raising up again of the fallen sons and daughters of men. Associated with the death and resurrection of the second Adam, the Lord Jesus Christ, are two gardens, namely, the Garden of Gethsemane, and the Garden of Joseph of Arimathea. It is admitted that the Lamb of the Passover was the antetype of Jesus, as the Lamb of God. The Lamb of the Passover was first slain by Abraham 'as Isaac's substitute, and afterwards annually at the brazen altar, in the precincts of the temple; and then the body of each of the lambs would be carried through the streets to the home of the owner of the lamb. While it was being so carried, the droppings of blood would be sprinkled along the streets. Jesus, the Lamb of God, was scourged, and led through the streets of Jerusalem. (Mark 15, 15; Mat. 26, 27; John 19, 1.) But the most astonishing of all is connected with the Garden of Gethsemane. In roasting the Lamb of the Passover, its fat streamed from it in abundance. The Lamb of God, in the Garden of Gethsemane, sweated drippings of blood before the fire of the wrath of the Jewish father of the Word, the Christ.

Each of the Druidic mounds and circles was a symbol of the whole earth as the Garden of the Sun, which the Lord himself had planted, and not any man. Jerusalem as Mount Zion, or the Mount of the Stone—it is still there, in the Mosque of Omar—was called a vineyard and spouse. Eden, and the Gardens of Joseph of Arimathea and Gethsemane, were each a symbol of the whole earth encircled by the sea, and was the very high mountain from which could be seen, symbolically, all the kingdoms of the earth. This is what is meant in Psalm 24:

The earth is the Lord's, and the fulness thereof;
The world, and they that dwell therein.
For He hath founded it upon the seas,
And established it upon the floods (tides).

Who shall ascend to the Hill (Mound) of the Lord?
Or who shall stand in His Holy Place?
He that hath clean hands and pure heart,
Who hath not lifted his soul unto vanity nor sworn deceitfully.

He shall receive the blessing from the Lord
And righteousness from the God of his salvation.

The figures employed relate to one of the Druidic mounds encircled by a trench full of water, to symbolise the sea around the earth as the Garden of the Lord. The sap of vegetation was supposed to stream up in spring and summer from the boiling of the Cauldron of Cariadwen, the source of the protoplasm, in substances of the vegetable kingdom. But it was passive in the seeds of those substances, until the fatness of the sun, coming as rays, amalgamated with it. When that amalgamation had taken place the process of development commenced. In Druidism, the effect of the rays, which is called heat in English, is called Gwyar (blood), and Giver-Es. or the oil of Hesus. This was in the East, in the feasts of Dionysus, otherwise Bacchus, the sun, symbolised by wine, which is called in the Bible the blood of grapes. In Number 15, 4 and 5, two pints of wine and bread were used, the wine as a substitute for the blood of the Lamb of the Passover, and, therefore, representing it, and the bread mixed with oil (Chrisma), both the oil and the wine symbolising the essence of the sun: Oil first to amalgamate with the passive sap of the earth; and wine as the result of the combined action of both on the seed germs of the Garden of the Sun, which the Lord had planted.—The sweat of Jesus eventuated "as it were (into) great drops of blood." Luke 22, 44.

It is deeply significant to find that the Hellenic Jews, or the LXX, translating the Hebrew text in Egypt, avoided giving the proper name P n l (Pan El), but gave instead, the words "Face of God." The God Pan was a well-known God in Egyptian and in the Greek Pantheons, and by omitting the name they avoided discovery.

THE TWO BETHANIAS.

ONE "BEYOND JORDAN," AND THE OTHER BEYOND JERUSALEM.

AN ANCIENT PARABLE EXPLAINED.

Dean Penrhyn Stanley states as follows: "It is with considerable hesitation that I lay stress on the name 'Bethabara.' All the oldest MSS, and nearly all the versions, read not ' Beth-Abara,' but 'Bethania,' and Origen, in his commentary on the passage, states that in his time this reading (Bethania) prevailed 'in almost all the MSS.' But considering the great improbability of the alteration of the familiar word 'Bethania' into the comparatively unknown 'Beth-Abara'—considering also that in the locality Origen still found the name 'Beth-Abara—considering finally that if the Evangelist had meant to distinguish it from the Judæan Bethania he would have distinguished this Bethania by words to that effect, it seems that Origen was right in altering the text, and being, as he says, "persuaded that we ought to read Beth-Abara." Those who read "Bethania" make it the House of Boats, in allusion to the Ferryboat. In the original Greek of St. John's Gospel 1, 28, the spot is alluded to as follows: These things were done in Bethania beyond the Jordan, where John was baptizing. In 2 Samuel 19, 18, the same locality is described as follows: "And there went over a Ferry Boat to carry over the King's Household." — Sinai and

Palestine, p. 310, note. It would have been better had Origen left
the text as he found it. How the verse escaped his Vandalic touch
is very curious. In Joshua, 7, the same spot is called The Fords.
It will be remembered it was at these Fords the Hebrew nation
crossed over Jordan dry shod into the earthly Paradise. To get at
the meaning of what John was doing here "beyond Jordan," that is
to say on the eastern bank of it, and, therefore, technically in the
"wilderness," we must refer to what the Jews did on the same spot
"beyond Jordan" at the end of their pilgrimage through the "wilderness." And Joshua said to the people, "Sanctify yourselves, for
to-morrow the Lord will do wonders among you." Joshua 3, 5.

They, in accordance with the ceremonial law, performed certain
rites of purification, which they called " sanctifying themselves," to
be fit to enter he earthly "Rest" beyond the River.

It is now known that the word "Baptism" signifies colouring,
as dyeing white, or any other colour. See Taylor's additions to
Calmet's Dictionary of the Bible. Now, John's "Baptism of Repentance" implied exactly the same thing as the Hebrews sanctifying
themselves preparatory to the crossing of the Jordan on the morrow.

In the Christian Church, becoming a member of Jesus's Church
is compared to becoming the subjects of Joshua and a member of
"the Commonwealth of Israel" in the earthly Paradise, on the
eastern side of the Jordan. Ephesians 2, 12. It seems that those
who might neglect to "sanctifying themselves," were excluded from
the privilege of crossing the Jordan, and that crossing into the
Rest was a corrollary or consequence of the other, hence the Apostle
says, "For as many of you as have been Baptised into Christ, have
put on Christ," an allusion to the white garment, the symbol of
sanctity, in the ancient religions. Be it carefully observed that in
crossing the Jordan the Hebrews did not wet themselves at all.
We are thus taught clearly that admission into the Church is not
through water.

To get at the meaning of all this we must revert to other ancient
religions. It is a remarkable feature of the Jewish characteristics
that while deficient in the creating or producing faculty, the Hebrew
excels in adapting the productions of others for his own use.

Now the story of the exodus from Egypt through the wilderness of Sinai, and across the Jordan into Palestine is based on an old world fable. It is a fable, briefly stated, to the following effect: There is below the earth another world. The world in which we dwell during the present life is divided into northern and southern hemispheres. Dividing the said hemispheres from each other is a line running from east to west. That line is called the Equator. It is often called a River.

The under world is similarly divided, and there is a River there corresponding with the said "River" of the upper world. Under the southern hemisphere of the upper world the corresponding one of the under world is called Hell, Hades, Tartarus, etc. The River of the under world is called Styx, and by the Druids Gwyllion-wy, or, Dark Waters of the Dove. Beyond this river of the under world, and corresponding with the northern hemisphere of the upper world, is a region called Paradise, by the Persians; Elysium, by the Greeks; Gwenydva, by the Druids; and "The Bosom of Abraham," as well as Paradise, by the Jewish Rabbins.

It was believed by eastern nations that all souls at the death of bodies passed into the under world through Hades, or Tartarus, called Sheol by the Hebrews. If the soul was a thoroughly bad one, the Devil (Pluto) claimed him as his subject, and detained him in Hell. But if during life a soul had slain abundance of the Egyptian sacred animals—that is to say, animals which before the invention of letters served to symbolise the twelve signs of the Zodiac, and the beneficient influence of the sun, through those signs, during the year—the Devil (Typhon, in Egypt) allowed such a soul to cross the River Styx into Paradise, but Satan took care to shut the gates after him, that he might never come out again. But it is now taught that Jesus, by virtue of his own immolation, descended into Hell, passed safely through it, pulled down the Gates of Satan, and visited "the captives in prison"; nay, more, "preached unto them," and, thereby, if they believed in him, gave them an opportunity to accompany him back to the upper world, and then to the Highest Heaven. The following is Dean Alford's version: For this was the Son of God manifested, that he might PULL DOWN the works of the

Devil. 1 John 3, 8. In the Cymric the translators render the words translated by Dean Alford "pull down," "that he might untie the works of the Devil." For Christ also hath once suffered for sins; the just for the unjust, that he might bring us to God, being put to death in the flesh, but quickened by the Spirit; by which (spirit) also he went and preached to the spirits in prison. 1 Peter 3, 18, 19. In the next verse St. Peter describes the Boat used by John in the ceremony of conveying the sanctified across the Jordan to the Rest of the Christian Church, and he compares the said Boat (Thebet) to the Ark of Noah; and Jesus and his Church, and Peter, James, and John, and the three Marys, to Noah and his wife, and their three sons and their three wives. In the time of John the Jordan no longer opened to allow the sanctified through "repentance" to cross to the rest of the Church, and it was indispensable, therefore, to use a Boat to convey across the Jordan—Styx,—and John performed the part of Charon as Master of the Boat of the Queen of Heaven. The nation was born from Egypt into the state of Nature. The open Red Sea was the substitute of the Sacred Boat of the Queen of Heaven (Isis I). Moses and Miriam were then the symbols of the Sun's Divinity and Nature (Isis 2). In short Moses and Miriam were the God-Father, and Goddess-Mother of the nation then symbolically born into the "wilderness." That is the meaning of the saying that they were "Baptised" to Moses in the Sea, and in the "Cloud," the cloud being the symbol of the Holy Spirit as the Father of the soul of each individual of the nation, and as souls and bodies, they were presented as a gift to Moses. At the Jordan we have the opening in the river as a variant for the Boat of Charon on the sacred Lake of Memphis, Egypt, and the Ark of the Covenant held up above the opening in imitation of the Mummy Coffin on the deck of the sacred boat, conveying the dead to the Rest of the Egyptian Catacombs on the other side of the lake.

In the Christian cult, the world stands for Egypt, each Church building for the opening in the Red Sea, the Font Miriam, and the space between the font and the chancel stands for the "wilderness," and the chancel itself for the rest of the people of God. In Welsh—a language in which are preserved the ecclesiastical terms of both the old philosophy and of earliest Christian ideas—a coffin is called Ark (Arch). The Church building is called Nave, or Navis, ship. It is the most ancient custom to place the coffin on the fore-part of the Nave opposite the chancel. Here the Nave and the coffin, on as it were its deck, symbolise precisely the same old-world ideas as the open Jordan and the Ark—the Mummy Case—held up in it on the shoulders of priests in the bed of the Jordan, with the Rest beyond the River. Between the nave and the chancel the consecration of confirmation is performed, and eligible can-didates, that is to say those who, like the Hebrews of old, have "sanctified themselves," are received into the Commonwealth of the Spiritual Israel with Jesus as their King and High-Priesthood in-carnate, for of the twain was made one new man. In the new sys-tem Jesus is Joshua as king, and is invested with the High Priest-hood which Aaron, and after him Eliazer, sacrificed symbolically each Day of Atonement, by slaying the He Goat, Pan-El, of Egypt, whose human upper part was symbolised by the white linen kirtle the High Priest carried on his own person, and sprinkled it with the gore of the slain He Goat, so that the High Priest appeared as if be-smeared with the blood of his victim of the altar.

The High Priest represented the God of Israel, who is pictured as follows : "Who is he that cometh from Edom, with dyed garments from Bozrah?" His garments are thus described as dyed crimson with the blood of the God of Edom and Bozrah, whom he has slain by his carnal symbol as the Ram and Bull and He Goat of Egypt.

The other He Goat of the Day of Atonement, and sent away to Azozel—so the Jews themselves call him, and not Azazel, as he is called by people who desire to bolster up erroneous views at the expense of truth—had a similar bloody kirtle to that worn by the High Priest during his sanguinary operations on the Day of Atone-ment. Jesus and Barabbas symbolised the Two He Goats, and the character given to Barabbas, namely a Robber, proves in what light the He Goat with the bloody garment tied to his horns, was regarded by the Jews, and by the Evangelists themselves.

We come now to the subject of the two Beth-Anias, called Bethany in English. Bethel and Jerusalem were the most notable places of Palestine. Long before Jerusalem came under the domin-

·ion of the Hebrews, Bethel, with its oaks and its sacred stones, was the centre of Hebrew national worship. In those days the entire country appears to have borne in the eyes of the nation the character of one great Elysium, with Bethel as its centre and rendezvous of the national worship. We have seen the nature of the associations of the Ford of the Jordan, a few miles to the east from Bethel, and having Gilgal between it and the celebrated sacred river. It is unnecessary to recapitulate here what we say as to the allegorical nature of the open river, and the Ark upheld above the level of the sides of the piled-up waters. The chasm itself was in the eyes of the allegorists, the Sacred Thebet, or Delphos (Womb), or miraculous Boat of the Queen of Heaven, consort of their God. Her other emblem was the great Stone, a Rocking Stone, which, like the sacred boat called ‚Argo of the Argonauts, could hear, and which stone was among the oaks at Shechem. Joshua, 24,27.

The Bethania on the Jordan was to the Bethel sanctuary more than the mere Ford and Ferry-Boat, it was also of the most sacred Thebet of their religion, whereon the Ark, symbolising the Mummy Case, had been held up before the eyes of their ancestors, to convey to them the lesson that, as they were transmitted from the wilderness of Sinai into the earthly rest of Canaan, so also would they find rest beyond Sheol in Paradise, beyond the River Styx of the under world. Thus the name Bethania beyond Jordan was preserved.

But in the course of time Bethel was abandoned, and Jerusalem became the rendezvous of the nation in both religion and civil matters. Successful efforts were made to make the temple and Mount Zion to be typical, not only of Palestine, but the whole earth. The tabernacle had two rooms, namely the Holy Place and the Holy of Holies, in the first was exhibited the Gold Crown of the God of Israel with fire burning in its orbit. It was a representation of the most awful apparition which Abram, as he was then known, beheld of his crowned God walking among the slain victims of the sacrifice: Egyptian emblems all—And it came to pass, that, as the sun went down and it was dark, behold a smoking furnace, and a burning lamp (in the margin, lamp of fire) that passed between the pieces. Genesis 15, 17. Then the two rooms were divided, one from the other, by a thick veil or curtain behind a blazing crown. In the Holy of Holies dwelt the Name of the monarch to whom the crown of fire belonged. This Name was represented by a mysterious Light called Shechinah, similar to an object sculptured on the holy places in the interior of the temples of Egypt. It appeared to Moses as the Burning Bush and a Voice in the Wilds of Midian. The owner of the crown "tried" to kill Moses while in obedience to the Voice he was on his way to Egypt, because his Son had not the Saturnian Mutulation, Ex. iv. 24. It was the Serpent-Rod that saved him!

Now the curtain, called the second veil, symbolised in the pattern of the True Tabernacle the same thing as the Jordan did, namely the under-world river Styx, dividing Sheol and Paradise from each other. To the East of the Temple another Bethania was named to relate to the Temple in the same allegorical sense as the Bethania "beyond Jordan" had done in relation to Bethel or Gilgal. In the ancient beliefs one had to return from Paradise across the river Styx, and up through the horrors of Tartarus to reach the upper world, and thence to ascend to the Highest Heaven. Moses was allowed the privilege of not dying, and therefore of ascending to the Highest Heaven from the Wilderness. Elijah passed to the East of the Jordan and the river opened as a substitute for Charon's Boat, to let him cross, and a heavenly chariot descended to convey him to heaven. He and Moses were many centuries later together on the Mount of Transfiguration, proving both were citizens of the Highest Heaven. Elijah's Cloak implied the same thing as the Dove and the Rod of Mars.

We now come to the most startling thing of all—Jesus after his triumphant return from the under world, himself ascended on high from the Bethania of Jerusalem, bearing captive captivity, that is to say, as many souls as were converted by him by his preaching to the captives of Pluto in the Under-world.

The sojourn of Jesus at the Bethania (House of the Boat) of Lazarus, Martha and Mary, on the eve of the Passover—corresponding with the time the Jews on the east of Jordan stayed to "sanctify themselves"—his triumphant journey over the Mount of Olives; the ripping of the heavy curtain from top to bottom—corresponding

J

with the ripping in the same manner of the waters of Jordan—
when Jesus's Divine Elohim passed through the second veil ; his subsequent return after his resurrection escorted by the Apostles, on
his way to Bethania of the Ascension, lend new and thrilling con-
siderations to the Bethania of Jerusalem.

JOHN'S BAPTISM OF REPENTANCE: AN IMPORTANT POINT CLEARED.

One of the most remarkable of the assumptions of the sanguinary Hebrew nation was that they were an exclusive people and a
holy nation "whose are the promises." They regarded being members of "the Commonwealth of Israel," as the highest distinction
attainable on earth. Canaan was Paradise on Earth, thus compar-
ing it to the fabulous Elysium of the Greeks, where the souls of all
good men and women pass after death and find "rest." But to
reach it they had to pass through Sheol, otherwise Hades, prefigured
by the "wilderness" of Sinai. Elijah, otherwise John the Baptist,
otherwise the God Pan himself, appeared in the "wilderness" and
furiously denounced the Jews of that day as a generation of vipers.
He invited them to repentance, and to observe the spirit, and not
merely the letter, of the law. He invited them to return to the spot
on the eastern side of the Jordan, where the fathers had, by sanctifying themselves, made themselves fit to enter the Holy Land on the
west across the Jordan. He invited that "generation of vipers"
to come to the sanctifying station of their ancestors, and after
repentance and going through the process of sanctifying prescribed
by the law of Moses, cross the Jordan at the very spot where their
forefathers had done, without even wetting their feet. We are here
confronted with the difficulty that if Jesus had no reason for repentance himself, why did he submit to John's outward sign of repentance and sanctification? It seems to imply that Jesus himself did not
differ from the rest of his generation till then. It is certain it was
after the events "beyond Jordan" with Elijah-John, he appeared as
the Word and the Power of the Spirit. For the business of John
"beyond Jordan" see Joshua, 3, 5.

ROCKING STONE AND CROM-LE-ACH.

The Crom-le-ach is a symbol of the earth, upheld over the abyss by the Adlais (Atlas), which name signifies the Echo of the Llev-Velus, Melodious Voice of the Word of the Creator. The Druids believed the earth stood still in the centre of the abyss, and that the heavens revolved like a wheel (rhod) around it. They supposed the Voice of the Word, as the Llev-Velus, echoed as far as existences are, and that the echo (Atlas) returned against the bottom of the earth's fabric, as a Divine power, and acted as a fulcrum in upholding the stupendous weight. This is the meaning of the expression in heb. i, 3, that the Word upholds all things.*

Underneath each Crom-le-ach are three stone pillars, acting as props "upholding" the horizontal stone resting upon their tops.

The three pillars symbolise the same as $\bigvee$, but the three pillars, representing its echo, are naturally placed in a reversed order. Thus we see the echo itself repres nts Hu Gadarn as two-fold in his nature. The voices of the earth were regarded as the filtered echoes of the Word's musical voice.

The Rocking Stone, it will be remembered, is the Kelwrn or Cauldron, containing the protoplasm, which being periodically fertilised by the seminal principle of the Word, personified as Jupiter, or Father Iu, oozes forth and imparts fertility to all things of earth, causing them to grow and develop; and in their decay and fall add to the fabric of the earth. And that the annual body of the sun itself came from the same Divine essence in the Kelwrn. It will be recollected what we state elsewhere respecting the Oriental heresy on this point, and why young Semele was imagined by them as the mother of the infant Bacchus, or the Sun, pages 57, and 91.

In Wales to this day a man or woman of superior attainments is called "Pen-y-Byd." The expression signifies Summit, Head, or Top, of the whole world. Jesus on the summit of a very high mountain, and on the summit of the Temple, and on the top of Circular

---

*Job xxvi, 7.

Mount Tabor, was on what the Ancients regarded in each instance the emblematic Pen-y-byd.* The same idea is conveyed by representing the God Brahma seated on the summit of the Lotos, upheld by its strong single stem above the water. It appears the summit of the conical mound, or Crom-le-ach, was permitted by the Druids only to the high priest—the Archon—who had been selected to undergo the rite of apotheosis. Jesus was selected twice, namely, after his Baptism by John and his admission into the high priesthood of the true Tabernacle, and at the close of his ministry, when both Moses (Bacchus) and Pan (Elijah) acknowledged him on the mount as uniting in himself their respective offices as Priesthood and King. On that occasion the Word as Father and Holy Spirit, did not descend in the semblance of a dove, as it did after his ascent from the Boat (Delphus) of John, when the "Voice of his Second Mother" was heard saying of the Divine humanity of Jesus, "This is my beloved Son, in whom I am well pleased: hear ye him." Matthew 17, 3.

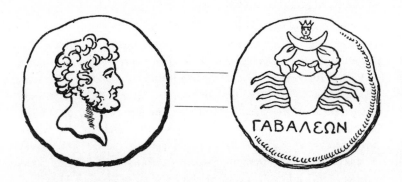

Medal of the city of Gabala, or Byblus, Phoenicia, on the seashore of Palestine. The Crab is shown holding up the crowned Babe Adonis (the Sun at the dawn of the new year) rising from the Galley, or sacred Thebet of the Queen of Heaven. See P. 50.

---

*Job xxvi. 7 ; Psalms xxiv, 2. Calmet's Bible Dictionary, plate 77.

The arms of Dunwich, East coast of England. The name is old British slightly altered· Correct: Din-Gwych or Grand Mound.

THE BATHKOL.

In studying the Hebrew esoteric mysteries one of which they term, the Bath-Kol, we must bear in mind that the compilers of the New Testament were adepts in the mysteries of the Kabbalistic school, and that in framing their narratives, they sought to prove the circumstances in the incarnation and public ministry of Jesus as the Messiah, were in agreement with the requirements of the Kabbala. Now, the mysterious Bathkol is a name meaning, the Daughter of the VOICE. Calmet states, "the generality of their traditions and customs are founded on this Bath-Kol." Now, the said Voice is that of the Queen of Heaven (Car:adwen). It is she whom Joshua associates with the great stone as its genius, in the Oakgrove of Shechem, and declares the stone had "heard all the Words of the Lord," Joshua, 24, 27. It will be remembered the oak beams from the Druidic oak grove of Dodona in the framework of the sacred Argo, or Sacred Galley of the Argonauts, were "possessed," and had a VOICE: "The Daughter of the VOICE" is shown in p. 50, and the Spirit of the sacred galley from which is the "second birth," is the winged Goddess behind her daughter, holding the Sun as Mabyn, in the Boat. In Welsh she in Anian, the Anima of Gwen or Venus. Vide Semele, p. 91. The Bath-Kol spoke "Hear ye him." "The

VOICE of the Goddess is heard in the Voice of Nature." It is clear the ancient Druidic saying is correctly, "Mae Llavar Duwies yn Llavar Anian."

When Jesus's Messiahship was completed by his apotheosis on the Mount of Transfiguration, and he was invested with the dazzling robe of Sol, the words now were those of a male God who said "Thou art my Son : this day have I begotten Thee." Heb. v, 5. Be it observed, no dove descended now. The Elohim or the twofold Word, as Father and Holy Ghost, were in him, and had previously descended in the semblance of a dove into his head. Jesus's carnal body had been begotten by the Power (Christ) of the Highest, thirty-three years before this second begetting, and his investure in a robe so white that "no fuller on earth can white them." Mark, ix, 3. It was the Queen of Heaven, called "the Spirit," who "drove" Jesus with the Christ in him (Dove), to be tempted by the Devil (Black Wings). This is adapted to the Druidic doctrine that Satan, being the fatherless elder son of the Queen of Heaven (Mam y Drwg), is ever jealous of the Elohim of the Highest, as the Light and Creator. Col. i, 16. In the "driving" she sends the Christ to a test encounter between him and his rival ; and to indicate her own impartiality, she "drives" the Christ to meet his antagonist. An excellent illustration given of the Jewish esoteric teachings, is that where Moses's Serpent (Christ as Wisdom) swallows all the Serpents of the Egyptian Enchanters.—Exodus vii, 12.

CHRIST THE FATHER OF ISAAC. CHRIST THE FATHER OF JESUS OF NAZARETH.

It is made evident that the Christian father, Justin Martyr, held that the Eternal Word was active among the Hebrews from the days of Abraham downwards, and that he was symbolised among them in divers ways. We find still higher authorities for the same assertion, namely, Moses, Isaiah, and St. Paul. As the most striking assertion in the eyes of Christians, we first quote the assertion of the apostle to the Gentiles. Referring to the miraculous water, which gushed out of the rock at Horeb, St. Paul states that the Rock was Christ, or Christos, that is to say, the emblem of the creating faculty of the Word, and that the said water was a spiritual one, and not an ordinary earthly water. In another epistle the same apostle states that Christ, as the Word, "is the image of the invisible God, the first born of every creature : for by him all things were created . . . and he is before all things, and by Him all things exist." Not only did he yield the essence water at Horeb, but He created all other things on earth and in the heavens above the earth, and it is His power that continues the existence of everything everywhere. We now come to a still more astounding assertion by Moses, namely, that the Rock, that is to say, the Divine power of the Word, the essence of the Christ, miraculously begot the Jewish nation : "Of the Rock that begot thee thou art unmindful, and hast forgotten God that formed thee."* Here the rock is God. How did the "Rock" beget the Hebrews? The answer is as follows : "And the Lord visited Sarah as He had said, and the Lord did unto Sarah as He had spoken, for Sarah conceived and bore Abraham a son in his old age." Genesis, 21, 1 and 2.

Then we find the Jews described as sons and daughters of the Rock ; that is to say, of the seminal element of him of which the Rock Pillar was the emblem. In the translation of the LXX of Deu. 32, 43, the blood of the Hebrew people is called "the blood of His sons." In the A.V. the word "sons" is substituted by the word "servants."

It will be thus seen that the Stone Pillar and the Ointment (Chrisma) of Bethel symbolised the Divine Father of the Hebrews as flesh and blood. And he says, "I am the God of Bethel." The same Divinity is said to have begotten Samuel.

We now come to the testimony of Isaiah, "Look unto the Rock ye were hewn, and the hole of the pit ye are digged." Then, as hinting the impossibility of Abraham and Sarah begetting Isaac in the ordinary way of nature, both the aged people are contrasted with the Rock, and the womb of Sarah as being inert.

*Deu. 32, 18.

We have omitted the "whence" inserted by translaters. In the translation of the LXX (300 B.C.) the same passage is rendered as follows: "Look to the solid rock which ye have hewn, and to the hole of the pit which ye have dug."

It is clear that the LXX did not understand the allusion, or that, translating in the land of Egypt, they wilfully corrupted the text to avoid detection by Egyptians and Greeks. It can be safely affirmed that the "Image" in the Temple of Diana at Ephesus alluded to by St. Luke in the Acts of the Apostles as having fallen from Jupiter, Father Iu (Christos) was a Rock Pillar.* But St. Paul had told the Corinthians that a similar Rock was the Christos, so St. Luke avoids giving the name by which the object was known to the Ephesians. St. John, after elaborately speaking of the Word as the Christ who is described by Moses and Isaiah as the Father of the Hebrews, states in reference to the flesh and blood of the Hebrews, "He came unto his own, and his own received him not." He himself thus eventually "became flesh, and dwelt among us, and we beheld his glory, the glory as of the only begotten of the Father, full of grace and truth."

Thus we are taught that Christ, the Word, was the only begotten of his Father, but Christ the Word was the Father of the Hebrews, therefore the Father of the Word was their Grandfather. In the foregoing we are taught that Christ begot Isaac by Sarah in her old age. Christ himself begot the body of Jesus by the Virgin Mary, through the inert agency of Joseph in his old age. When Jesus, the man, was, in accordance with the law of Moses, of the necessary age to be made high priest, thirty years old, the two-fold Word as Christ and the Holy Spirit, that is to say, the Father Christos and the Holy Spirit, descended into his head in the semblance of a Dove \|/ ; the body, like the Staff, the Rod, and the Rock Pillar, symbolising the seminal Christ, and the Wings, the Holy Spirit, the Druidic A-Wen. The wings and the horn of an unicorn; the burning bush, and Rod of Moses, symbolised the same divinities as the body and the

*Acts 10, 35

wings of the Dove. The meaning of the name Elijah is My God
IA. He is intended by the writer of his history to be understood as
an incarnate Deity, and to convey that he was the messenger of the
Father of the Christ, that is to say, according to the Jewish Pantheon,
the master of Elijah who killed the son of the widow of Zarephath,
with whom he lodged.* Elijah's departure from the earth
is like the departure of a God. He became incarnate again through
the inert instrumentality of Zacharias and Elizabeth. As we show
elsewhere Elijah is intended for the God Pan—the Pan El of Genesis
31, 32, and 33—whose haunts were the wilds, and his wanderings
took place at night time. Both Jesus and John, described as re-
lations, were the offspring of the Seminal Word, called, instead of
Christos, Gabriel, or the Voice of God the King, meaning Saturn,
placed blasphemously for the Almighty. Elijah came now, according to Justin Martyr, to proclaim and anoint the incarnation, Jesus,
as both high priest and king on earth; and he as Pan returned,
having delegated the priesthood of the half man and half goat, to
the Royal young Nazarene. But, as immortal Gods, both Moses and
Elijah afterwards interviewed the young hero who was about to suffer. This interview took place on the Mount of Transformation. Caiaphas had to be at his station in the Temple as the Cut-throat of
Saturn.

"HE IS THE HEAD OF THE BODY OF THE CHURCH."

As the result of incorrect pointing, the omission of the "of" in
translating the Greek text, and placing a comma after "body," together with ignorance of the figures employed by St. Paul, the
Christian world has been perplexed as to his meaning in the above
passage. Now, in the Gentile world the figures of solar mythology
were probably better known than anything else· It was universally
believed that in the western ocean was a barge called in the east
Thebet, and in the west, among other names, Arch (Ark), and Arech
by the Greeks, and Navis by the Romans. From this the name

*1 Kings xvii. 20.

Navis was given to the church, as the ship of the mysteries conveying the souls of the saints to the realm of Elysium, otherwise
Paradise and Gwenydva in Druidism. The sun was universally called
a Head, and in Druidism Pen Taliesun, or Taliesun's Head, and the
Head of the Bards or Druids. The said Navis goes also in Welsh
by the name Pair Cariadwen, or the Cauldron of Holy Love. Golgotha signifies The Head's Place.

The said Galley was supposed to be full of the miraculous essence,
called by Huxley protoplasm, with which, as sap, the earth was and is
gradually supplied and built up. In spring, when the fermentation
of the earth commenced, the Druids said that the cauldron of Cariadwen had begun to boil, under the fertilising influence of Hu Dad Eilir,
or the Christos in the sun's head. That sun received a new body every
year between December 25th and 27th, constructed miraculously
in the said Ark or Navis by the action of the same Divine Christos,
who, on being deprived of his tabernacle of the year before, had
sought and obtained refuge in the Ark itself, and by his fertilising
influence there upon the Essence in the Ark of the Goddess, again
reappeared a radiant head in which he himself ascended on high to
serve the earth with light and life. That is the simple meaning
of the above passage, only that he uses it as referring to Jesus.

The said Ark or Navis is alluded to by Jeremiah as the Queen
of Heaven, which as the source of the essence by which the earth
and the body of the sun were annually constructed, had become ob-
noxious to Saturn, since Saturn had become identical with the
Destroyer Typhon, otherwise Pluto, the Black Wings (Avagddu) of
the Druids. The following is the description of the Hebrews' attitude towards the Queen of Heaven: "We will certainly," they
say, "do whatsoever thing goeth forth out of our own mouth"—
into their stomach—"to burn incense unto the Queen of Heaven, and
to pour out drink offerings unto her, as we have done, we and our
fathers, our kings, and our princes in the cities of Judah, and in
the streets of Jerusalem: for then had we plenty of victuals, and
were well, and saw no evil." Jeremiah 44, 17. Then there is a
reference to making cakes to glorify thereby the Queen of Heaven,
whom the Druids held was the source of the material essence of

which all eatables and drinkables were made by the co-operation of the Word in the Sun. But in v. 27 the prophet represents the God of Israel crying in consequence, and saying of the Hebrews, "Behold I will watch over them for evil and not for good."

The hot cross buns of Good Friday are the said cakes to the Queen of Heaven still retained as a popular custom in honour of the boiling of the Cauldron of Cariadwen and the consequent streaming up of the sap, causing the earth to sprout forth and producing food for man and beast. It will be recollected that the crescent moon called Llun by the Druids was supposed to be a monthly-produced image of the Ark, to strengthen the faith of humanity, and evidence of the existence of the said Ark or Navis moored underneath the earth.

We perceive here that the original Triad of Egypt was based on the Seven personifications of the Sun while travelling over the Seven planetary lines during the Solar year, and before the invention of the Zodiac with its Twelve Signs.—Herodotus, Euterpe, Section iv.

In associating the Dove (Amen Ra) with Pan, the Ninth, we perceive an effort on the part of the Egyptian priests to restore the ancient purity of their symbolic religion, by discarding the Typhonïan third person, which the Royal Shepherds' nation had thrust upon them during their domination over them, lasting 511 years. Then we find Moses making Pan subordinate to Typhon, and naming him Abel, or Father of the Sun.

EGYPT AND SYRIA.
Amen Ra.

Old Osiris.   Young Horus.   Young Isis 2

—

THE WORD, SYMBOLISED BY THE DOVE ABOUT TO DESCEND ON THE INFANT HORUS.

—

In the sculptured figures given in Montefaucon's works, Osiris's head is missing. On referring to page 100 of this volume, the reader will see the same three and Pan, and old Osiris on the back of an ass We have restored the head to the above figure. Lucian, who was born in A.D. 24, wrote a book on the Syrian Goddess, and in p. 16, states that in the most sacred part of the temple of Hieropolis, the Holy City of Syria, were three figures. The middle one had a golden Dove on its head. "Not only," states he, "no name is given to it, but the priests say nothing concerning the origin or form. It is called THE SIGN. He is referring to the Golden Dove. The Chair of Glamorgan still calls the like sacred sign Y Nod CYVRIN (The Mystic Mark). It is still the sacred protective mark of the Government. See Payne Knight's Symbolical L. S. 220.

OLD OSIRIS, YOUNG HORUS, AND DOVE.
OLD JOSEPH AND YOUNG JESUS.
A GREAT MYSTERY EXPLAINED.

We should, in contemplating the above illustration, bear in mind that according to ancient religious philosophy, the Mind or Word of the Most High signifies the Lord of David in Psalm cx., and the latter is called Hu Gadarn in Welsh, referred to as the Lord and Elohim and Gods, and the title signifies in English, Invincible Hu or Iu, and from this is derived the Latin name, Jupiter Iu-Pater or Father IU. The Mind, or Word, is twofold (Gods), having in addition to the masculine essence of Paternity, also a Soul; and the two essence and soul are called Elohim or Gods. One is the Father of material things, including all bodies of flesh and blood, and the other the Father of all souls or intelligencies in all their degrees of progression towards perfection. Samuel dead is described as Elohim. Sam. xxviii. 13. In Bardism, the Father Spirit is called A-Wen, or Holy Wings. The Body and Wings of the Wren or Dove—both birds were used as symbols of the twofold Word—symbolised the complete Logos or Voice of the Most High. We say the Hebrews mistook the jealous and cruel old God, Saturn, for the Most High, and came to represent the twofold Word, which they called Elohim, as the Word, or Voice, of Saturn. In the history of Saturn attacking Jupiter, represented as his Son, we have the fact amply confirmed. In the addition to the twofold Word and the Sun, we have the sun itself personified three times, and Seven times, during each year.

From the station of the Sun on June 25th to his station on December 25th are the Seven lines of the planets or the paths the planets travel over across the firmanent in the course of the twelve months of each year. Those Seven paths have three principal stations. The upper line of those the sun is on on June 25th, the next is the line of March 25th; and next is that of December 25th. The sun is in Gentile religions personified in each of the said three and seven stations, and those three are the trinities and seven Gods of all the Gentile nations of antiquity. In the Christian religion we have the twofold Word in the Sun (Son); and the sun

himself was Jesus, with the Dove Elohim in his head.   In Peter,
James and John, we have the solar triad represented.   In the seven
men of honest report, Acts 6—3, we have the sun on the seven lines
above mentioned represented.   In days after the ascension, we have
the sun of righteousness taking the role of seven back to himself as
follows :—And unto the Church of Sardis write these things saith
He that hath the seven spirits of God, and the seven stars.—Rev.
3, 1.

(1) Iona or Jonah signifies Dove, and the Great Fish, which
swallowed Iona or Dove, is one of the three Oriental Symbols of the
instrument of the Queen of Heaven, namely : a Rocking Stone, a
Boat, a Dolphin, a name signifying Delphos, a Greek name signifying the womb, the womb in this instance being that of the Queen
of Heaven, mother of the Sun's baby body.   P 92.   Being a spirit
it was anciently believed that she used a boat, imbued with her own
spirit, to (1) convey the feminine sap from some world unknown to
the known one, (2) to succour the Sun on his nightly descent on the
Western Ocean, and (3) to convey souls away from this world.
The two others signify the same thing as the Thebet
(Boat).   It was believed the body of each sun was annually
murdered in the air on each December 25th before he
was able, owing to old age, to reach his usual nightly abode in
the boat of his mother, but that the Word in the guise of a Dove
always succeeded in escaping from the dying sun into the ark or
boat, shaped like the crescent moon.   Pages 17 and 71.   There the
Word (the Dove) was supposed to be reclothed in a new body, and in
page 50 we see him newly re-born as the Mabyn Arthur, from the
boat, and in the arms of Gwen, the Goddess Nature, his sister, who
acts as his nurse.   In page 92 we see the Dolphin emblem used instead of the crescent boat and rocking stone.   The Bards calling
the boat Llun (Image) and the Latins, deriving their name of the
Moon, namely Luna, from the Druidic Llun, and the Solar Boy
being described as in the Llun, gave rise to the old legend of "the
Man in the Moon."   The Dove is the Sign,—the Prophet Iona,—
referred to in Luke ii. 29, 30. ; Mat· xii. 38, 39, 40.   It is also the
Sacred sign $\vee$ (2) We explain fully elsewhere the meaning of the

monogram IAO (pages 96, 97, etc.).   In the Iolo MSS., pages
308—9, we find most remarkable expressions on this subject:—

> Ac Addav,—-Duw Nav, dy nawdd;—
> O dasc Alpha a'i dysgodd—
> Y gerdd gyntav, llathr Duw Nav llwyd,
> A genau doeth a ganodd."

Translation:—

"And to Addav (Sun) came the lesson—God Nav thy blessing!
It was taught by Alpha (the Word) and it was the earliest polished
    melody of holy God,
And by a wise mouth it was canticled."

Then we have introduced into the venerable poem, Christian
ideas mixed with Druidic ones..   This happens so frequently in
very ancient Welsh poems, as to convey the conviction that the
Druids glided from Druidism into Christianity almost without knowing it themselves.   They occasionally write Elphin for Alpha. Rev.
i. 8.   We have thus an attempt to discard Hu Gadarn.   The use
of the name Alpha in the foregoing is a proof the Druids had been
attracted by the declaration of Jesus that he was the Beginning
(Alpha), and that, to illustrate it, he had applied to his existence as
the creative Word, untold ages before he had created the human
body of Jesus to dwell on earth.   Therefore, the Druids called the
Christ, apart from the human Jesus, Alpha, instead of the more
ancient name Hu Gadarn.   Then the ancient Bard states of the
Sun:—

> "Pont Hu, ac yn gu gywir,
> O gwn wawd ac e'n wir;
> A roes Duw o'i ras del
> Er gwobr yn ngenau Gabriel:
> A Gabriel yn Air gobraff;
> Da y gwn gred a'i dyyg graff.
> O'r Nev Gatholic ei naid:
> Fawr gynydd i Mair Ganaid.
> Ysbryd Tad, urddad aurddellt:
> Glan a Mab, goleuni mellt:
> O'r TAIR llythyren Air teg:
> Byw vyrain yw vy anreg.

Translation :—

The conveyer of Hu : blessed and true :

And I know his praise and his truth :

Given by God graciously to impart activity

As a gift in the mouth of Gabriel :

And Gabriel, himself a powerful Word, sharp and keen-
sighted,

From the Catholic heaven his leap :

Great increase came to Holy Mary ;

Father—crowned with flashing golden rays—

Holy Ghost and Son—lightning lights :

The Three Letters constitute one fair WORD :

Living, infinite, is my Largess.

We treat of the Three Letters in another part of this work
(p. 97), and submit that the said Three Letters are the monogram
IAO, or the signs of the Trinity in Unity. The name of the composer of the long poem, of which the foregoing are brief extracts,
was Rhys Goch, of Snowdon.

The foregoing, most of it a recapitulation of what has been said
already, we deem essential to insert here to enable the reader to
understand the illustration at the head of this chapter.

In the East, as already pointed out, religious philosophers came
to suppose the sun's physical body—and because it is an object seen
by the eyes   it was supposed it is   composed of the same
substance as the earth itself—they concluded the sun's body—a
new one every year—was conceived by Nature (Gwen, or Venus)
somewhere in the bowels of the earth, and that Nature's gestation
of the Sun-Baby began each year on March 25th, a date still called
in Welsh almanacs, Dydd Beichiogiad Mair y Cyhydedd (the day
of the impregnation of Maria of the Equinoctial line). The employ-
ment of the name Maria (from Mare, the Sea) instead of Gwen, is
an indication that the early Christians, in Britan, sought to per-
suade the Druids that the words referred to the Virgin Mary's conception, and that the Mabyn, Taliesun, was Jesus, and not the
personified Sun. The apparent reason for fixing upon March 25th
was, because that is the time of the year the annual fermentation of
the earth is supposed to begin in Western Europe, where the reli-

gious ideas relating to the Sun's personality appear to have originated. Those who established the belief, pointed out that the Sun's power annually declined after September 25th, and that the climax of his decrepitude was attained on December 25th, when, as the entire ancient world believed, Pluto (Satan), called Black Wings by the Druids, always in his murderous efforts to get at the Word (Elphin) of Coelus Kelu, slew the Sun's physical personality in the air, the attack commencing always at noon on December 25th, and the struggle ending in favour of Pluto, the poor Sun's dead body then dropping into the Ocean, but the Word always escaping into the Ark or Boat, of the Queen of Heaven, his second mother, according to those who supposed Gwen, or Nature, was the mother of the Sun's physical body. In these two mothers we have the origin of the doctrine of Generation and Re-Generation. Jesus underwent both. (Hebrews v. 5).

Now, in the East it came to be believed that the aged Sun by the fertilising influence of the Word in him, even in his old age, symbolised by a dove, was the father of each new year's new Baby-Sun. But now came the puzzling question, which must have perplexed many an ancient Egyptian priest after the Shepherd Kings had confused matters, namely, how the old sun which had perished on the previous December 25th, could be the father of the new Baby-Sun of the following March 25th. It appears the difficulty was got over by supposing the old sun (Osiris) of the previous year had not perished on December 25th, as had been taught, but on the following June 25th—longest day instead of the shortest day—and that on March 25th he had became, in old age, the father of the Baby-Sun (Horus) by the instrumentality of the Word-Dove within old Osiris, in the same way that Abraham, in his extreme old age, became, by the act of the Word, he himself being the passive agent, the father of Isaac. That this was yearly repeated, one year after another, ad infinitum. If the reader will refer to the Proto-evangelion (Apocryphal Gospels) (C.8), he will find this given in the history of aged Joseph, the Dove, and the Youthful Virgin Mary. We are told in the history of Sarah, "And the Lord visited Sarah as he had said, and the Lord Did unto Sarah as he had spoken, for Sarah conceived, and bore Abraham a son in his old age, at the set time of which God had spoken to him." Gen. xxi. 1. That Isaac was the son of God is taught in Deut. xxxii. 18, and Is. li. 1-2, and St. John's Gospel, i. 11, is certain. This is the foundaton of the assertion of the Hebrew rabbins that the Jews are a Holy nation.

The entire Christian world have lost the primitive idea of the Ancient respecting the existence of the Queen of Heaven. The Spirit of the Church whose symbol on earth was the Nave-Building, or Arkite Boat, was her visible presence. She is the spirit on the Jordan from which Jesus was "born again." It was she, the second mother of Jesus, who "drove" him into the wilderness, and he was there forty days (hours), tempted of Satan ; and the angels ministered unto him." The voice which had said, a few minutes before, "Thou art My Son : this DAY have I begotten Thee," was that of the Holy Ghost, the Father of his Soul (Psyche) : the Christ was the Father of his body by a daughter of Royal David : thus the seed of David and David's Lord (Ps. cx., Luke xx, 42) had comingled. It is further stated that the "Voice" added in reference to Jesus who was king from his birth, "Thou art (now) priest forever after (the same) order as Melchisedek." Heb v. 5, 6. Justin Martyr states, the incarnation of Elijah-Oannes was for the purpose of anointing Jesus, the King of the Hebrews, to be also the High-Priesthood ; for the high priest was a separate identity apart from the he-goat and linen kirtle of the Day of Atonement.

The sojourn in the wilderness during 40 hours correspond with the Word's absence in Tartarus and Paradise, during which 40 hours his body was in the hollow sepulchre underneath the great stone, resembling the hollow under the great stone in the Holy of Holies, where the high-priesthood was each Day of Atonement 40 hours entombed. In the Druidic religion Satan, otherwise Black Wings (A-Ddu) is the elder son of the Spirit (p. 4) Queen of Heaven, the Sun being the younger of the two : Black Wings regards the Sun (Taliesun) as an usurper, and is after him to destroy him, called by Isaiah, Lucifer, or Giver of Light. What appears to be intended by Mark, etc., is to convey that the Queen of Heaven drove the Sun on earth with the Elohim in his head—Light of the World— to test the grit of the just completed Messiahsip, by putting him in conflict with his murderous rival, who ruled the world before Lucifer appeared in the firmament, and lit the universe with his electric lamp. The test proved eminently satisfactory, and Jesus returned in the Power of the Spirit, to Galilee; and there went out a fame of him through all the region, round about. Luke iv., 14· It will be remembered the Wilderness was symbol of Tartarus, or Hell, where Satan was supposed to retain his rule which he had lost on earth.

THE ARMS OF BRIGHTON

The CASQUE showing the sacred Argo in two forms: side view, with bars as seats across. The sun rising therefrom. Shield showing sea and Dolphin. the Babylonian emblem same as Delphos the Womb of Queen of Heaven.

ARMS OF PORTSMOUTH.

The Sun rising from the sacred Ark of Druidism.

THE TWO MOTHERS.

One of the most difficult matters to understand is the mysterious doctrine of the two mothers referred to by theology. In the New Testament the two births are described as one of the flesh, and the other of the Spirit. Both mothers must be of the feminine gender. "That born of the flesh is flesh; that born of the Spirit is Spirit." St. John's Gospel, iii. 6. The allusion in John i. 13; 1 John iii. 9; ic. 7; v. 1; v. 18, to a second birth of "God," (instead of God should be Goddess) signifies the Nave Church as the Spouse of Christ. Most people confound Christ, the beginning of the crea-tions of the Most High, his Father, with the young Hebrew, Jesus of Nazareth, who "was made flesh," and who, therefore, was "born of the flesh." But the Christ was born of the Most High's "bosom" before any flesh had existed. Rev. i. 5; iii. l'. Christ is called the Power of the Highest. St. Luke i. 25. Observe, the Holy Ghost is mentioned there, too, as in union with the Christ-Power. Christ is the Power of the Highest, as the Creator under the Highest. Col. i, 16. Both Christ and the Holy Ghost form Elohim, or Gods, after which pattern man was made substance and soul. The name Christ, in Greek Christos, and in Latin Christus, signifies Oil, and in Pagan worship the name was given to the Staff or Stone Pillar (Priapus) because anointed with the symbolical holy oil. When the Greeks of Antioch understood what the new sect was teaching, they gave its adherents the name by which a similar sect had been known among themselves from time immemorial. Acts xi. 28. That was the way the Hebrew names Messiah, otherwise Elohim, came to be called by a Greek instead of a Hebrew name· That Divine Oil, a fertilis-ing fluid from the Word of the Highest, the Druids, described com-prehensively as three drops, as described in p. 8. He is the fertili-ser of all ova, by the instrumentality of his male agents on earth, therefore, "we are his offspring." St. Paul agreed with this. Acts xvii. 28, 29. Under the system of Moses, this oil was symbolised by wine and oil. Deut. vii. 13. The symbolical oil was mixed with dead, or unleavened bread, in honour of the fabulous Saturn whom the Shepherds in Egypt had placed on the throne of the Highest, and, strange to say, as the Father of Elohim, the Christ and the Holy Spirit.

The Jews, following the Shepherds, burnt eggs, and do still at the Paschal supper, in honour of Saturn, the Destroyer. The jealously of Saturn of Christ is given in every history of Saturn and Iu Pater, or Father Iu—the Hu Gadarn, of Druidism. Now comes the most difficult thing to make clear.

(1) The oil Christ is the Power of the Highest.

(2) The Protoplasm in the Arkite Galley of the Queen of Heaven is the original passive essence, apart from the Spirit Queen of Heaven herself, as the oil Christ stands apart from the Highest.

(3) The Arkite Galley, or Cauldron, of the Queen of Heaven (Cariadwen) is moored beneath the earth. From it, in Spring, steams up through the earth the protoplasm, and then through roots, and coming into contact there with the Sun's rays, it is fertilised by them·

(4) All the old nations believed that at the end of each solar year, anciently December 25th, the Sun's corporeal body perished, and in p. 17, we see the Dove, his body symbolising the oil-Christ; and its Wings, the Holy Spirit, fleeing to the refuge of the Arkite Boat of the Queen of Heaven.

(5) That the Oil Christ, represented by the Dove's body, coming into touch with the protoplasm in the Ark, generated thereby each year a babe Sun, which the Druids called Mabyn, Taliesun, Arthur, Merddyn, etc.

(6) In the East a most disastrous mistake was made, resulting in throwing the Druidic teaching into confusion, and two mothers and two births of the sun were the result.

(7) In the East it was at first taught that the Goddess Nature (the ascending sap) was the mother of the sun's flesh; for they believed the sun was flesh and blood. But as we explain in the story of Young Semele (p. 91), this led to the Sun (Bacchus) being represented as the son of his own sister, and Semele was substituted for Venus, as the mother of his flesh. Moses—who assumed the role of the two-mothered Sun in the Grand National drama he was writing—had observed the absurdity, and represented Miriam, his sister, as his foster-mother, and placed Pharaoh's daughter instead of the Queen of Heaven.

(8) The East next came to represent the Arkite Boat of the Queen of Heaven, as the Mother of the Sun's soul or the Holy Ghost, instead of Generator of Souls from her spirit.* They thus separate Oil-Christos, otherwise Jupiter, Eros, etc., from each other as separate personages, instead of being body and Soul of Elohim, or the Word, or Mind, of the Highest. The Sun, as the son of Semele, was "born of the flesh;" and water of the matrix was used to symbolise that birth. The birth of the soul—called second birth—was from the Arkite Boat, of which most ancient sacred lakes in Wales carried one of its Arkite symbols. In the second birth of Jesus, the Dove-Elohim descended into his head, as if he were the sun on earth. These old erroneous ideas of the ancients are valuable only as showing the foundation of creeds, derived from the earnest speculations of the Druids and Chaldeans, who, no doubts, were Druids. In the illustration, young Horus is the young sun of the flesh. The lady is either Venus (Isis 2) or Semele. The import of the Dove will be now clear. See also p· 217.

---

*In the following, the Father referred to is the Christ of the Druids, namely, Hu Gadarn:—

"After the Peal of Music at the beginning,
The Holy Ghost was with the Father."

The Holy Ghost is called, in addition to A-Wen, A-Dda, or Good Wings.

Prince Aneurin in A.D. 550 writes:—

"On the first day, the Crowned Babe
Sang a Canticle in Elysium (Gwenydva):
And the Holy Ghost descended from On High,
Accompanied by Pealing of Worlds,
And the Holy Ghost assumed activity."

Bardism, pages 38, 39.

In the translations we have endeavoured to give the sentiments in the idioms of the English tongue. It will be seen that the letter A. in A-Wen, and A.-Dda are dealt with as, in each instance, a pair of wings, one of the ancient emblems of a spirit. The sounding descent of the Holy Ghost on the Day of Pentecost, resembled the sound of descending rushing wings, cleaving the air. "It" alighted on the head of each apostle, and "it"—the pair of wings—radiated from each head "like tongues of fire," as Shechinah.

THE GOD PAN AS A SATYR ACCOMPANIED BY A DOVE.
ALL FULNESS IN HIM.

In the Bible the God Pan is referred to in Gen. xxxii· 31, in Hebrew, under the consonontal form P—N—L, which in full is Pan-El. This translators render both Penuel and Peniel. El in Hebrew signifies God. Herodotus, who was born 443 B.C., states "the Mendesian (Egyptian) women would not sacrifice Goats of either sex, out of reverence for Pan, whom their traditions assert to be one of their Eight Gods, whose existence preceded the twelve Gods" (or the twelve signs of the Zodiac personified as Good ones). "And Egypt esteems Pan as the most ancient of the Gods." If the reader will refer to the seven and twelve Gods respectively, whose history is given in this work, as the personification, of the Sun in the seven planetary spheres, and his subsequent personifications in the twelve signs of the Zodiac respectively, he will find that the seven persons, and including the sun's own personality, eight in number, preceded the twelve—the seven were the personified emanations of the Word in the sun, the agent of their transmission. It will be borne in mind that the seven days of the week are based on the earlier system of seven, and that the Sunday sphere of the sun is the line traversed by the sun on the longest day of the year, which anciently was June 25th, which was the Syl-Gwyn (Whit-Sunday) of the Ancient Britons. The middle day of the week corresponds with the line of the celestial equator, and Saturn's day with the shortest day, December 25th in old calendars. It seems certain either the Egyptian priests ignorantly misinformed Herodotus, or that he misunderstood them, for the he-Goat (Capricornus) does not belong to the seven Spheres, but is the Sun in the Ninth signs of the Zodiac, counting from Taurus (Apis or Bull). The sun on the seventh sphere was personified as Typhon (Saturn) in Egypt by the Royal Shepherds, and as Pan—one being the seventh, and the other Ninth, corresponding with December 25th—and hence the great rivalry which was supposed to exist between Saturn and Pan, and he, the Ninth, was annually put to death on the cross of the sky on December 25th. p. 71.

Typhon is Arabic for Anarchy, or Deluge, a name still in the Oriental name Typhoon : a terrible storm· Noah (Pan) signifies

Ninth or Ninius.   In the history of the Deluge we have Ninth represented as a Righteous Man, upon whom and his family Saturn-Typhon takes pity, and preserves them from the universal Typhoon. And with Ninth is preserved the Egyptian symbol of the Word of God, namely, the dove, and also the symbol of Black Wings (Typhon), namely, Raven, and all in the Ark, called Thebet in the Bible, the Egyptian symbolical Matrix—the Argo-Delphus—of the Spirit Queen of Heaven, one of whose symbols was the Crescent Moon; another an Egg; another, each Rocking Stone; Ceubawl (a Canoe) and a Coffin, which is still called Arch in Welsh; and, finally, the church borrowed the symbol and called the church Nave or Navis (a Galley).   In 1 Chronicles xxiv 10, Pan is called Abijah, or My Father is IA, or the Dove, for the letter I in IA here is given to be inserted in the fork of the sign V (Wings), anciently called A. Abijah was the title of the course of the priests to which belonged Zacharias, the reputed father of the re-incarnation of Elijah, called Oannes—Man and Dolphin, as p. 50—the Baptist who, like Pan, was peculiar about the loins, and in his unnatural wild habits.*

In the mysteries it was taught the Word (Dove, p. 17) was, after his escape from the murdered and wrecked old sun, the Father-Christos of the new Crowned Babe, regarded as a Sun or Son, fertilising by his Divinity as Seminal Logos, the feminine essence in the Crescent-shaped Ark of the Queen of Heaven on the Western ocean. The reader will bare in mind we are dealing with the speculations of ancient philosophers, and not with actual facts.

On the return of the Jews from Babylon, the twelvth zodiacal position is assigned to Abijah (Neh xii, 4).   This error arose doubtless in the confusion caused by the ordinance of sacrificing the He-Goat and sprinkling his blood on the linen kirtle of the

---

*Elijah.—There was a common tradition among the Jews that Elijah was Phineas, son of Eliazer, the High-Priest, and that the Prophet, who lived among men, sometimes under the name Phineas and sometimes under the name Elias, was not a man, but an angel. P. Bayle, Vol. II., p. 18   Calmet states the name Phineas is from the Hebrew Pana.   Thus tradition retains the association of the character with the high-priesthood, with the supernatural, and with Pana.   The final a in Pana is superfluous.

High-Priest, who acted as the bier—called the body of this death—
of the sacrificed high-priesthood, on Sept. (Tisri 10) instead of Dec.
25th (Thebet or Ark Month). In Gen. xil. 21, Pan—the Ninth—
is represented by Naphtali, and to prove the Hebrews knew this, we
find a city near it, if not in the territory of that tribe, named Paneas.
In Gen. xil. 21, Jacob describes Naphtali as a Hind, the very name
given to the crucified Pan in the title of Ps. 22, which was recited on
the cross by Jesus (p. 71). The words of Jacob that Naphthali was
"a HIND, let loose," refers no doubt to the He-Goat "let loose" on
each Day of Atonement as a prey to Azozel. In the tragedy of
Jesus, when the circumstances of the Passover and those of the Day
of Expiation are described by the Evangelists as having been observed together on the former named occasion, Jesus is both the
Lamb of the Passover and He-Goat, and Barabbas is the "Hind, let
loose," or in the erroneous translations the "Scape-Goat." The
Christian Father Eusebius, secretary to the Emperor Constantine,
about A.D. 300, states on the authority of Plutarch, that, in the
reign of Tiberius Cæsar, a loud voice was heard in the Ionian sea,
crying, "The Great Pan is dead!" and that God in that manner intimated to the Gentiles the death of Jesus. Vide Bell's Pantheon :
Name Pan. The words of Eusebius are only valuable as showing
that the high-priesthood of the Jews, in the opinion of the most
learned of the early Christian Fathers, was identical with Pan as a
sacrifice to the God whom the Jews worshipped by sacrificing other
Gods to him, and by way of glorifying Him, as God of Gods. The
ancient Greeks had been made to believe the God Pan had once
assumed the form of a hare. It appears this fable had reached the
Druids and induced them to regard the hare as most sacred, as the
Brahmins do monkeys, because they believe the fable the God
Brahma once assumed the form of a monkey. Readers of Tacitus
will recollect that the statement the British Queen Boadicea sent
from her war chariot a hare when her army was about to engage the
Romans near New Market, Flintshire.

There may be another explanation as to the reason why the
Egyptian priests of Heliopolis—the early home of Osarsiph otherwise Moses, told Herodotus Pan was eighth God. According to
the astronomical law, called the procession of the equinoxes, the sun

on each March 25th rose 8000 or 9000 years ago in the Zodiacal sign of the Twins. Then the sign of the He-Goat would be the eighth sign, and therefore would be the Eighth God or good. It will be recollected we point out that on December 25th the ancients believed the sun, apart from his tenant, Hu Gadarn, was slain on the cross in the heavens, and that in forty hours, he was succeeded by a Young Babe Sun under as many names as there were ancient languages.

Now, the sun as old Pan, was succeeded by a young Pan (p. 34).—Zacharias was the predecessor of the young Pan, John the Baptist. It is stated in the Apocryphal Gospel that old Zacharias was slain between the altar and the Temple. Dr. Lightfoot points out that according to the Babylonian and Jerusalem Talmuds, Zacharias was slain on the day of Atonement and therefore simultaneously with the sacrifice of the He-Goat at the altar by the high-priest, and the sending the other He-Goat away to Azozel. (Protevangelion, 16, and footnote). Thus Zacharias symbolised carnally old Pan. Dr. Inman states the name Zacharias signifies, the Watchful Old Sun. This took place in the regular order, young Pan being, in the corrupt Druidism of the East, the son of Old Pan, instead of Son of the Word, symbolised by a dove in the East and by a Wren in the West. Both of John's parents being old, the incarnation of their child was more strange than the incarnation of Jesus by the agency of the Lord of David by a young daughter of David (Ps. 110). In p. 34 we see the He-Goat humanised as young Pan, and the young Ram humanised as the Infant Jupiter, otherwise Jove (Jesus). If it was correct to call Jesus the Lamb of God, it was correct also to call John the Young Kid Goat of God· In the very ancient illustration in p. 34, both the animals and the two young Gods, are shown as both in each case. Truly the ceremonial law had "shadows" of things to come, and not the very "Images" of them. John-Elijah was the God Pan himself, having become incarnate for the purpose of transferring the high-priesthood, through the agency of descendants of Aaron, as both John-Elijah's parents were, and to add it to the tribe of Judah, in the person of the King Jesus, while Caiaphas was still Aaron, the slayer of the high-priesthood, and also the Kingship, as represented by the eldest son whose substitute from Isaac downwards was the Lamb of the Passover, and the Lamb the emblem of the Sun in the Zodiacal sign of the Ram (Aries) on March 25th (Nisan 14th. Faber, in his work on the Mysteries of the Cabiri (Vol. I., p. 161) states on the authority of Livy and Macrobius, that Pan had a Dove (the Egyptian symbol of Amen, or the Word of God) associated with him. It will be recollected that when John-Elijah transferred the high-priesthood, while Caiaphas still represented Aaron, a Dove descended on Jesus. Here the Dove was transferred from John-Elijah-Pan to Jesus. Jesus was King before that event, but it was then the Elohim—the Hebrew name for the combination of the dual word as Essence and Holy Soul, after whose image all mankind were created in the beginning—descended into his head. The Dove (Elohim) is referred to as follows:—"And the Spirit of God Brooded upon the face of the waters" (Embryo). Gen. i. 2. The word Brooding—the act of a bird over an egg—is inserted in the margin of the recently Revised O.T. The Elohim states in verse 27 that they who Brooded said, "Let Us make man in Our Image:" that is to say, of Essence and Soul like Ourselves, namely Christos (Seminal), Holy Spirit (Soul)· The First was symbolised by the Dove's body; the Second by his Wings. The "Brooding" was over the Argo-Delphos, or Galley-Womb, of the Queen of Heaven (Isis I), here compared to an Egg. In Genesis i, 2, the Galley ((Thebet or Ark) is called "Face of the Waters." The Chrisma is called "water" in Exodus xvii, 6, and 1 Cor. x, 4. Illustrations, pages 17, 24, 50.

The descent of the Dove on the head of Jesus, implied the descent of the Urim and Thummim into him as the high priesthood joined the Kingship which he already possessed as the Son of Mars—as the lineal descendant of King David, of the tribe of Judah, we find the epistle of the Hebrews proclaiming in the next verse that now Jesus was completed, and he therefore was proclaimed by the Dove as Father-Spirit.

> Thou art a priest (and King) for ever,
> After the same order as Melchizedek."

This teaches us the earthly sonship of Jesus was not complete till he was invested also with the high-priesthood: indeed it was

then the "twain was completed as one new man." Eph. 2, 15th.
In Colossians the apostle states that it is he, whom the Dove symbolised, created all things and that he was the first produced—born as a
Word from the Mind or bosom of the infinite Divine first Lord referred to in Ps. cx.   He was before all things, and all things by Him,
are held together (Greek). Col. i, 17.   To be Christians we must
believe, first, the Almighty sent forth from Himself a separate identity called His Voice (Logos), and that the Voice,
as the vehicle of his Word, assumed a separate personal
identity other than his source, and was apart from the
Almighty himself; was a dual agent; a fertilising essence
and Soul; that he was thus the Father of all material things and
of all animated lives or souls.*   Secondly, that the Word, as Divine
Chrisma impregnated a young Jewess named Mary of Nazareth, and,
in that manner, assumed the earthly form of one of his own creatures
as body and soul.   Thirdly, that when the miraculous Son was
about thirty years of age two supernatural events came to pass in
relation to him : first, the God Pan descended, and was incarnated
by the instrumentality of a son and daughter of Aaron, and after
waiting until the Royal Son of the lineage of King David, by his
mother's side, was thirty years of age in accordance with the law of
Moses as the proper age to be made a high priest, that is to say
of the required age to don the priesthood, emblemised by the linen
Kirtle, and the he-Goat of the Day of Atonement, and called "Hind,"
Pan ordained him to represent him on the earth : at the same time
the Elohim descended, in the guise of a Speaking Dove, into his head.
Thus had Jesus become King as regard his relation to David through
Mary, and Father, Son, and Holy Spirit as regard his relation to
the Creator Elohim.   (Christ, Holy Spirit, and Son).   This is
what the apostle means by the words, "For he was well pleased

---

*Christ our life (lives).   Col. iii, 3.

"The ancient copies differed from Jerome's, for one of
them, the learned Faustaus, a native of Britain, who became Bishop
of Reitz, in Provence, endeavoured to prove that Jesus was not the
Son of God, till after his Baptism." The Gospel of the Birth of
Mary : introduction Apocryphal Gospel.

that in him (Jesus) all fullness should dwell." Greek. The One "well pleased" is the Christ, as his father. Col. I, 19.

We can see plainly that the writer was thinking when penning the foregoing, of the Druidic belief that each new Sun as a substance was the joint production of the Winged Word and the feminine essence in the Crescent shaped Nave (Church) of the Queen of Heaven, for the sun being alluded to as the Head of Taliesun of the Bards, the apostle states Jesus is the Head of the Church or the sacred Boat. See p. 50. Here is the secret of the meaning of Golgotha.

THE GOD PAN AND JACOB: THE NIGHT SCENE IN THE FOREST.

It is patent to every student of the Hebrew writings, that the Hebrews never doubted the existence of the Gods of other nations. What the Hebrews asserted, and implicitly believed, was, that their God was chief of all Gods and Lords.—"God of Gods, Lord of Lords." Herodotus states the Egyptian priests deemed Pan as the most ancient of Gods, and even of those eight who are accounted the first Gods.—Euterpe, 145, section. He adds that the Greeks deemed Pan as the youngest. Thus we see that Herodotus had not been initiated into the Greater Mysteries which taught that the corporeal body of each Pan, as the personified sun in the Ninth sign from Taurus, only lasted till December 25th in each year, and that in 40 hours from sunset on the twenty-fifth, till sunrise on the twenty-seventh, a young Pan (Son) appeared. The time is to be measured in the latitude of Greenwich. Thus the Egyptians took into account Old Pan, and the Greeks young Pan, in other words in the corrupt Oriental mythology, one Father and the other Son. But the compilers of both the O.T. and the N.T. were thoroughly initiated, but concealed the mysteries of the words forty hours by forty "days" and often forty "years." Noah or Ninth is Pan, and the Deluge is the forty hours of Anarchy which was supposed to prevail during the reign of Typhon, during the said forty hours, between the death of Old Pan, and the birth of Young Pan, his successor. Now, Pan is not called God in the account of his wrestling with Jacob in the woods at night, but Man (Ish.). But the Seventy translate P.N.L. God's Face. The following is the explanation: Jacob, like the rest of the nation in Egypt, called Royal Shepherds, worshipped Saturn under the Arabic appellation, Typhon. Pan was, like Elijah, supposed to dwell in caves, and to roam the wilderness at night. Here he and the Typhonian, Jacob, met accidentally and Jacob caught hold of him, and a desperate struggle took place between the two. Jacob proved the stronger, and Pan, finding day dawning, asked Jacob to let him go. Pan admitted Jacob had conquered in the struggle, and in our translations, the word used to denote Jacob's victory is "prevailed." Then, Jacob, a Saturnite, having "prevailed," by the assistance of his terrible God, Pan acknowledges his own defeat, by calling Jacob, Israel, the Phœnician, and therefore, also Hebrew name of Saturn in that remote period. The only one Jacob is said to have met was one he calls Ish or Man, but he adds, "I have seen God face to face." It is certain we should read "I have seen a God face to face," and that the LXX translation in Egypt substituted Face of God, for the P.N.L. of the text, to guard against detection by the Greek and Egyptian scholars of the time. It is said Isra-El signifies Prince of God. But Sanschoniathon, the ancient Phoenician writer states it was the Phoenician name of Kronos, who is Time personified, who is confounded with Saturn, with the result that to Saturn is often given, most erroneously, the name Kronos from the Greek Chronology. Vide Cory's Ancient Fragments, p. 21.

TWO MOST SACRED HORNS.

THAT OF THE ANOINTED AND THAT OF NATURE.
ONE THE TRANSMITTER, THE OTHER THE RECEIVER.

By referring to pages 34 and 100, the reader will see illustrations showing two gods. In p. 34 is shown two infant Gods, one younger than the other. The younger is being fed from the Cornucopia or Horn of Plenty, by a Goddess. The Cornucopia is the symbolical counterpart of the Linga, otherwise Phallus, emblem of the Sun's rays, collectively considered as a fertiliser of the seed germs of Nature, personified as Gwen-Venus. The sun pours into the earth, and the earth pours out. The ancients state this Horn was given by Jupiter, or Father Iu, to his nurse (Gwen). Here is Father Iu placed instead of the sun's separate carnal personality. He, however, is but an agent of the Word. On referring to 1 Sam. xvi. 1, we find reference by the Christ himself, Who is Jupiter, to the Horn of Christ. "Fill thine Horn with oil," said the Lord to Samuel—as the said Lord's delegated authority—"and go : I will send thee to Jesse the Bethlehemite : for I have provided Me a King among his sons." Here is what took place : "And Samuel took the Horn of Oil and anointed him (David) in the midst of his brethren." In Psalm i, 12, David describes his new relationship to the second Lord referred to in Psalm cx. and in Mark xxii. 44. The following is David's descripition of his new relationship to the eternal Word : "The Kings of the earth set themselves and the rulers take counsel together, against the Lord, and his Anointed" (David himself). Kiss the Son (David again) lest he be angry, and ye perish from the way." Psalm ii. "David is (was) not ascended into the heavens ; but he saith himself : "The Lord said to My Lord," etc. "Therefore, let all the House of Israel know assuredly, that God (Christ) hath made this (Greek) whom ye have crucified (Jesus) both Lord (second Lord of Psalm 110) and Anointed (Christ)."Acts ii. 34. Jesus was of the Essence of the second Lord, and, therefore, bore the same relation to him as a son does to his father. Where theologians have gone wrong on this question is by not understanding that the Chrisma from the Horn in the hand of Samuel, was an imitaton of the real Sunbeam and its Chrisma, employed by the Lord of David, to fertilse the Ovum of the Virgin Mary to create the body of Jesus himself, for Christ to come and dwell in it on the earth. On the mother's side Jesus was "the son of David," and therefore the King. But by the father's side he was the son of David's Lord referred to in Psalm cx and Matthew xxii, 44, 45. The genuine Holy Oil is the generating essence of the Logos Sperm, named Three Drops (Tri Diveryn) by the ancient philosophers of Western Europe. p. 8. The Baby God, who is being fed by Gwen (Nature) in page 34, is the same Infant God (Sun) in the arms of the same Gwen in page 50, and is on the back of the Dolphin in page 92. He is the Sun as a Crowned Mabyn on December 25th at his first creation, but 40 hours later in each of his succeeding regenerations. He is Arthur-Sun renewed. His soul has returned in the Boat of p. 17, where it enters the Infant Head prepared for his, or their, reception, as the twofold Divinities —Elohim—Gods—John's Gospel, x. 34-38. See also Mark xii. 36 ; Luke xx, 42 ; Acts ii, 34 ; 1 Corinthians xv, 28 ;Hebrews i, 13 ; 1 Peter iii, 22. The Prince of the Apostle refers to the Christ and not to the Son of Mary ; unless we are to understand that Jesus after his resurrection from the dead, had become absorbed in the Christ—the Second Lord, so pointedly referred to in the foregoing references. We find that such absorbtion is referred to in the instance of the prophet Samuel, who, after his death, is called Elohim, or Gods. It appears that Samuel himself was regarded as an incarnation of the Second Lord of Psalm cx. (1 Samuel xxviii, 13). Indeed, the history of the miraculous circumstances associated with his mother's conception leads one to infer that a Divine Father of Samuel is implied. We have the two horns alluded to by Hannah his mother in connection with the miraculous generation of Samuel, her son. But while she alludes to herself as a cornucopia, the Stone Pillar (Rock) is the masculine symbol employed. 1 Samuel i, 11, and 19 ; C. ii and 2 ; Luke i, 40, etc. These facts throw a new light on the cabbalistic significance of Samuel being deputed to pour the contents of his horn of holy oil on the head of David* as conse-

---

*"And Jacob rose up early in the morning, and took the STONE that he had put as a pillow, and Poured Oil upon the Top of it" (a Phallic rite). Deut. xxxii 18. ; Gen. xxviii. 18 ; ixl, 24.

crating him King, and joined to the Word in the substance of the Messiah through Mary. Samuel is associated with the VOICE in governing Israel. 1 Sam. viii. 7. The VOICE (Christ) asserts that He led the nation from Egypt. Judges ii. 1., and Heb. xi. 26. It is clear that whenever the name Elohim (Gods) is employed in rela- tion to Deity in the Old Testament, the twofold Word or Amen Ra is intended. Those Elohim were mystically symbolised by the Rod of God in the hand of Moses, and by the Cloud, Shechinah, the Urim and Thummim, etc. See pages 93, etc., and 102. See Calmet, Vol. II. 584. The Bathkol, or daughter of the Voice, is the Voice of the Church as the Echo of the Voice. Ps. xxii. 3.

TWO SUBORDINATE GODS.

In the foregoing chapter we have the secret of the doctrine of the Trinity again explained. We have the twofold Word as Father, and Holy Spirit or Soul, and the Sun as the Son of the Father, called Jove, or Jupiter. See p. 96. Now, it will be observed that one of the infant Gods in page 34 is the God Pan as an infant, and is the elder of the two. The other infant God is the infant Jove or Jupi- ter, as regards his body. The He-Goat at the foot of the very ancient illustration, is the original emblem of Pan, and the Lamb, the original emblem of the "House" of Jove or Jupiter, and the two animals were undoubtedly placed where they are to convey the lesson as to who the two infant Gods represented. That they represented two signs of the Zodiac, namely, the Ram of March 25th, and the He-Goat of December 25th. The two animals were originally the signs of two of the "Houses" of the Sun in his annual progress through the twelve signs of the Zodiac. Then came the un- fortunate practice of humanising the animals or Houses followed by idolatry. It seems that the illustration in p. 34 was intended to check the tendency which had been observed to regard the personi- fications as veritable two distinct Gods, and not, as originally in- tended, merely stations of the sun in his annual progress through the twelve signs, and the two animals were placed in the illustration to arrest the attenion of those who might be in peril of being misled by the humanised figures. But the Jews fell into direct opposite error : they came to regard the said two Gods as real ones, and the Lamb and the He-Goat as representatives of the two, and both as hateful to their God, and that to please him, slaying the two symbolicals as such, would be highly pleasing to him. Pan-He- Goat is the emblem of the sun's "House" on December 25th : the Lamb Jove that of the sun on March 25th. Aaron and his descendants as the ministers and slayers for the God Saturn, killed a Lamb on behalf of each ten of the nation, on each March 25th. (Nisan 14 in the Jewish Calendar). In slaying the He-Goat we find very peculiar circumstance : (1) Removal of the date of the He-Goat (Capricornus) from December 25th to September 21 (Tishri 10th). This removal is to give the Autumnal Equinox, or December 25th, to Saturn, the Sun on the Seventh planetary sphere on December 25th, which in the East had been made identical with Typhon, whose emblem among the Phœnicians and the Shepherd Kings was a Black Boar. (2) The Hebrews in a most mysterious way came to regard the God Pan, whose symbol was a He-Goat, as their own representative as a nation. It seems we have the reason for this in the act of Jacob meeting him in the forest at night, and the God imparting to him his blessing. Genesis xxxii. 31. The God Pan made Jacob lame like himself. P. 88. It is certain, the Jews hold in deepest reverence the sinew which was touched by the God of the forest, in the hip of Jacob. They likewise refrain from eating flesh of Boars or any other swine, as the Royal Shepherds did in Egypt. Now Jove and Pan are symbolised by Jesus and John the Baptist. The Jews here abandoned the animal symbols and adopted the human personifications instead and in p. 34 we have the figures that the ancients guarded against being regarded as two Gods, by placing the Lamb and the He-Goat at the foot of the illustration. (3) Another peculiar thing is, that the Egyptian symbol of the Word of the Most High, called Amen Ra, namely, the Dove, (p. 65), is in the Jewish cult associated with the He-Goat Pan, instead of with the Taurus—the sacred Bull Apis of the ancient Egyptians. p. 65. As we have shown throughout, the Jews adored the Word under various disguised names, from their earliest times down to the time the Dove descended on the Head of the Young King of Nazareth, who is associated with Pan-John—

called Oannes or Man and Fish, the Fish being the emblem of the Boat of the Spirit, Queen of Heaven, who was the Mother of his High-priesthood. The Virgin, of the line of David, his mother as King; but the Queen of Heaven was the mother of the High-priesthood, and her Womb was the sacred Boat, whose emblem appears to have been rowed across the Jordan by Oannes, for the Fish (Delphos-Womb) is associated with him in his compound name. As Eli—I.A., we are to understand the words My God the Dove. See pages 50, 97. We now come to a remarkable observation made by St. Paul. Jesus became by birth, as David's descendant, King of the Jews; but he was consecrated to the High-Priesthood by Oannes-Eli I.A. In these names we have as profound a mystery as the profoundest mystics of the Nile Valley ever invented. Oannes signify Man and Fish. In Eli I.A. (Jah)—the I the body, and the A the Wings of the Dove—we have my God the Dove. This is all consonant with the style of mystic teaching of the Talmudists. St. Paul, in Ephesians ii., refers to some two meeting in Jesus. Formerly those two were at variance. The Gentiles were represented by one, and the Jews by the other, associated with both of whom was the ceremonial law. Both united in Jesus—he is "our Peace." The apostle is referring to the two separate identities. In Jesus the two became one. The rival factions were in him reconciled—Jews and Gentiles met in him—and he, therefore, is "our Peace." The apostle is referring to the Royal Ram and He-Goat—Monarchy and High-priesthood—the first represented by the Lamb of the Passover, killed and eaten as enmity by the Jews, and the He-Goat, killed at the altar of the Temple, was always burnt beyond the gate of Jerusalem. Leviticus xvi. 27; vi. 30; Hebrews xiii. 11* In conformity with this ordinance Jesus, as King and High-priesthood, died beyond the gate. But neither as the Lamb was he roasted and eaten, nor as the he-goat was he burnt. The other He-Goat, commonly called the Scape Goat, but really an offering to Azozel—Satan, with the Sins of all on his head, was represented by Barabbas, or, Son of the Father. Both He-Goats had to be even of

*2 Cor. v. 21.; Gal. ii. 15-21. The "Minister of Sin" was he who sacrificed him, who was "made sin for us."

RENEWAL OF THE HIGH PRIESTHOOD OF THE HEBREWS.

The Benediction of the Cohanim. Showing the Horns of "The Hind of the Dawn."
Explanation in the text. Vide also pages 88 and 89.

the same name. The roasting was imitated by the "bloody sweat."
Luke xxii. 44.

We have seen that Jesus died "beyond the gate," or camp, because beyond the gate, for some unrevealed reason, the He-Goat, as
Pan's representative, was burnt on each day of Atonement, together
with the Bull representing both Apis and Baal. We may point out
here that at Ab-Rhi (Avebury, Wilts) the Barrow of the Sun,
called Silbury Mound, is likewise "beyond the Gate" or sacred circle
of the Temple. Further, it is exactly under the meridian, or the
line north to the south, of the Temple Circle, which is a mile in
circumference. The mound is exactly under the Zodiacal sign of
the He-Goat, and, therefore, under the awful scene—an imaginary
one it is true, but during many ages believed to take place annually
at noon on December 25th in the air, and depicted in page 71. In
page 17 we have the Word flying as a Dove for the refuge of the
Ark of the "Queen of Heaven" of page 71. This is the scene so
tragically described in Psalm xxii, where occur the doleful cry of
unutterable woe : "Eloi, Eloi, lamma sabachthani," etc., Mark xv.
34. In the title of the Psalm we have who is the subject of those
moving sentiments of the Psalm, that they are those attributed
to "The Hind of the Morning Dawn." The Hind is a figure of
the God Pan, and in Druidism is substituted for the He-
Goat. In the Mabynogion "Hunting the Deer" (Dear), Hart
(Heart) is often referred to in those ancient dramatic novels of the
Ancient Bards. To be as mystical as possible, the Hebrews, while
sacrificing the He-Goat on the Day of Atonement, at the close of
ceremonies they, to this day, describe with their open fingers of both
hands lifted up to their foreheads, the Horns of the Hind, as a
token that each Jew—each son of Jacob—was represented by the
Hind, which had died in the air. Pan was renewed by a succeeding
Young Pan, after the death of each old Pan, and this in 40 hours
after the death of the Old Pan (p. 34).

The forked fingers of each hand is held one hand on each side
of the top of the forehead, as symbols of the two forked Horns of
the Hind or Stag. The ceremony is regarded as being one of the
holiest functions of the Sons of Aaron, who are called Cohens. The

ceremony is now called, The Benediction of the Cohanim or Cohens. All the congregation stand in awe while the ceremony is performed, and hide their faces in the folds of their Tallises or Prayer mantles. It is to be noticed the Day of Atonement is on Tishri 10th, when the Moon is ten days old, and, therefore, crescent shaped. That corresponds with our September 21, Old Style. The High Priest, having sacrificed the He-Goat and sprinkled his blood on his own white kirtle, and thereby symbolically slain the God Pan, entered the Holy of Holies, and passing to the South-east of the Zion Stone there, descended a flight of steps underneath the said Stone. This would be done just before sunset on that day. At sunset the eleventh day of the Civil year commenced. On the evening of the thirteen+h, the Feast of Tabernacle commenced. At Sunrise on the morrow, the ceremony called "The Benediction of the Cohamim" took place. The fourteenth correspond with September 25th. There are circumstances which indicate unerringly that the high priest, acting as the bier of the symbolical high-priesthood, descended into that symbolical Crypt-Grave beneath the Stone-Zion; that the high-priesthood was supposed to be there dead, till sunrise on the morning of the fourteenth. That the high-priest divested himself of the bloody white kirtle, and then re-ascended the steps, and re-appeared with the renewed high-priesthood on his own sacred person.* This is the meaning of the particulars about the careful manner the grave garments of the new high-priesthood of the Christian religion, saturated with his own blood, were carefully folded and left behind him in the sepulchre under another great stone in the "True Tabernacle." See Isaiah i. 18; Hebrews x. 5.* The other He-Goat "for" Azozel, had a like blood-sprinkled kirtle fastened to his horns. Thus the Hebrew high Priesthood of the nation, was renewed by the return of the new Pan, symbolised by the ascent of the High-priest carrying upon his shoulders the new white linen surplice of Druidism. In descending, the linen garment was

---

*See how the difficulty is got over as to priesthood and the sacrificing high-priest. St. John x. 18.

*Called, "the body of this death." Romans xii. 4, 24.

thick with the sprinkled blood of Pan and Apis. But the blood
thereon having been accepted by him, shown in p. 71, with the
Spear, the high-priest donned a clean surplice as white as light.
When Jesus was on the high mound, and there consecrated the
High Priesthood incarnate, apart from the High-priestship, whose
function was to annually sacrifice the emblem of the God Pan and
then burn him "beyond the gate," Jesus's "raiment became shining,
exceeding white as snow; so no fuller on earth can white them.'
Mark ix. 3. Those were the robes prepared for his pontifical office.
When the apostle Paul said to Ananias he was a "whited wall," he
alluded to his priestly surplice. It will be particularly noticed that
on the Mount of the "ordination" of Jesus were Elijah and Moses.
Aaron was represented by Caiaphas, whose duty was to sacrifice the
high-priesthood each Day of Atonement. The kingship was represented by Moses. True to the ancient myth, both Moses and Elijah
were Old, and now the young Nazarine was about to undertake the
office; both were about to resign according to mythology on
account of old age. He thus assumed the two characters shown in
page 34, and died as both, but rose from the dead as both, and after
forty days—still the old plan is followed, only that "days" instead
of hours are introduced—he ascended to heaven as the universal
monarch, and the universal High-Priesthood. He was slain as both
to satisfy him whom the Shepherd Kings, and after them the Jews,
called Father of the Christ, or the Word. We show him with a
spear in page 71.

The Surplice of the High-Priest, as he descended into the Cave
Grave under the Great Stone in the Holy of Holies with a Shaft-pit
in it, symbolising the passage into Hell, was bloody.* He divested
himself of it, and donned one "white as snow." He then, in the prescribed time, leaving the bloody ones behind reverently folded, for
the blood upon it was "a sin offering" or sin offered, vicariously, and
yet the sin is called "holy."

Jesus was clothed in white grave garments, besmeared with his
own blood. The blood upon the grave clothes was the essence of

---

*See pp. 72 and 73.

his nature, therefore, the said grave garments were most reverently folded, apparently by him who descended from heaven, rolled away the great stone over the Cave Sepulchre, and then sat upon the great stone. The angel's countenance, states S. Matthew, was like lightning, and his raiment white as snow. It appears that at the time the Jews carried on their national worship at Bethel, the Dead Sea to the South, with its sulphurous exhalation, was the mouth of Sheol, or Hell. That sea was supposed to be the site of Sodom and Gomorah. Dean Stanley states that according to the Midrash, the Jordan flows from the Dead Sea with its sulphur and smoke, "into the mouth of the Leviathan." "Sinai and Palestine," p. 293. That appears to be intended as a figure of horror.

TWO YOUNG GODS GROWN AGED—PAN AND OSIRIS.

The two young Gods of page 34, are in page 100 shown having grown old. The Mabyn (Boy Sun) who is being fed by the Goddess Gwen (Nature) from the cornucopia in page 34, is, in page 100, shown riding a donkey. The other Young God, with his extremities like those of a He-Goat, is in page 100 shown very old, and stretching forth a wreath to Gwen, who is in Egypt Isis 2, and married to Osiris, the aged one riding the ass or donkey. In front of the ass is walking the Mabyn-Sun called Horus in Egypt. It will be observed that now he is of an age to walk unaided, and not requiring being fed from the Cornucopia any longer, and is now carrying his cwn feeding bottle, which is an Eastern wine skin-bottle. He is the Son of Old Osiris and Young Isis 2. Here the reader should read what we state respecting Venus (Gwen) and Semele: why the latter was placed by mythologists in the station of the former, and she in the station of Ceres (Tynghedwen) in September, or Harvest time. (Pages 25, 30, 31, 79). The illustration in page 127 gives an earlier group of symbols of Egypt than that in which Nature (Gwen-Venus-Semele-Isis 2) is represented as the mother of the Mabyn-Sun, as regards his corpus apart from the twofold Word called in Egypt Amen Ra. There cannot be any doubt the illustration in p. 127 dates from before the conquest of Egypt by the Shepherd Kings and the introduction into the country of Typhon worship in the place of the prior pure theocracy of Egypt. As we point out elsewhere, the result of the action of the Shepherd nation was to introduce Typhon into the Triad of Egypt. (See "Abel," page 80), and making the Triad thus : —

Osiris, Horus, Typhon ;

instead of   Osiris—Isis 2—Zydik.*

Before them were : —

The Most High and Isis I, Queen of Heaven (Cariadwen).

Horus, or the Sun as an Infant God, must have been—in the earlier system of Egypt, before the disturbing influence of the Shepherd Kings was introduced—the Son of Isis 1 and Amen Ra, the twofold Word called Elohim. Isis 1 was the Spirit Queen of Heaven, whose visible representative was the Thebet-Boat or Ark-Baris (p. 87 and 50) or as a Dolphin (pages 92 and 127).

Amen Ra in the Sun as a Head is shown in p. 96, and as a Dove on the back of the Sun as Baal Apis (Bull) in p. 65. In the original religious system of Egypt, based on Britannic Druidism, the Sun (Horus-Taliesun-Arthur-Adonis as a Babe, Son, or Mabyn) was regarded as an infant until March 25th. Then he would be in a condition to don the Toga Virilis, and marry Gwen (Nature— —the Earth), and to have offspring.† On March 25th, the sun would be on the Celestial Equator, and Gwen on the corresponding terrestrial Equator. The Goddess Gwen now is under the influence of the fertilising emanation imparted to her Ova or Seeds—called "the seed of the Woman." Then he passes up towards the Tropic

---

* It is a remarkable fact that the late Mahdi of Ethiopia, or Soudan, gave the name El Zydik to his son, who, with the Khalifa and ten Emirs, was slain at Omdebrikat, 180 miles from Khartoum, at the latter part of November, 1899. El Zydik signifies the God Zydik. It is known the old Mahdi, his father, asserted that he was "the expected one," the Messiah of the whole earth. The fact he gave the name of the third person of the ancient triad of Eypt, prior to the advent there of the Shepherd Kings, appears to indicate the continuation of a hazy tradition about the earlier astro religion of ancient Egypt lingering still in Ethiopia. (Vide "Mysteries of the Cabsri," vol. I., p. 50).

†This teaching, misunderstood, led many in ancient times to marry their own sisters.

of Cancer, traversing, including the Equatorial line, four lines, each ten time, making a total of 40; then descending to the Celestial Equator he, from September 25th to December 25th, traverses the remaining three ten times each sphere, making 30 rounds, or a total of 70 rounds during the Solar year. This is the Key to all the 70's of the Bible and other ancient religious records based on the apparent movements of the sun up and down, during the year. Like the seven sons of Jesse, three out of the seven were Chief ones, so also here, three of the seven solar personifications were Chief ones, and those are called in Latin Septentrio, or Three in Seven. Those are the triads of all nations of antiquity, but the Shepherd Kings made that the Seventh, the last of the Triad, was Typhon Saturn, and that he was the Most High! (See "Abel," p. 80). We must refer the reader also to pages 84 and 34 for the key to the mystery of the two infant solar deities.

Pane, wife of Pan, and Baby.
Prototypes of Elizabeth and John Baptist. p. 88 and 89 ; 34, 100. Montfaucon, vol. II.

AGED ZACHARIAS AND AGED JOSEPH—OLD PAN AND OLD OSIRIS. p. 100.

There are two old men, and two mysterious events, in the history of the laying of the foundation of the Christian religion. The old men are Zacharias (Pan), the father of John the Baptist, and Joseph (Osiris), the husband of the Virgin Mary (Isis 2). The events are, the visit of the angel Gabriel to Zacharias in the temple at Jerusalem, and announcing he and his aged wife Elizabeth, who never had had a child, would have a baby in due course from that day. The other event, which took place six months later, when the angel Gabriel visited a young Jewish Virgin called Mary, in the Village of Nazareth, and announced to her she would have a Child by the Power of the Highest, which is Christ as one of the two Elohim (Gods). Luke i, 11, 25 ; xxvi. 35. Joseph is the venerable God Osiris on the ass, and Zacharias is the venerable God with the He-Goat extremities, shown in the illustration on page 100, and their two sons in p. 34. The peculiar loin vesture of the son of Pan-Zacharias, his camel hair cloak, and woodland wild habits of John Oannes, or Man (Ish)—the description of Pan in Genesis xxxii. 24—identify him with Pan. The 'rest of the name Oannes signifies Fish—the Dolphin instead of the Thebet Boat, or Baris, and adroitly called "Spirit" in reference to the apotheosis of Jesus from the Thebet by John's agency. The visit of Mary to Elizabeth is the foreshadowing of the union of the Kingship of Jove and the Priesthood of Pan in one person, as the Lord Jesus Christ. On the Mount of Transfiguration Moses and Pan Elijah sanctioned the union of the two orders. We have now a perplexing problem before us. As often intimated by us, the last of the three Sun personifications, corresponding with December 25th, represented as very aged, decrepid, and weak, came in Oriental countries to be regarded as the father of the succeeding year's Mabyn, or Baby Son (Sun). Thus Abel, which name signifies in the Shemitic language, Father of El or Helios (sun), but El is generally used to signify God, and Ab-El to signify Father of God. But Abel is the third of the Egyptian Triad—Osiris, Horus, Typhon (Saturn), and given as Cain, Seth, Abel. All Egyptologists know, that in the mythology of Egypt it is stated Typhon slew his brother Osiris. But Moses reverses this, and represents Cain (Osiris) slaying Abel (Typhon). Then Set, another name for Typhon, and rendered Seth in translations, is substituted for Horus (the Mabyn of Egypt of the Shepherd Kings' epoch), and Set is given as the Father of the line of Noah, who is in the Ninth (Ninus) from Set. The pedigree of Noah is not a human one, but is the stations of the sun during the year as follows:—(1) Bull, (2) Twins, (3) Crab (4) Lion, (5), Virgin, (6) Balance, (7) Scorpion, (8) Archer, (9) He-Goat. Those are given in Gen. 5th as human beings as follows:—Seth, Enos, Cainan, Mahalaleel, Jared, Enoch, Methuselah, Lamech, Noah. Now takes place a very curious thing. The twelve signs of the Zodiac are completed by a triad, described as the three sons of Noah. The three signs are:—When the Bull (Apis, Baal, etc.), was co-incident with March 25th, the three signs Waterer, Fishes, Lamb-Ram, the sun's three stations, would be as periods of the year as follows:—Waterer, from December 21st to January 20th; Fishes, from January 20th to February 18th; Lamb-Ram, from February 18th to March 20th. It will be observed that since about one hundred years before the Christian era, the sun rises on March 20th (25th in each of the four Seasons' Stations, as given in the Julian Calendar). Let the reader refer to the astronominal law called the Precession of the Equinoxes, and he will see and under-stand why each Zodiacal sign in its relation to the sun is thrown back to the right, and affecting all the twelve signs. The sun in those three signs are by Moses personified as:—

Japheth, Shem, Ham.

The same plan, taking three out of the twelve, is adopted in laying down the foundation of the Christian system of religion. Like Adam, the father of the 12, beginning with Seth, and ending with Ham, we have Jesus, the second Adam, with 12 disciples, three of whom are:—

James, Peter, John.

Now, to agree with the earlier Triads.

Osiris, Horus, Typhon,
Cain, Seth, Abel,
Japheth, Shem, Ham.

the Christian triad ought to have been Peter, James, Judas—the accursed, like Ham was. And of Judas it is said:—

> While I was with them in the world
> I kept them in thy Name:
> Those that Thou gavest Me I have kept,
> And none of them is lost, but the SON of Perdition.
> That the scriptures might be fulfilled.

St. John's Gospel, xvii. 12.

This refers to Psalm cix., and in the Septuagint version, which was the popular one in the hands of the Jewish masses, the 8th verse is as follows:— Set Thou a sinner against him,

> And let the devil stand on his right hand:
> When he is judged, let him go forth condemned:
> And let his prayer become sin:
> Let his days be few, and let another take his office of
> Overseer.
> Let his children be orphans, and his wife a widow.

It appears that by the word "Overseer" the accursed of the Psalm is identified with Judas, because he was the Overseer-Cashier of Jesus.

"Then saith one of His disciples, Judas Iscariot, Simon's son, who would betray Him, Why was not this ointment sold for three hundred pence and given to the poor? This he said, not that he cared for the poor, but because he was a thief, and carried the Bag and bore (carried) what was put therein." St. John's Gospel, xii. 6. In verse 6th of Psalm cix., are these words: "Let the Devil stand on his right hand." This expression refers to the station of Cain, reversing the order as in the first Hebrew Triad in Genesis. This transposition, placing Evil in the station Good occupied in the scientific arrangement of the earliest religion, justifies the observations of Tacitus, the eminent Roman historian of the first century. "As for Moses," he writes, "in order to secure the nation firmly to himself, he ordained New Rites, and such as were contrary to those of other men." Here follows a statement of the very greatest importance: "All things are with them profane which with us are sacred. And again, those practices are allowed among them, which are by us esteemed most abominable."—Tacitus, B.V.C. IV. The practices alluded to are obviously Circumcision and gelding in honour of Saturn. How little Josephus may be trusted when in his rage with Apion for stating Antiochus discovered the head of an ass in the Temple, when in Exodus xiii. 13, the sacrifice of the eldest male ass is enjoined. What has caused endless perplexity to theologians is the following : (1) Failing to realise that the Hebrews worshipped Saturn, as if he were the Almighty. (2) That Elohim, one of their names for the twofold Word, were, or was, worshipped by them as IAO, or Jehovah. That Elohim are, or is, Father Iu (Jupiter), given out as being Saturn's Son, and being also Psyche, or the Holy Ghost. (3) That Elohim (Gods) are symbolised by I-A (Jah) in the I.A.O., and that the O is the symbol of the Sun as a Head. (4) That Saturn is regarded as "jealous" of Jupiter his "son," and that, to mollify Saturn for the annoyance, the Sun, by the work of generation by the instrumentality of his agents, as men, women, and animals on earth, he must have sacrificed to him certain of the sacred living emblems of generation among the ancient Egyptians. Those are given in Leviticus xii. and Exodus xiii. 13 ; Genesis xv. 9., etc.

NOAH AND TYPHON—NOW CALLED TYPHON
ALSO TYPHUS.

It is only those who have studied the ancient methods of religionists of hiding their ideas as greater mysteries, and only allowing them to be conjectured through the veil of parables, or allegories, called Lesser Mysteries, can realise the difficulties to get at the true meanings of the parables or allegories, which alone remain, to the public, of the mysteries. At Jerusalem, the college of the greater mysteries of the Old Testament was called the Cabbala. The teachings of this Cabbala are preserved in the Talmuds of Jerusalem and Babylon. It is evident that Jesus was an adept in the knowledge of the Cabbala by his question founded on Psalm cx., namely, If the Messiah (The Christ) was to be the Son of David, how could he be David's Lord? And also his conversation with Nicodemus (St. John iii. 10). Ibid 10, 18.

We have seen that Noah is-the personified Sun in the Ninth sign (Ninius) of the Zodiac. In Hebrew his name signifies Nine or Ninth. Thus we find that Noah is the God Pan, the Sun on December 25th in Capricornus, or He-Goat, in the Ninth sign of the Zodiac.

Now, Saturn is the Sun personified as the Destroying Typhon on the Seventh planetary sphere on December 25th. The Shepherd Kings had, as we have seen, thrust into the religious system of Egypt Typhon-Saturn, and Typhon—preserved in the name Typhoon—is Arabic for Anarchy or Deluge. In Phœnicia, Typhon under the figure of a Wild Boar, was fabled to have mortally wounded Adonis (the Sun) on Mount Libanus on March 25th. In that story the murderer, who had assumed the form of a Wild Boar, was called Pluto. In the Roman Triad he is, like Typhon, in the Egyptian Triad of the Royal Shepherds, and given in the following order :—

Neptune, Jupiter, Pluto.

We know the above is the true order, because Jupiter, whose "House" is the Lamb Ram (Aries) is in the system co-incident with March 25th, while Neptune with June 25th, and Pluto with December 25th.

"A tidal phenomena at the estuaries of certain rivers is called 'Bore.' When a river expands gradually towards a very wide mouth, and is subject to high tides, the spring flood-tide drives an immense volume of water from the sea into the river; the water accumulates in the estuary more rapidly than it can flow up into the river; and thus is gradually formed a kind of watery ridge stretching across the estuary, and rushing up towards the watery ridge is many feet in height." This rush of water is called a Bore (Boar). It appears that the ancients did not understand the cause of the phenomenon more than they did that of the tides, and attributed it to the act of Pluto, whom they symbolised by a Wild Black Boar. The victory of Pluto-Boar over the sun was supposed to take place annually on December 25th, and a Boar was killed on each December 25th to imply by the sacrifice detestation of the Sun's murderer. This is the origin of the Boar's head in heraldry, and serving the head of a Boar on Christmas Day in the palace of the monarch of Britain and at the University of Oxford. In Egypt the adherents of Osiris sacrified Boars in his honour and in contempt of Typhon, another name or title for Pluto. The eastern idea that Satan was associated with Swine is implied by the story of a legion of Evil Spirits taking refuge from the twofold Word in Jesus of Nazareth in the land of the Gadarenes (Mark v. 11). The Druids also had the Satanic and Plutonic Boar to which they gave two names, viz., Twrch Trwyth and Bawdd. In everything of the character of a symbolical nature, they gave a different name to the religious and ordinary appellation. (Twrch Trwyth signifies the Boar of Chaos). Bawdd (now Badd, th as in thou), is the common or secular name of Boar in Welsh. The Welsh name Badd is the root of the English Bad. We have to this day in Wales many localities, associated with the "Hunting Twrch Trwyth." From this we infer the Druids hunted Black Wings (their Pluto) on each Christmas Day. In the ancient Records of Wales we have a story, to the effect that a Bawdd (Boar, or Bore) went (myned) over the land, and all men and women were drowned, except Duw Ban (High God) and Duwies Vach (little Goddess); that they made their escape in an Ark (pages 17 and 5).† The Bawdd is Pluto's Wild Boar; the Ark is the Boat (Thebet) of Cariadwen, Queen of Heaven; the High God is Hu Gadarn, the twofold Word of Coelus the Most High; the little Goddess is Dien, the Druidic Diana, who is Gwen or Venus in incipient babyhood (weak) at the winter solstice; for it appears that not only the Sun, but also Nature, was symbolised as an infant at the winter solstice.* It appears thus the Druids symbolised both by a male Wren and a female Wren, and that in the East two Doves were used in a like manner, and this is proved by the sacrifice of "two turtles or two young pigeons," as commanded in Leviticus xii. 8, as an atonement to the God of the Jews for the offence against him of having begotten a child, although that was done by the human agents of the Elohim, the twofold Word.   In

---

*The Crescent over the forehead of Diana is the Image of the Sacred Boat. p. 71.

†"Archæology of Wales," Vol. II. pages 59 and 71.

the account of Noah's Deluge we have the Dove, but also the Raven, a symbol of Typhon the Destroyer, the Raven being another symbol of Black Wings. The Ark (Thebet) of Noah's Deluge, as we have often said before, is no other than the mystical ship or Ark of the Druids, which they imagined journeyed to and fro between this world and the mysterious world beyond the Western Ocean, and extending underneath the earth and reaching to the Eastern ascent therefrom, from which all the raw embryotic substances came, and comes still, for Springtime, in the Ark, to the range of the scope of natural laws, the operations of the Ark being called by divers nations by different names. The Greeks, we repeat, called it Delphos (Womb), because this Divine Ark was supposed, like an egg, to be the transport conveying the embryotic substance that, fertilised by the tenant of the sun by the agency of the sunbeam, was the mother of all substances, whether in the constitution of the earth, or of all carnal beings of flesh and blood on the earth. This is the groundwork upon which the tragic story of Noah's Deluge has been built upon. (p. 17). The story of Jonah (Iona—Dove) in a Great Fish, is based on the same founda-tion—(p. 92)—and actually the stone sepulchre of Jesus with a hollow space under it, is a Rocking Stone, rocking in imitation of the supposed action of the mysterious Ark of the Queen of Heaven, during her journey to and fro between the world in which we dwell and the world beyond it.

A coffin, it will be remembered, is still called Ark (Arch) by the Welsh people, because a coffin was regarded as a symbol of the said mysterious transport Ark of souls, on her return voyage to the Land of the Blessed, decked with flowers, implying its native clime! This, too, is the origin of Easter rites and Flowering Sunday.

There are many lakes in Wales, and, doubtless, others in all parts of Great Britain during the Old Briton's supremacy, where local religious rites and dramas were performed at certain seasons of the year, and which were intended as descriptive of the great events which were supposed to be taking place on the ocean, between this and the other world.

Celtic authors, oblivious to this fact, have been unable to comprehend the meaning of the lake legends of Britain, although bearing traces of the same meanings and common origin.

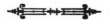

LLANGORS LAKE, NEAR MERTHYR, GLAM.

It appears that Llangors Lake above Merthyr, in Breconshire, was one of the sacred lakes on whose waters were performed, in days of old, the story of the Ark of Cariadwen, annual demise of the old sun, and the escape of his soul (Hu Gadarn, otherwise Elohim, Amen Ra, etc.) for safety into it; that a Wren—indeed, two Wrens, as explained above—were employed as symbols, escaping from Black Wings (a Raven, called Sea Crow in Druidic mythology) into the said sacred Ark. That they were carried in the Sacred Arkite Boat from S.W. to S.E. of the Lake. The older name of the lake is Llyn Sav Addov, corrupted to Addav, Eddav, etc. In Welsh Sav signifies to stand, and also a resting place. In the same language the name "Llyn" is now synonymous with the English name Lake. But Llun (Image) is the primitive form of the name as in Dydd Llun (Monday), the Crescent moon as the image in the sky of the holy Ark of Cariadwen on the Ocean.

We find that the Symbolical Ark was called among other names Llun, and Llun Sav means the Resting Place of Hu Gadarn under the name A-Ddov or the Tractable Winged One. See Jones's "Breconshire" (p. 243) for more about this Lake.

The white water lily, whose stem was the Druids' symbol of Taliesun's (Sun's) naval cord, is still found in vast quantities in this once sacred Lake. Now, it was believed there was a cave in the sea in the direction of the point of the Sun's setting on December 25th, and a passage from its mouth to the Land of the Blessed. (See the whole of pages 72 and 73).

THE LEGEND OF LLAN-Y-GORS LAKE.

(From Davies's "British Druids;" p. 155).

"In ancient times, it is said a door in a Rock near this Lake was found open upon a certain day (December 25th) every year. Those who had the curiosity and resolution to enter, were conducted by a secret passage which terminated in a small island, in the middle of the Lake. Here the visitors were surprised and enchanted with the prospect of a most enchanting Garden, stored with fruits and flowers. The inhabitants were Fairies" (Y Tylwyth Teg). In passing it may be mentioned the Fairies were the Angels, the Divine messengers, of Druidism. We now proceed with the quotation :—

"They (the Fairies) gathered fruits and flowers"—ministering angels—"for their guests, entertained them with the most exquisite music, disclosed to them many events of futurity, and invited them to stay as long as they should find things agreeable. But the island was sacred, and nothing of its produce was to be taken away. The whole of this scene was invisible to those who stood without the margin of the Lake. Only an indistinct mass was visible in the middle ; and it was observed that no bird would fly over the water, and that soft strains of music at times breathed with rapturous sweetness in the breeze of the mountain. It happened upon one of these annual visits an impious wretch, when he was about to leave the garden, put a flower with which he had been presented, into his pocket ; but the theft boded him no good. As soon as he had touched unhallowed ground, the flower vanished and he lost his senses. Of this injury the Fairies took no notice at the time. They dismissed their guests with their accustomed courtesy, and the door in the Rock was closed as usual. But their resentment ran high. For though, as the tale goes, the Fairies and their garden undoubtedly occupy the spot to this day—though the birds still keep at a respectful distance from the Lake, and some broken strains of music are still heard at times, yet the door which led to the island has never re-appeared. And from the date of the said sacrilegious act the Kymric Britons have been unfortunate."

It will be recollected one of the legends of a similar import, states the birth-place of Tegid (Sun) is in the middle of Bala Lake, meaning the Ark of Cariadwen, of which that on Bala Lake was the emblem. At Borth, Cardigan Bay, the Sun, old and young alternately, is called Taliesun, and the Lake is the sea between there and Arklow (Arch-Le), meaning Place of the Ark, on the coast of Ireland, as the western station of the Ark of the solar drama. See Adonia in Bell's "Pantheon" for description of similar performances as were enacted between Borth and the coast of Ireland. It appears the Island of Ramsey, St. David's Head, formerly called Ynis y Bru (Bree), or the Delphos Island, was the emblem of the Isle of the Blessed, and the arm of the sea between it and the mainland the emblem of the Styx (Gwyllionwy, the Jordon of Wales).

We invite the reader to refer here to p. 58, where is given by Dean Penrhyn Stanley a description of a Cave and Passage in the form of a wynch or shaft, on the ancient site of the Holy of Holies within the second veil of the Tabernacle at Jerusalem. The Mahomedans believe to this day the pit, shaft, or wynch, is the way to Paradise, and they have a legend to the effect that one once descended there to Paradise, and in addition to many other romantic particulars as to what the man saw there, they say he brought back with him a leaf of one of the shrubs of the world of immortality, and that the leaf is in Mecca to this day. This tradition is very much like the incident mentioned in the story of Llangors Lake legend given above. The Cave of Apollo at Delphos—Womb of Cariadwen, which the Cave, like the Ark, symbolised—the Cave of the Nativity, etc., will occur to the mind of the reader. Each of these Caves was a symbol of a grave and a birthplace. The Christian world continue to so regard each grave to this day. Over each open grave it is said of the dead: "It is sown a Natural body; it is raised a Spiritual body." Thus each Grave is a Chamber of Death, and a Birth-place. There cannot be any doubt the Crypt below the floor of a Church was a continuation of the Cave of mythology, and that each fresh member of the Church—Nave (Boat)—had to pass the ordeal of the Crypt, as symbolising he had passed into death by descending into the Crypt, and had raised into a Spiritual life by ascending from the Crypt. That the apostle alludes to the rite of the Crypt by the words, "Therefore we are Buried with him by Baptism into Death; that as Christ was raised up from the dead by the glory of the Father, even so we also should walk in newness of life." Romans vi. 4; Col. ii, 2. It will be remembered what is said elsewhere as to why a part of the Church edifice is called Nave (Boat); the Crypt seem to represent the hold of the Galley or Boat. In Welsh the word Baptism in the above verse is Bedydd, or Badydd, which signifies the Arkite ceremony, while Bedyddio is the verb stating the act itself. The apostle alludes to the Stone-Cave, underneath which Jesus was buried, as the early Crypt of which all others were symbols. In the same way all Shell grottos with a candle in it was a symbol of the Cave of the Sun near the margin of the Ocean with the Soul (the Word) of the Sun in it. The Christmas "Box" has a similar symbolical signification. The word Bapto, the root of the English name Baptism, signifies dyeing white, or any other colour, and it implies, making holy. (See p. 49, 50). In the Greek version of St. John's Gospel, i. 28, we have Bethania (House of the Boat) and not Bethabara, as in the Authorised Version. We see that Jesus was introduced into his public ministry from the House of the Boat on the east of the Jordan; but into his spiritual existence after his resurrection from the dead, from a Crypt-Grave in the True Tabernacle. See also Joshua iii. 5, 6, 7, for the origin of the function—John observed the old rites on the very same spot in introducing Christianity to the Commonwealth of Israel.

We have in the introductions of Jesus the following: (1) As a child born in a Cave from his mother's womb. (2) From John's Boat, called most esoterically a Spirit, the "Spirit" being the Queen of Heaven, whose symbols in the East were Dolphin, a Boat, and a Rocking Stone, into his Public ministry. (3) His death and burial underneath a Vast Stone in a Cave, and his return from Paradise through Hades into a spiritual body, and then his resurrection. Those stages are by the Church represented as follows: (1) Birth from the mother, (2) made a child of Heaven by Baptism and Confirmation: (3) death and burial and resurrection, symbolised by de-

scending into the Crypt and ascending therefrom to "newness of
life," compared to life in heaven. Then we have the earlier solar observances. (1) Birth of the Babe sun from Semele; (2) His birth
from the Sacred Arch or Boat. (3) His ascension into the sky. In
the case of Moses (1) Birth from his mother (represented by Miriam),
(2) Born of the Arech or Thebet of Bulrushes, whose Spirit Genius
is a Princess of Egypt. (3) Moses's ascension to heaven from the
Bethania of Bethel and the Jordan. We detect the like plan in the
history of Joshua. (1) Hosea; (2) Joshua; (3) Ruler of the
Hebrews. The LXX. state that Joshua was the son of Nave (Boat or
Arech (Ark) The Rabbinical version, which is the same as our
A.V., state Joshua was the son of Nun. This is the Hebrew for Fish.
It will be recollected that we point out the Orientals symbolised the
Presence of the mother-spirit, Queen of Heaven, by both a Great
Fish and a Great Boat, which was, says Herodotus, symbolised on
the Nile by a basket-like Boat. See pages 87, 127.

At the close of his life Joshua, in Druidic fashion, erected a
great Stone in an Oak Grove at Shechem, and referring to the Queen
of Heaven, whose invisible spirit animated the mastless and sailless
Thebet or Argo, which the Rocking Stone symbolised, told the
people the stone in the Oak Grove had heard every word of the promises the Lord had made to them. The Great Stone was the inland
emblem of the Nave or Navis, his second mother in the same sense
as Pharaoh's daughter by the instrumentality of the Thebet of Bulrushes of the Nile was the second mother of Moses. Joshua xxiv.
26, 27. That Stone was afterwards the Coronation Stone of the
Hebrews. Judges ix. 6.

We now return to consider the meanings associated with the
Great Stone, Cave, Room under it, and the Shaft descent from the
room. It is evident we think they signified the same things as
similar objects did among other nations. It is clear Mount Zion
or Mount of the Stone, was sacred from time immemorial, and
untold ages before the "pattern Tabernacle," called Maesgwyn in
Hebrew, which is pure Welsh, and meaning literally White Ex-
panse, and signifying Holy Place.

As often stated (p. 138) that Holy Mound or Holy Hill, symbolising the whole earth surrounded by the sea—such was the belief of all ancient nations, as symbolised by the Shield of Achilles, described by Homer—the Great Rocking Stone, the Cave underneath it, the stone being called Zion, and the Shaft in the floor of the Cave, must have been visited often by many successions of Melchisedeks, Priest-Kings, during many rolling centuries before the time of Abraham. It is intimated that with a terrible cry—a cry that shook the whole earth—something, it is not stated what, shot out of the mouth of Jesus as he died on the cross, then darted with irresistible Divine force, ripped the second veil of the Holy of Holies, from top to bottom as the Jordan had done, and the Red Sea had done as the effect of the Rod of God in the hands of Moses; and the Cloak of Elijah had ripped open the Jordan. (p. 111). The Urim and Thummim which appear to be other attributive names in addition to Elohim, like lightning darted forth down from Golgotha, tore the veil, and entering the cave-crypt of Arawn,* darted into the aforesaid pit, the old gullet of the blood of the sacrifices, then passed through Hell, across the river Styx which both the Jordan and the second veil symbolised, pulled down the doors of Pluto, and then joined the Captives in Paradise, otherwise Abraham's Bosom. (See bottom of p. 141). It was now Jesus underwent the work promised in the synagogue of Nazareth he announced was his work to accomplish. But the beautiful poem of Isaiah, of which the announcement is a quotation, refers to the termination of the Babylonian Captivity. Luke iv. 17, 19; Isaiah lx. and lxi.

---

*Aran is the Hebrew for a Wild Goat.

THE SABBATH, A DAY OF REST; AND NOAH'S DELUGE.

SACRED TO THE GOD SATURN WITH THE SCYTHE.

One of the most subversive errors in dealing with the ancient religions of the world is, taking for granted that the Seven planets of the earlier astronomy were named after Seven Gods. Each name was given to the sun as an attributive as from June 25th to December 25th, he travels, as was anciently supposed, the lines the sun journeys over across the heavens, from his rising to his setting as explained in page 67.

The Jews name the planet Saturn, or originally the entire line traversed by that star, and the sun also on December 25th, etc., ten times as the quota of the seven-times ten, is called in Hebrew, Cochab Shabbath, or the Sabbath Star. (Dr Inman's "Ancient Faiths," Vol. II, p. 504). We have here Saturn on December 25th in the Seventh position, and associated with the Seventh day of the week, the Jewish Sabbath. As we have often pointed out, the said seven have three principal stations of the sun. Those are the journeys of the sun across the heavens on June 25th, March 25th, and December 25th. In Egypt, in the time of the rule of the Shepherd Kings, which lasted 511 years, were personified as Osiris, Horus, Saturn-Typhon-Seth, or Cain, Seth, Abel. The reason why Seth is placed second in the Hebrew triad is given elsewhere. The Sunday is the first day of the week, and is the first of the seven. In the calendar of the Druids, June 25th, in every year is Syl-Gwyn, literally, White-Sunday, but meaning Holy Sunday. In English, the Church translated the name from the older British, and called it "Whit-Sunday." During many centuries past, in this country the Solar style has been abandoned for the lunar one, and Whitsunday made moveable, like the Jewish Pentecost, and in A.D., 1900, Whit-Sunday falls on June 3rd.* Some Oriental nations ended the old year at sunset on June 24th and commenced the new year forty hours later at Sunrise on the 27th. Thus the Old Sun as Tammuz (Osiris) died annually. Ez. viii. 14.

---

*Old Pan and Son, page 190.

At the end of the forty hours from the death of old Tammuz (Sun) a baby Tammuz was supposed to be born from the sacred Boat of the Queen of Heaven, or, in the case of those who had adopted the Fish substitute for the Sacred Boat, from the Dolphin, p. 92. The reader will here pursue the chapter on Old Osiris and Young Horus, etc. See also p. 84. We particularly invite attention to what is stated on the subject as to the marvellous correspondence between the resurrection of Jesus on March 27th (Nisan 16th) and the new birth of the Egyptian Horus or Old Osiris renewed.

We have the Old sun slain in the air by Saturn-Typhon under different names and among different nations. As Arthur, otherwise Taliesun, on December 25th. He is also called Aran by the Druids. Aran is the Shemetic name for a wild He-Goat. We believe the name is derived from the Keltic, and that it is correctly, Arav (Slow) and refers to the slow condition of the sun when in the sign of the He-Goat, because the ancients used him as a symbol of the sun when he was supposed to be weak, and therefore Slow at the end of the Solar year.

The Egyptians during the dominion of the Shepherds in Egypt, described the Old Sun under the name Osiris, slain by Saturn Typhon on June 25th. The Phœnicians observed the death of the Old Sun under the name Adonis on March 25th.

The Syrians observed the death of the Old Sun under the name Tammuz on June 25th. To this day the month of June is called Tammuz is the Jewish calendar.

In each instance the birth of a Mabyn, or Baby Sun was supposed to take place forty hours later. It is perfectly manifest that the entire solar fables originated among the Druids. (1) They had concluded the sun's body was a material substance, and the fact he travelled made them believe he was a living being. (2) The fact that his powers seemed to decline as he descended down the sky of the southern hemisphere caused the Druids to regard the periods from Sep. 25th to Dec. 25th as the period of the sun's old age. The gradual lengthening of nights, and the shortening of daylight, the Druids attributed to the increasing weakness of the Sun's body to act as transmitter of the light from Hu Gadarn (the twofold

Word or Winged Mind of Coelus) within his Head; for the Sun was regarded as only the Head of the God and his rays were his hair.

(3) After December 25th the Druids observed that the light from the sun began to increase in length daily, but they could not believe the old solar body which had declined to the shortest day, December 25th, was the same body as that rising with the dawn of the new solar year, and daily grew stronger and effulgent.

(4) Then came the idea of an old sun of one year and the young one of the next. And that the life of each Sun as a corporeal identity only lasted one year. But all nations agreed that the Soul of the Sun as an emanation of the Highest never dies, but at the wreck of each sun escapes to the Sacred Boat of the Queen of Heaven, as shown in the illustration on page 71.

Now comes a still more astounding thing. For some reason, probably the reason is to be discovered in the consequence of the earth's latitude where the Druids inhabited at the period the ideas took practical form as a religion, the sun did not appear there above the rim of the southern horizon on December 26th (St. Stephen's Day), and the Druids concluded as the result that an interval of forty hours elapsed between the death of the Old Sun and the birth of the Baby Sun, his successor.

This period of forty hours is the "rest" of the Seventh Day—the Sabbath of the Hebrews. It is indicated by the forty "days" Noah was in the Ark, with the Dove and Raven, symbols of the Word of Coelus, the Most High, and Black Wings, or Satan, the destroyer, with the feminine essence from the other world with which, fertilised by the Word, Elohim in Hebrew, and Hu Gadarn, etc., in Druidism, all creatures of flesh and blood were, and are, ever created. p. 24. It cannot be doubted this was what Solomon's Molten Sea symbolised. (I Kings, vii. 23). And the egg which the Jews have roasted on each Passover table.

In pages 88, 71, 34, we describe the God Pan under the figure of the He-Goat as the personified Ninth sign of the Zodiac, while the Deluge is the Anarchial period which was supposed to prevail during the interval between the death of the Old Sun and the Birth of the Mabyn Son, his successor. During the anarchial period of forty hours when the Dove was in the Ark, the Raven dominated the world, and went on with the work of disintegration. The Raven is Typhon or Typhoon. He is the Black Boar or Bore, the Twrch Trwyth of Druidism. Because during the anarchy of forty hours, Time itself was suspended and no chronology possible, Typhon became, in the confusion of creeds having their origin in Druidism, Kronos or Time, to be regarded as identical with Saturn-Typhon, the destroyer, and it came to be said that Time, like Saturn, swallowed his own children.

The story of Iona (Dove) in a Great Fish is the same as the Dove in Noah's Thebet, an Egyptian name for the Ark of Bulrushes, another emblem of the sacred Boat of the Queen of Heaven. In the story of Moses and the Ark of Bulrushes, Pharaoh's daughter is substituted for Juno, a name meaning female Dove, Queen of Heaven, p.87.

We now come to a fact one almost dreads. The Lord Jesus in his Kist Grave forty hours, while his Christ is absent in Paradise, mean the same as Noah and Dove in the Ark, and Iona in the Belly of the Delphian Delphos, commonly supposed to be a Whale. It appears that at some early period, the Druids of Western Europe, as we see in the fact of Twrch Trwyth, or Boar of the Suds, otherwise, Chaos or Anarchy, or Di-Lyw, meaning Governless Universe, the British Druids admitted into their system the Boar emblem of Satan-Pluto of their friends, the Phœnicians. For in the ancient Records of Wales we have the following :—"One of the three misfortunes of the Isle of Britain—the bursting of Llyn Lion, and the going of a Boar (Bawdd) over all the lands, and all people were drowned, except the High God (Duwban) and the Little Goddess (Duwies Vach)." In the text the names are spelt Dwyvan and Dwyvach. But it is clear to everybody familiar with the Kymric tongue that the first name is masculine and the second feminine, and that "Dwy," the first name in each of the compounds is Duw (masculine) and Duwies (feminine). It is further evident the two are Hu Gadarn and Dien or Diana, who is the infant Goddess, Gwen as a Baby Girl, the consort of the Boy Sun, the Mabyn of the Mabynogion, or Druids, as adherents to the Son of Hu Gadarn, or the Christ and the

Queen of Heaven by the instrumentality of her sacred Thebet or Boat. In the Keltic Researches, p. 157, we find Bawdd erroneously translated "the overwhelming of the face of all lands." The translator mistook the noun Bawdd (Boar) for the verb boddi (drowned). We are further told the High God and Little Goddess made their escape from the Boar in a naked ship, that is to say, a mastless Boat, whose moving impulse was the spirit of Cariadwen, Queen of Heaven. In the next paragraph we have a further reference to the catastrophe in the words that there was a roaring fire, and the earth was rent asunder down to Tartarus (Annwn), and almost every living thing perished. "Myvyrian," Vol. 12, pages 59 and 71.

THE TRINITIES OF THE ANCIENT WORLD.

TWO PAIRS OF TRIADS.

In Druidism and in those ancient creeds derived from Druidism of the Stone Age, there were two pairs of Trinities. The first were the Essence and Soul in the Sun. These the Druids called Hu Gadarn and A-Wen. Then the Sun himself was the Son, Son of the said Essence, and the Queen of Heaven, represented by the Navis or Thebet, Boat, Coracle, Delphos (Womb), Nun (Fish), Ceubawl (Cybele), Argo, and known by other symbols, such as an Egg, called Mundane Egg, etc. In British this sacred symbol of the vehicle of the Queen of Heaven was called Clain Neidr, or, in English, the Passive regenerating embryo of the Serpent. During the long ages before the invention of letters, ideas, it will be remembered, were communicated by the agency of emblems, such as pictures and live creatures. A spirit was symbolised by a Serpent, because, like a spirit, it travelled without feet and hands. Wings were used in the same sense. The Serpent here associated with the Egg-Symbol of the Baris or Boat of the Spirit, Queen of Heaven, is her emblem as the Genius of the Boat, propelling it by her will. Bryant in his

"Analysis," vol. II. p. 319, states, "the Syrians used to speak of their ancestors, the Gods, as the progeny of Eggs." Here in the course of ages, the Syrians, having lost their teachers, the Druids, came to speak of "Eggs" instead of one or two eggs, the emblem of the Sacred Barge, or Baris of the Great Royal Lady of Heaven, whose Son (Sun) was called by the Druids the Crowned Babe. Cwyn ap Nydd, or the Holy One, son of Nydd (Neith) the Turner of the Solar Wheel. (Vide Introduction). The reader is invited to refer to the Rev. E. Davies's "Rites and Mythology of the British Druids," pages 205 to 212.

It is most surprising to read how very near the eminent Welsh writer came to the truth. He identifies the said Egg, the Ovum Anguinum of Pliny, with the Ark of Noah. Had he said the Ark and the Egg were two different emblems of the same thing, namely, the Navis or Boat of the Queen of Heaven, now represented by the Nave of each Church building, he would have been correct. Pliny states on the authority of Druids, that this Egg had the capacity of "floating against the stream," a way of intimating the Boat which it represented, was animated by an invisible power.

Now, the other triad or trinity is the Sun personified thrice in the course of each year, namely, on Spring Day, the Longest Day, and on the Shortest Day, anciently on March 25th, June 25, and Dec. 25th. In the old Solar map based on the seven lines, this Triad would correspond with the Sun on Whitsun day O.S., Woden or Mercury's Day, and Saturn's Day. But in the Zodiacal map of the Sky or Nev, with Cancer, Ram, and He-Goat. In the Christian foundation, the triad is based on the three zodiacal three signs, otherwise the three apostles would have been the first, middle, and last of the "Seven men of honest report." Acts vi. 3. It is known that Peter, James, and John (Oannes—Man and Fish) were of the twelve disciples. In accordance with the Egyptian triad, Osiris, Horus, Typhon or Set, otherwise Saturn, Judas Iscariot would have occupied the third position in the Christian triad. But most deftly and designedly, John is made to occupy the third station, and there representing two characters, namely, the human nature of Jesus and his church, for the Fish in his name is the

Phœnician Delphos or Dolphin, representing the visible Nave or Navis of the Goddess Cariadwen, Queen of Heaven. Each of the following Triads represents the Sun in one of the foregoing three stations during the Solar year.

Behind each group of Three is to be understood the Word of the Most High operating through them, exactly as the "Excellent Spiritual knowledge, and understanding," in Daniel, in Babylon, operated through Shadrach, Mesach, and Abednego, the names of a triad of Chaldea given to the three Hebrew lads, Hananiah, Mishael, Azariah. To Daniel was given the name of the Queen of Heaven, Beltes-Zhazzar. In other words the personified Church of Bel or Baal, the personified Sun. It is precisely a combination as Oannes, otherwise John. The Babylonian feminine titular name which he bore induced Dean H. Prideaux, of Norwich, to infer Daniel was in immediate attendance on the Queen Mother in Babylon. Vide "Connection of the History of the Old and New Testaments." In the House of Commons the old British arrangement is preserved to this day. There the Speaker, seated high, is supposed to inspire the Three clerks in front of him. The following triads are all, except the Druidic ones, based on the corrupt system which the Royal Shepherds thrust upon the Ancient Egyptians, where Typhon, under various names, is placed in the third station, that of December 25th.

It will be observed we use the name Baris above as one of the names of the Boat-Shrine of the Spirit Goddess Cariadwen, Queen of Heaven. This was one of its Egyptian names. In great processions of Isis I. in Egypt, a Baris was carried as an emblem of the thing itself, which all nations believed to roam the Ocean for the Sun's accommodation, etc. Bryant, on the authority of Nicolas Damascenus, states it is the name of the Mountain in Armenia on which the Ark of Noah alighted. In Herodotus's "Euterpe," section 96, in his particulars about Egypt, he states the Baris was an Egyptian name of a Boat. This makes it clear that Ararat in Armenia bore a Rocking Stone, and being the emblem of the sacred Shrine the mountain itself came to be named Baris, and that upon this Moses engrafted the legend, that the Ark of Ninus

or Noah had alighted there after the subsidence of the waters of
the Deluge. St. Peter identifies the Navis Church with the Baris.
1 St. Peter iii. 20, 21. In passing we may state that the Canal
encircling the vast arena of Avebury, Wilts, being emblematic of
the Ocean round the earth, probably a lunette-shaped Baris floated
upon its waters on festive accasions.

Britain.

(1) Planydd—Alawn—Gwron.

(2) Nevydd—Nav—Neiv—Iona, or Boat and Dove.

Greece.

Poseidon—Zeus—Dis or Hades.

Roman.

Neptune—Jupiter or Jove—Pluto.

Persian.

Ormudz—Mithras—Ahriman.

Phœnician.

Phos—Phur—Phlox.

Egypt.

Osiris—Horus—Typhon.

Bablyon.

Daniel, endowed with the Logos.

Daniel v. 12. Ibid III. 25th.

Shadrach—Mesech—Abednego.

Daniel i. 7.

India.

Brahma—Vishnoo—Shiva.

In the Britannic Triads, we have a trace of some early devia-
tion from the original Triad. Possibly we have here a trace of the
sedition we read of, which resulted in the revolt of the Scythians
against the Cimmrii, causing the latter to seek a new home in
Britain. Probably the immigration was small at first, but eventually, with the exception of the Galatians, all arrived in Britain, and
proceeded to practice the patriarchial religion of Chaldea and Mesopotamia. The first Triad of Britain are as follows in English :—

Planter—Full Wings—Hero.

The Second: Celestial—Father—Boat and Dove.

It is represented Saturn (Black Wings), was averse not

only to reproduction, but to creation in general. His Kingdom
was night, and his rule, death. But after he came to be represented as being the Father of a Son, Jupiter, he came to be represented
as married to Rhea, Cybele, etc., but deadly averse to any offspring. But the old Satan had Jupiter by Rhea. He was furious.
He, true to his savage and destructive nature, sought his son (Hu
Gadarn and his Soul, Awen) for him to eat him. Rhea (Cariadwen)
hid the Son, and wrapping the emblem of the Shepherd of Israel,
namely, a stone obelisk in a garment, and telling the monster the
parcel was Father Iu (Iu-Pater), Saturn devoured the Stone. Gen.
49, 24. The Son grew up and dethroned Saturn. The entire
ancient world believed this story of the great blood sacrifice. Christianity is based on the assumption that in Jesus, the Son-Father, gave
himself up to Saturn, and yielded himself to the death of the Cross,
to satisfy the Father of his Father, namely, Saturn. Ps. cx. No
man can find in this word a holier task to perform than tearing
away from public worship, the bloody rags of Saturn worship!
Nothing can be more horrible than that the living serpent of
Midian was slain to satisfy the rage and appease the wrath of the
fiery dragons of the wilderness! St. John's Gospel, iii. 14. And
that he was made Sin for us!

THE GARDEN OF EDEN.

It is highly probable the name Eden is a corrupt form of the
ancient Keltic, Y Dinor, The Mound. The Druidic sacred Mound,
with a Sea around it, as the water trench around the circle of twelve
stones on Mount Carmel, is described in the translation of the LXX.,
symbolised the earth standing out of the Ocean and encircled by it.
The Mound, being a symbol of the whole earth, was described as
the Garden of the Sun, its Husbandman. It was the Garden which
the Lord Himself planted. In Western Europe, Britain, surrounded
by the Ocean, was the Garden of Hesperus, the Greek form of the
name Taliesun, or the Sun. The Mount near Edinburgh called

"Arthur's Seat," is in the Gododin, the earliest British poem preserved in the Roman alphabet, called by the Bards, Coelbren y Moneich, or the Alphabet of the Manks, is printed "Ei" Din, or, "His" Din. In Welsh the personal name Hu is pronounced "Ei." At first, great difficulty was obviously experienced by the British writers in arranging the Roman letters to represent the sounds of the native language. The dual forms, Ch, Ph, Dd, Ll, Ngh, Nh, Th, with other orthographical monstrosities in composition, was the result; things which have had a deadly effect on the career of the venerable language of the ancient Britons. Arthur, as often stated, is another title of the Sun, and like George—St. George—signifies Husbandman, or Gardener, as Adam and Noah were. The name Hu Gadarn, it will be remembered, was the name the Druids gave to the personified masculine essence in the Sun, therefore, he was the Druidic Jupiter, or Father Hu, rendered "Ei." His Soul was A-wen, or Holy Spirit, the A. being a hieroglyphic or sign, of a pair of wings. Both Essence and Soul were supposed to be inside the Sun, called the Head of Arthur, otherwise Taliesun or Hesus. It is profoundly interesting to find that at the Modern Athens are preserved in the local names, Hu's Din ("Ei" Din), and a solar titular name of Sol himself, namely Arthur. The river there is called "Eden," and the town "Edin." Both illustrate the tendency of the British "Ei" Din (Hu's Din) to assume the forms "Eden" and "Edin" on the tongues of strangers to the old language of Britannia. The also elaborate allegory of the Garden is stationed on the Mound Jerusalem. (See page 138).

Jerusalem is called a Vineyard. Isa. i. 8 ; Cant. i. 6 ; Jer. xii. 10-13 ; Gen. ix. 20 ; Joel ci. 12-13. In the West a sacred Mound was also called the Orchard of Taliesun ; and the poem regarding its Apples can be read in the "Myvyrian Archæology of Wales," Vol. I., 150. Mer-Ddyn, meaning the Sun as rising from the Mer or Mor (Sea) is made to say—

> Am ysgwyd ar fy ysgwydd, a'm cledd ar fy nghlun,
> Ac yn nghoed Celyddon y cysgais fy hun.

> My shield on my shoulder, my sword on my hip,
> 'Neath the Trees of Caledonia I slept my nap.

The allusion is to the Apples Sanctuary, as being a place so safe that the Priest of the Sun could there sleep in safety. It is highly probable the allusion is to Arthur's Seat, near Edinburgh.

The essence of the apple was used in the Druidic Sacrament, in the same sense as the essence of the grape was used in the sacrament of Bacchus. This gave to the symbolical apples of the Druids a most sacred character (p. 10). In England it is called "Lamb's Wool." In the following the name Aval (Apple) has the word len, from llen (scholarship), joined to it by some copyist, half bard and half monk, ignorant of the meanings underlying the figures employed by the original composer :—

> Aval len, beren bren, sydd vad ;
> Nid bychan dy lwyth—sydd ffrwyth arnat ;
> A minau wyv ovnawg, amgelawg, am danat,
> Rhag dyvod y coedwyr, coed gymmwynwyr,
> I gladdu dy wraidd, a llygru dy had,
> Vel na thyvo byth Aval arnad.

Stanza 6th.

> Sweet apple : learning : a Tree that is fair :
> Thy crop is not small : the fruit that is on thee,
> And I am anxious about thee,
> Lest the woodmen, hewers of trees,
> May bury thy roots and corrupt thy fruit :
> That thou mayest no more bear one apple.

He is referring to Druidism and encroachments of Chrirstians.

Now, Mount Moriah, was even in the days of the Jebusites, one of those numerous "patterns" of the True Tabernacles, scattered over the surface of the earth in ancient times. The Real, or True Tabernacle, was the whole earth with the vault of the sky, called Nev by the Druids, and Knep by the Egyptians, for its bell-like roof The curtains were blue, and bespangled with stars. P. 138. Each of those Mounds or Mountains was an emblem of the whole earth, otherwise "the Garden of Eden."

Ancient maps give the situation of Eden to the West of Mount Baris (Ark), otherwise Ararat, in Armenia. It is to the North of Mesopotamia. In Mesopotamia are Chaldea, Shinar, Babylon, called Babel in the Bible. The Chaldeans were in Babylon a priestly caste. From Ur of the Chaldeans admittedly Abraham came forth. There are Haran, Niniveh, or Ninus. To the South are Babylon, Tadmor, Damascus, Nazareth, Carmel, Tabor, Jerusalem, and Egypt. On the North of Mesopotamia are springs of the Murad Euphrates flowing from the East to join the main Euphrates in the West at Keban Madden. To the North West of Ararat springs the River Gihon, and passing above Ararat, flows to the Caspian Sea on its Western border. Gihon is now named Araxes. Farther West, and to the South of Pontus, or the Black Sea, is the spring of River Pison, now called Kizil Ranak. There cannot be any doubt the River Hiddekel is the Tigris, "which goeth eastward of Assyria." The name Euphrates as flowing from Eden decides the matter that by Eden is meant the Mount Baris or Ararat, as emblematical of the whole earth as the Garden of the sun. Ararat Mountain was used as a Gorsedd or Throne of worship by the Chaldeans, who were Druids, and Moses, while borrowing their ideas, was honest enough to indicate the Armenian locality from whence he was borrowing. Genesis ii. 14-14. For Ethiopia in verse 13th read Cush, which is the name in Hebrew of the country indicated, and meaning that watered by the River Gihon or Arexes. (Calmet). About 50 miles above Babylon the Euphrates and the Tigris rivers, both flowing from the Eden mountains of Armenia, come within 30 miles of each other. A Royal Canal 40 miles in length, slanting from the Euphrates on the West to the Tigris on the East, was constructed. It was used by the Romans in the Seventh Century, but under Mahommedan rule it has fallen into decay. The rivers named flow far east of Damascus and Jerusalem and Arabia into the Persian Gulf. The Euphrates is about 1,600 miles long, and is navigable to the sea 1,193 miles.

The old maps place the Garden of Eden on the West of Mount Ararat, Armenia, in the regions of the fountains of the rivers above mentioned, and it appears they are perfectly correct. In the great plains between Mesopotamia and the lower reaches of the Euphrates, Moses gives the earliest home of mankind. He calls the said plains Shinar, Babel, etc. Genesis xi. There they, we are told, built the extraordinary tower. Verse 4.

Moses introduces the Deluge allegory between the Garden of Eden period, and the immigration to Shinar. We have explained the import of the Typhoon novel. Then in the pedigree of Noah or Ninus, after whom Niniveh, in the district of Shinar, was so named, Moses proceeds to give the descent of mankind from Typhon-Set (Seth) through Noah (Ninth-Noah-Pan). Nothing was more natural than for mankind to first congregate together near Eden, and here we find them at Shinar so friendly with each other as to dread a separation. We will show directly that in Moses's Deluge narrative, he employs two figures as the native places of mankind. (1) Eden; (2) Ark. These imply the True Tabernacle and the Navis—Church of the Queen of Heaven. Those are represented by the Gentiles and "the Commonwealth of Israel." They really imply the Oriental birth of the flesh and regeneration. Jesus died in the Garden, or True Tabernacle, but he rose from the dead from the Navis (Ark), represented by the hollow grave below the great Rocking Stone in the Garden of "Joseph of Arimathea." This name is thrown in as a gauze veil over the Greater Mystery. Vide 1 Peter iii. 20, 21. Indicating that in the early days of Christianity, some of its adherents were aware that Mount Moriah, or Mount of the Stone (Zion) was an Eden, we are told by Calmet's "Dictionary of the Bible," Jesus was crucified on the Tree of Knowledge of Good and Knowledge of Evil. This is what is meant by the Good "thief" on his right hand and the "Bad thief" on his left hand. The Three Crosses represent One Tree, like the Cadeuces of Mercury. Mercury is the personified Sun corresponding with the station of the middle day of the week above the line of the Terrestrial Equator—and the serpent on the Northern side of the pole is opposing the progress of the serpent representing Evil from coming farther towards the region of the earth over which in summer and autumn exercises a beneficent influence. One Serpent represents Summer and the other Winter. Jesus on the cross faced directly West, and therefore his back was exactly towards the East point of the earth and sky.

The fact that Jerusalem was one of the countless symbolical Eden, or Hæ Din, is seen in what is said that in early times it was asserted that the Tree of Knowledge of Good and Evil was used as a footbridge over the Kedron brook, south of Jerusalem, and that it was used to make with it the cross of Jesus.   (Calmet).

Much confusion has been introduced into theology by the way the words of Gen. iii. 24, have been translated.   The Rev. Wm. Cooke, M.A., in his "Enquiry," etc., p. 12, states the words translated "And He placed at the East of the Garden of Eden, Cherubim (Kerubim), and a Flaming Sword, which turned every way, to keep the way of the Tree of Life."   The said writer tells us the Hebrew words mean Irradiation of Glory.   The Cherubim are identical with those, one on each side of the Shechinah or Effulgent Glory.   (Calmet).   This indicates that the Cherub on the northern side of the Shechinah represented the same idea as the Penitent thief did on the right hand side of Jesus, and the impenitent thief on his left hand side, the same idea as the cherub on the southern side of the Shechinah.   The exclusion from Eden, otherwise Paradise, meant the same thing as the exclusion of everybody except the High Priest, and even he, unless he brought on his white kirtle and in a bason, the blood of Pan-He Goat, and other "Gods" of Egypt.   Leviticus xvi. 14, 15.   Thus the Royal Shepherds engrafted on the worship of Amen Ra, or the Christ and Holy Spirit, as taught in Egypt, the awful worship of Typhon-Saturn, the Destroyer.   In Druidism the Shechinah is called Llygad Goleuni, meaning in the English idiom, Fountain of Light, the Hebrew Ain of Light.   The Sun on March 25th is meant.

Very probably the vast populations of Chaldea, Shinar, Mesopotamia, Armenia, were in extremely ancient days in the habit of ascending Mount Baris or Ark (Ararat) to worship.   The Baris there was no doubt a Rocking Stone, rocking in imitation of the motion of the sacred Argo of the Queen of Heaven, the Baris being the Delphos, or the instrument which the Spirit Queen employed to convey the crude element to build up the earth and all flesh and blood, therefore, Moses describes all carnalities coming out of the Ark-Baris, and descending from the Baris on Mount Ararat.   This is the reason why the ancient world believed the Garden of Eden was in Armenia, with the river Euphrates flowing from it

We now come to Moses's Scientific plan of creation.

Garden of Eden.

Adam and Eve.

Cain, Seth, Abel (Pluto).

The Ark.

Noah and his wife.

Japheth, Shem, Ham.

Pluto is another name for Typhon, otherwise Saturn (Boar).

Paradise—Palestine.

Abraham and Sarah.

Abraham, Isaac, Jacob—Israel.

Palestine.

Jesus (second Adam), His Bride.

James, Peter, John.

Mary, Mary, Mary.

There is a striking peculiarity about the pedigrees of Cain and Seth. Cain's pedigree is based on the Seven planetary signs stretching from June 25th to December 25th from North to South.

The pedigree of Seth is based on the twelve signs of the Zodiac. The Three named apostles are of the twelve, precisely as the Three sons of Noah complete the number of the twelve Zodiacal signs, Abel being Typhon the Destroyer would naturally be averse to pro-creation, and no wife is alloted to him. But slyly, he is introduced under Typhon's other Egyptian title, namely Set (Seth). A wife is alloted to him, and thereby Set-Typhon is represented as the Father of Mankind, yet retaining all the ferocity of Typhon. Abel was identical with the first God mentioned in Ps. cx., and Ex. iv. 24, and xv. 17. It was the Rod emblem of Amen Ra, otherwise the Christ, in the hand of Moses that, acting as a Mediator between Typhon and Moses, saved his life in the inn. But Zipporah, wife of Moses, further mollified the savage God by marking the child with Saturn-Typhon's Mark.

CYMMRY, CIMMERII, CIMBRI, CIMRI.

The practice of English people of giving the S sound to C, which in Ancient British in common with all other ancient languages, has the sound of C in Can, Come, etc., has caused the initial C in the names at the head of this chapter to be rendered as Simmrii, etc. It is well known to scholars that the inhabitants of Wales have always called themselves Cymmry, pronounced Keemmre. Strangers call them Welsh, and the Principality, Wales, while the natives name the country Cymmre: a difference of spelling for the sake of distinguishing the country from the nation itself. It is only necessary to remind the reader that all ancient history agree that the Cimmrii once occupied the countries from the .Danube to the Caspian Sea, on the east, to the north of Persia. To the south of them would be Mesopotamia, Assyria, Nineveh, Babylon; to the south east would be Persia.

In the midst of their territories would be Armenia, "the Garden of Eden," Mount Ararat, otherwise Mount of the Baris, or Ark. The Cymmry still call a coffin Ark, as a symbol of that which the Druids imagined conveyed the souls of the dead to the Fortunate Isles (Isles of the Blessed) beyond in the west in the direction of the setting sun. The name of the Supreme Being among them is Celu, pronounced Kelee. It means, like the Greek Agnosto Theo, Unknown God. The nation is often called Celtæ, or Celts, after their name of the Almighty. To this the Greeks gave the form of Cœlus. We will not trouble the readers with the historical particulars given by Herodotus, Strabo, and others, as to the reasons why the Cimmerii or Celts left the banks of the two Euphrates, Pison, Gihon, or Araexes, and the north of Mesopotamia, for Britain. And we must point out that the Crimea is still Cimera in classic literature, that the Bosphorus (Constantinople) is still called Cimmeria, and that Moses in Genesis x. names the Cimmrii, or Celts, descendants of Gomer, son of Japheth, eldest son of Ninus, or Noah, the builder of Niniveh: that is, if we may say that Noah is the same as Ninus, a solar personification. The name Gomer is the genitive case form of Cymro, but mis-spelt, so here we find Moses nodding.

It can be seen in our table of Triads, Japheth is like Cain, etc., placed first, corresponding with the station of the Sun each June 25. Therefore, Moses places the descendants of Japheth and Cain to the north of Shinar, Plains of Mesopotamia. Moses must have written long after the Cimmrii, or Gomerians occupied the remotest isles of the north west of Europe, for he locates them in the Isles of the Gentiles. Their immigration to the far north-west, with their sacred Nod (Mark— $\vee$) gave to Moses the idea of describing them as "fugitives and vagabonds in the earth." Aye! they are still at it, and Colonising the distant places of the world. Gen. iv. 14 ; vi. 1, 2. Homer alludes to them as being there near the Kingdom of Night, in his time. It is highly probable that the Cimmrii occupied the regions of the Black Sea, etc., long after the most enterprising and most powerful of them had established a strong government in the British Isles, but occupied also during many centuries afterwards the parent hives on the banks of the rivers mentioned.

The Gauls, or Galatians, of Asia Minor, were probably a powerful remnant of the great and cultured people who had established themselves in Britain and France. In Galatia we find the Druidic and Gorseddic system prevailed. They were governed by Twelve Tetrachs, assisted by a senate of Three Hundred, called Aesach, or Shield of the Nation, but literally, of the Progeny, or Ach, the A circumflexed. The Twelve were, and are still called Rhaith, hence Law is called Cyv-Raith, Twelve Jurymen Rhaithwyr, a Rector is Rhaith-Ior, or the Rhaith of God.

We are aware historians state that the Galatians were a remnant of those who invaded Italy under Bren-us (King-Brenin). Jerome, who flourished in the fourth Century, states the Galatians in his time spoke the Celtic (Welsh) language. St. Paul in A.D. 52 must have heard Cymraeg daily, and in his Epistle to them against Judaism, he alludes in the beginning of the third chapter to the Solar Crucifixion which from the days of Ararat downwards was observed by them, as being antetypical of Jesus's Crucifixion at Jerusalem. Vide also Rev. xi. 8, Revised Edition.

Plutarch, who was born either in the reign of Claudius or Nero, wrote of the Cimmrii or Welsh, that they inhabited Scythia,

Pontus, or Eastern countries of the Black Sea. Then Plutarch states they also inhabited a country, "the elevation of the Pole (North) is such, that by reason of the declination of the parallels, it makes almost a vertical point to the inhabitants, and their day and night are of such lengths that they serve to divide the year into two equal parts." March 25 and September 25th. He further states the inhabitants passed from the East through Europe: that they were a warrior race: that under Brennus they invaded Italy, and that their march was like that of a devouring flame, and that nothing could resist their impetuosity. Plutarch states they bore separate distinguishing tribal names. Those inhabiting Western Europe had kept themselves so much to themselves, that when they burst upon Italy, no one knew who they were. Another author states they came from a Scythian Island. Plutarch states one of their distinguishing names was Celto Scythians. But Plutarch states that the Celts and Scythians mixed with each other but that they quarrelled over religion, and the Scythians proved the stronger. It is further intimated the Celts were in the habit of crossing Europe to the West, in the spring of every year.

We have in the foregoing enough to prove the early connection of Britain with Chaldea and Mesopotamia, Assyria, etc. We can now understand why the Old Testament is so full of references to Oaks, the stone circles of Bethel, Gilgal, and foot of Mount Sinai. (Ex. xxiv. 4). What is the meaning of the Zion or Great Stone of the Holy of Holies, now enclosed by the Mosque of Omar, Jerusalem, and why is the Messiah called "The stone of Israel?" Gen. xlix. 24; Isa. xxviii. 16; Deut. xxxii. 18. Because Moses, or somebody in his name, drew his system of religion from Druidism, and Saturn worship of the Shepherd Kings; and engrafted on the latter the doctrine of the Druidic Logos, or the Word.

"Lords and Commons of England.—Consider what nation whereof ye are, and whereof ye are the Governors: a nation not slow and dull, but of a quick, ingenious and piercing spirit; acute to invent, subtle and sinewy to discourse, not beneath the reach of any point the highest that human capacity can soar to. Therefore, the studies of learning in her deepest sciences have been so ancient and so eminent among us, that Writers of Good Antiquity and able judgment have been persuaded that the School of Pythagoras, and the Persian Wisdom, TOOK BEGINNING FROM THE OLD PHILO-SOPHY OF THIS ISLAND, Britain."—Milton: "The Liberty of Printing."

According to the earliest records of the Britons, they originally came to Britain from Deffrobani; "where Constantinople now is." Deffrobani may mean Dyffryn y Banau, or the Watershed of the Lofty Peaks. The Rev Edward Davies, in his "Celtic Researches," p. 551, states: "The contemporaries of Herodotus had a confused idea, that the Hyperboreans (Britons) were to be found some-where upon the northern confines of Europe and of Asia." This was a correct inference for their earliest home was in Armenia. For the same reason the Celts, or Cimmrii, are called also Scythians.

THE DRUIDIC CRUCIFIXION.

THE ANNUAL TRAGEDY AT AVEBURY, WILTS.

The British Isles are full of Druidic remains. They are met from Penzance to John O'Groat's House, and from Dunwich in the East to the Island of Aran, or, more correctly, Arawn, on the West coast of Ireland. But the two most notable of those relics of the past in Britain are those called by English people Avebury and Stonehenge in the middle of England. With regard to Avebury, it is a mile in circumference. Around its rim is a canal which is now dry and full of undulating mounds of turf heaps. In those grow trees. But the ancient outline of the canal is perfectly distin-guishable. Rising to a height of about fifty feet from the outer rim of the canal, is an artificial mound sloping back all round the canal. Upon it are clearly traced the terraces of seats in the surface of the slope all round, and looking over the canal on to the great arena enclosed by the canal and circular lofty rampart. The arena covers a space of about 32 acres. A ring of lofty blocks of stones, exactly 100 in number, formerly ran along the rim of the arena, all round, along the edge of the canal, but above it. Inside the arena stood two great circles. One had an outer circle of thirty lofty blocks of stones, then inside that circle another circle of similar blocks, twelve in number. In the centre of the double circles was a tripod of great stones 15 feet in height, with an immense block of solid stone lying on the top of the said threepillars, which we have called a Tripod.

The second circles were exactly like the other, but instead of a Tripod, those had in the centre a vast cylindrical pillar or obelisk, eight feet in diameter and twenty feet in height. The Tripod and block on top was a Cromleach. The pillar was called Maen Said, or Stone Linga.

"SILBURY HILL," OTHERWISE, SOL BARROW, OR BIER OF THE SUN.

Exactly south of the aforesaid stupendous circle, and three quarters of a mile from its southern edge, is an artificial Mound. Close to its base it measures 2,027 feet in circumference. The sloping height is 316 feet, or 16 feet and 100 yards. Its perpendicular height is 170 feet. The diameter of the level area on its top, is 120 feet. The Mound covers five acres of land. It was there when the Romans made the military road from London (Llan-Din) to Bath, or Bathon, as the Old Britons named the city. For that road in its approach to the Mound from London, makes a sudden curve to the south, to avoid it. In British or Welsh this vast mound is called Cludair Cyvrangon (Bier of the Mediator). The present Welsh for Bier is El-Lawr, or Sun Down. The name for Coffin is Arch (Ark), which, like the Nave of a Church, convey the soul of the dead to the realms of eternal summer bloom. The beautiful custom of the bedecking the symbolical Ark or Coffin with flowers, implies that the real Ark of which the coffin is a symbol, is bound for the world prepared to receive the perfected soul "beyond the river."

Cludar is literally Carry Upon, and is evidently the earlier form of the name of what is now called El-Lawr. Each dead in the Ark in the funeral procession conveyed to the mind of the bereaved friends that the dead had simply passed through the like ordeal of dissolution as Taliesun, otherwise Arthur, underwent on December 25th (21) every year, and that his soul, symbolised by the Wren in an Ark carried on an El-Lawr, returned again, clothed in a body blazing with glory or halo. It appears that during the long ages, when the Druids lit a funeral pyre to consume the body of each dead, a Wren was carried enclosed in each Ark or coffin, and this practice came down to within living memory. In England a wax candle was carried in front of the coffin to symbolise the soul of the dead. It will be seen in the first of the Druidic Triad given in the preceding page, that the third is Neiv Ion or Iona, or Boat and Dove. No mention is made of the dead body of the old Sun, Arawn.

But it appears the Druids at Avebury (Ab Rhi-Son of Rhi) sought to refer to the sacred remains of Arawn with great reverence, and at a cost estimated as amounting to what at the present day would be £20,000, piled up a symbolical sepulchre to him, and called it the Bier of the Mediator : for the sun was regarded as an intermediary between all humanity, all living things and created substances, and Black Wings of Druidism, who is Satan, called Saturn, Typhon, Pluto, Set, Siva, Ahriman, Typhoon, Anarchy, etc. And whose empire was Night, and whose Rule was absolute till the Sun (Taliesun) was created and ascended into the firmament. Isaiah refers to the latter as follows : "How art thou FALLEN from heaven (heavens), O Lucifer (Giver of Light), SON of the morning?" Isa. xiv. 12. In Rev. xxii., 16, Jesus is represented as identifying himself with Lucifer by saying, "I am the Root and Offspring of David—the Bright and Morning Star." As the habitation of the Logos, it is said, I will give him the Morning Star. Ibid 2, 28th ; 2 Peter i. 17-18, 19. In Rev. 11, 8, we read of the Druidic Circle, being a symbol of the circle of the whole earth, as the "Great City," which, Spiritually, is called, Sodom and Egypt—both had the Druidic Circle, and so had Mount Zion—Ps. xxiv.—"where (Sodom and Egypt) their Lord was Crucified." St. Paul alludes in Galatians

(iii. I) to the Solar Crucifixion among the Britons of Galatia, and as being typical of the crucifixion of Jesus, whom we have seen is called by John and Peter "The Morning Star." He is, too, Tammuz of Ez. viii. 14, only he is represented crucified on June 25th, the longest day, instead of December 25th, shortest day in the old style. It is plain the early Christians in Britain knew that everywhere except in Syria, Tammuz was represented as annually put to death on the cross, described in p. 71, on each December 25th, for the Christian Church of Avebury is dedicated to St. Thomas, who is placed by the church as a substitute for Tammuz:

> St. Thomas Grey, St. Thomas Grey,
> The Longest Night and Shortest Day.

Juvenal who laughed at everything, sacred and profane, alluding to the supposed annual death of the sun in the air on each December 25th, ridicules the idea by saying the sun's carcass falling into the ocean became "meat for Oysters." It appears that the Cross of p. 71 was erected on the summit of Silbury Hill on December 25th every year, and that the weeping and wailing myriads of Druids and Druidesses stood on the northern side of the Mound, and the moment the sun at 12 o'clock of that day reached the line of the meridian, it was inferred the murderous attack of Black Wings upon the sun commenced. Then a scene like that of men and women took place, wailing for Arthur, otherwise Taliesun, looking towards the south instead of towards the north, as the Syrians did "for Tammuz." In the case of the crucifixion of Jesus, the wailing Galileans gazed towards the east, for his crucifixion took place on March 25, at the hour of 12 o'clock, when the sun was in the centre of the vault of the heavens, exactly where the lines of the cardinal points cross each other. This to this day is the shape of the Cross of the Eastern Church, called the Greek Church. The Evangelists knew all about the solar two crosses, for by describing the darkness which prevailed they identify the dying of Jesus with the dying of the Morning Star. It is extremely curious that in the touching narratives of his death the time is given in correspondence with the time of Sunset in Britain on December 25th (3, 53), and not 6 o'clock and 18 minutes, the time of sunset on March 25th. Now, in Druidism, the darkness is assumed to last from December 25th at 3.53 in the afternoon, till 8,7 o'clock on the morning of the 27th. This is the one whole day Ioan (Dove) was in the Delphos (Fish), and Jesus was in the Crypt of the Great Rocking Stone, symbol of the Arkite Boat of the Queen of Heaven, his second mother.

We find the secret of the mysteries of the Egyptian figures of the illustration (p. 156) is unearthed as follows : After the Shepherds in Egypt had placed Abel (Typhon) in the third position (December 25th), and death of old Osiris (Sun) was observed afterwards on June 25th, and the child Horus (Sun), his successor, was annually miraculously created on the previous March 25th, therefore, Horus is represented as an infant with his aged father, Osiris, on June 25th, the new date of his death since the Shepherds had come by violence to monopolise by thrusting Abel into the ancient station of Osiris on December 25th. This accounts for old Osiris riding, and Horus walking, in p. 100, being saluted by Pan, personified He-Goat, and likewise old.

But now comes a more wonderful coincidence. Jesus died on Nisan 14th, and rose from the dead—young again—on Nisan 16th, or March 27th. We here find his birth from the dead co-incident with the birth of Egypt's infant Sun Horus, and Joseph, disappearing like old Osiris did, and as old Zacharias did after the advent of John.

"Our Old Man was crucified with him" is a figure of speech borrowed by the writer of Romans vi. 6, who had the death of old Osiris in his mind at the time. But no ingenuity could give forth that Jesus died as an old man, and rose from the dead as a Baby Boy or Mabyn, except by saying he died as old Adam and rose as second Adam. Calmet states that the Mahomedans say the skull of old Adam spoke on Golgotha to Jesus, the Second Adam. But the old God of Egypt annually died on June 25, three months after the birth of his Son Horus. In consequence, the "old man" is joined to young Jesus in his death, and it is the old man that undergoes corruption ; but there is reference to the new Baby Sun Horus as Jesus from the dead in the words "new man,"

Eph. iv. 22, 23, 24. It is forgotten the apostles were writing to nations to whom the Solar allegories of Egypt were the most familiar things of their religions.

The reason why the Virgin Mother of the Babe Son (Sun) was represented as Young was, that it was necessary to represent her as in her conceiving period of life, to be able to bear the Solar Child, whereas man continues even in old age to be a fertiliser of "the Seed of the Woman." But in the instance of Sarah—so favoured were the Jews—her old age, etc., was no hindrance to her conceiving by the act of a Divine Lord. Gen. xxi. 1. This was present in the mind of Isaiah when he compared the womb of Sarah to a mere hollow pit, and the one who brought Isaac thence to a Stone Pillar, the Druidic Egyptian symbol of "the Anointed" as the Divine procreator. 1 Chronicle i. 23; Is. li. 1 and 2; Deut. xxxii. 18; 1 Cor. x. 4. See Semele, p. 25 and 29, 44, 79, especially p. 90, etc. The Assumption or Translation of the Virgin Mary (August 15) is the Roman Catholic substitution for the Festival in honour of Venus, under her title of Ceres, the Tynghedwen of the Druids. Until the fourth century the church observed August 15th as the anniversary of the death of the Virgin, making it coincident with Nature's quietus, or falling asleep.

But it appears Sarah is intended to occupy really the station of Cariadwen (Cybele, Isis I, Ketos, Delphos, Boat (Thebet); Argo, etc.). It will be recollected Cybele (Cariadwen), Queen of Heaven, being a Spirit, and existing before matter or its essence, was first formed in scientific frames, had not the characteristics of sex, therefore Cybele's priests were all gelded, and wore scarlet, the colour of blood, as an euphemistic symbol of the feminine essence which Cybele (Ceubwl-Boat) brought from over the seas to the regions where the elements came under the influence of the operation of constructing laws of the universe. Thus, Sarah, like Cybele, "the mother of the Gods," the Consort of the Ancient of Days, was herself devoid of the sexual carnal instinct, yet she conceived and bore Isaac, the miraculous child, by the co-operation of the Angel Messiah.

We remind the reader the Seminal principle of the two-fold Word, and which is called Jupiter, was symbolised by a Stone Pillar, called "Rock," in the English translation. Deut. xxxii. 18, 30,31, and 1 Cor.

x.4; Gen. xlix. 24. That was the emblem of Christ made flesh in Jesus as the fertiliser of seeds, including "the seed of the Woman." Keturah, Abraham's second wife, who is called his concubine, appears to be intended to represent Nature, in the same way that Miriam does, and to pose as the foster-mother of Isaac, in the same way that Miriam is represented as the foster-mother of Moses. In Egypt those Goddesses were Isis I. and Isis II. The latter, the Mother and sister of Osiris-Horus, or the Sun in his two characters of old and young ultimately. Abraham is represented by Sarah as incapable to beget Isaac; but many years later he begets six children by Keturah. The scribe, while desirous to represent Keturah as fruitful Nature, forgot the description given as to the condition of Abraham long before in the lifetime of Sarah (Gen. xviii. 12,17; Ibid xxi. I), or he wished to convey Sarah was mistaken.

Ket-Urah is a name very much like Ked, a Druidic title of Cariadwen. The pupil of a Cat's eyes were regarded as like the shape of the sacred boat; that apparently was the reason for giving the name to Pussy. But, if our conjecture be correct, the name is inappropriate to the second as Nature. But like Isis I. and Isis II. there were Cariadwen I. and Cariadwen II, the name of the mother being given to Nature, her daughter, whose usual name is Gwen, or Venus. Spring buds are still Cat-kind.

THE STONE KIST OF ELPHIN, AND THE STONE SEPULCHRE OF CHRIST,

CURIOUS COINCIDENCES.

In the year A.D. 517, Maelgwyn Gwynedd succeeded his father, Caswyllion Law Hir, on the throne of North Wales. In A.D. 546 he was crowned King of Britain. This so far seems based on historical grounds. But in the next account of his career we find ourselves in the labyrinth where history and Druidic mythology are mixed together, for it is stated that he succeeded Arthur, a title of the sun, and meaning the same thing as George, namely, husbandman. Apparently an Archdruid as such as was customary, uses his title as representing the sun on earth, calls himself Taliesun. He writes as follows:—

> Myvi sydd Ddewin,
> A priv Vardd cyffredin;
> Mi adwaen bob corsen
> Yn ogov Gorllewin,
> MI RHYDDAV ELPHIN
> O FOL Y TWR MEININ.

> Translation.
> I am a prophet,
> And the principal public Bard;
> I am familiar with every shrub
> In the Cave of the West;
> I'll liberate Elphin
> From the hollow
> Of the Stone Kist.—Myv. Vol.I.,p. 34.

Then he foretells about the king. It will be borne in mind that the Druids is here speaking in the character of him whom he, by his office, as the Archon, represents in the Druidic Church. It will be noticed he says he is familiar with "every shrub in the Cave of the West." On referring to the story of Llangors Lake, it will be seen the Druid is referring to the perennial blooming shrubs of Gwenydva, or Paradise, the entrance into which was where the sun sets in the South West on December 25th. Elphin is Alpha, a Greek name introduced with Christianity, and employed as a substitute for Hu Gadarn, the most venerable Druidic name for the two-fold Word of God—Kelu (Cœlus).

We are next confronted by the difficulty as to how Taliesun, or the Old Sun, could "liberate Elphin from the hollow of the Stone Kist." Obviously, the reference is to the ecclesiastical ceremony of liberating the next Mabyn Taliesun from the hollow chamber under the Rocking Stone, used in this instance instead of the Bol-Groen (Belly-Skin), that being a more realistic emblem of the instruments.

Boat and Dolphin used as emblems of the Delphos of the Queen, named Cariadwen, Ced, Gwr-ach, and Nyddrig. It will be recollected it was an angel who opened the Kist Stone of the Elphin (Alpha) of Revelation i. 8. See St. Matthew xxviii. 2. And doubtless a ceremony of a like meaning was practised in parts of the country where lakes were not conveniently available. The Shell Grotto often seen in England, with a candle burning in it, is a symbol of the Kist Stone with Alpha, the Light, in it. The "Corps Candles" of Wales no doubt had their origin in the Custom. And the Christmas Box, like the Easter Eggs, is another survival of the emblematical Stone Kist of Elphin or Alpha. Panlora's box with "Hope" at the bottom, is the same symbol. So is also "Daniel's Den," which, like the Grave-Kist of Jesus, was "sealed." Dan. vi. 17 ; Mat. xxvii., 60, 66.

THE STORY OF ELPHIN AND TALIESUN.

The story of Elphin, and Taliesun as a Mabyn, is to be seen in the Myvyrian, Vol. I, p. 17. There we find it stated that Elphin was the son of Gwydd Naw Garau Hir. In old fragments the "Naw" is often rendered No. The name in English is, Long Legged's Ninth Presence. This was an eccentric name given to the Sun in the Ninth sign of the zodiac on December 25th, counting from the sign Taurus. Therefore Gwydd Naw, or No, is a Welsh name of the God Pan. It is probable the allusion to Pan's legs is due to two causes. (1) The Sun's rapid daily journey across the great field of the heavens ; (2) the peculiarity of the legs.

In the Iolo MSS. Pan is called Haner Dyn, or Half Man, the lower half being Goatish. We come next to the error of regarding Elphin (Alpha) as being the son of Pan or Gwydd Naw Garau Hir. Here the old sun as Pan is mistaken for Kelu, the Agnosto Theo, or the Unknown God, of the Athenians. We find another error illustrating the tangled wreck Druidism sustained during the fierce conflicts with the Roman Empire, and the succeeding contest with Christianity, namely, attributing the resurrection of Elphin from the Stone Kist grave, to Taliesun, or the personified Sun. This is like saying that the resurrection of Christ from the dead from the Stone Kist of Joseph of Arimathea, was the act of Pan-Jesus, for the name Christ is the Greek name of the Logos Spermaticos, or the material essence of the twofold Word of Agnosto Theo. We are his offspring. The enemy of Alpha, or Elphin, was Black Wings, or the Evil Spirit, whose empire is Night, or Darkness.

It is further erroneously represented that Maelgwn, Gwynedd, is Elphin's enemy. Here King Maelgwn is placed for A-ddu, or Black Wings. Dr. Davies, Mallwyd, in his dictionary, states, Mael is a form of the name Malen : one of the Three Graceless female triads of the Ancient Britons, the antitheses of the good Three Graces, consorts of Arthur (the Sun) at his Court. It is quite possible some ancient scribe in the course of the Dark Ages, finding one named Mael was the enemy of Elphin-Alpha, jumped to the conclusion he must have been King Maelgwn. Another fertile source of error was mistaking the names as those of real personages, instead of titles given to abstract personifications. Further, down to the present day we have traditions about fairies associated with sacred ancient mounds in Wales and Ireland. In the last named country the Celtic Fairies are called Little People. In parts of Wales they are Tylwyth Teg, or the Fair Tribe of the Tabernacle. In Glamor gan the designation of Fairies is, Bendith y Mamau, or Mothers' Blessings. See page 45. The traditions to which we refer are undoubtedly echoes of the remote past in Britain's annals, when, like Egypt, religious instructions were largely imparted by means of the dramatic art, and in which performances Divine ideas were represented in the forms of dramatis personæ in character, for the Druids were great ritualists. Fairies were the angels of the Celtic tribes, and in the Druidic Gorsedd of Bethel, Jacob beheld them descending to the earth over a ladder, to their avocations, and returning in the same way. He saw, too, as Justin Martyn points out, Alpha-Elphin standing on the heavenly ladder. Genesis xxviii. 13.

Jacob poured the oil on the top of the Stone Pillar representing the creating function of him who had stood on the ladder ; and the Stone Pillar was the emblem of Christ, otherwise Alpha, Elphin, Hu Gadarn, Amen Ra, Menw Hen, Minos, the First of the Creations of God, the Ancient of Days.

Another positive proof that the compiler of the extraordinary mixed story of the "Myvyrian Archæology of Wales," is the statement that Tegid Voel was the husband of Cariadwen. In pure Druidism, she is, like Isis I., the Queen of Heaven. Tegid Voel signifies in English, Tegid the Bald, and is a title of the Rayless Sun in the depth of Winter. Tegid is in full Teg-y-gyd, or All Fair. and appears to convey that the Sun in his annual old age is still "altogether lovely." One would expect the said compiler, after stating Tegid Voel to be the husband of Cariadwen, to state that Tegid Voel to be the father of Taliesun, whom he does state was Cariadwen's Son. But it is made evident that the mysterious "Three Drops" which Cariadwen swallowed when she swallowed Gwy-Iona Bach, who himself had swallowed the "Three Drops," were, as one generating power, the Father of Taliesun, as the Mabyn Sun or Son, as a corporeal substance. See p. 8-13. It is further stated in the very interesting tangled story in the said page 17, that the Baby Son, Taliesun, was found in a Skin Coracle between the Dovey and Aberystwyth, on the sea shore of Cardigan Bay, evidently opposite the well known village called Taliesun. Of course, the story is a compilation written by a Druid-Christian scribe, who did not understand that the traditional story was simply a distant echo of the olden time, when the Druids of Wales observed the birth and the tragic death of the sun annually by an aquatic dramatic performance between Borth, Cardigan Bay, and Arklow, Ireland, in the same manner as the Phœnicians did the annual birth and death of Adonis (Sun), across the Mediterranean, between the Mouth of their river Adonis and Egypt. Vide Adonia : Bell's Pantheon.

In the Dihuddiant Elphin, p. 20, of the "Myvyrian," we have allusions to "Iessu" (Jesus) in the following lines : —

> Pwy wyr canu
> Ger bron Iessu,
> Yngwydd y Tri Llu,
> Pan vo'r barnu?

Translation.

Who can imagine the chorus
That will be sung before Jesus
In presence of the Three Hosts
On Judgment Day?

Those lines enable us to conclude the tangled narratives here under consideration, were compiled during an early period of the history of Christianity in Wales. In another part of the verses of Taliesun, while yet a Baby-Boy, to Elphin-Alpha, we have as follows:—

Tydvwlch Cyvwlch,
A goreu vywlch,
    Ar van Caerau;
Gan Vynyddawg
Bu adveilawg
    Eu gwirodau;
Blwyddyn hiraeth
Er gwyr Cattraeth.

Translation.

Tudvwlch made a friendly breach,
The most excellent breach
In the place of fortifications;
But Mynyddawg and his army
Were ruined through their liquors;
A year of woe and sorrow
For the loss of the Cattraeth Slain.

The writer appears to refer to the battle of Cattraeth as then a recent event. That battle on the Solway Frith, most disastrous to the Britons, was fought, it is conjectured, about A.D. 570.

By the following verse, which is the fourteenth in the Ode of Varieties, Myvyrian, Vol. I., p. 93, we see what was the view of the Druids down to the sixth century, as to who was the father of Jesus as as incarnation:—

O'r Gwenith gwyn-fraint,
A'r Gwin, rhudd, rhwydd-vraint,
Y gwnair Corph Cywraint,
    Crist fab Alpha.

Translation.

Out of the holy wheaten grain:
And the red generous wine,
Is constructed
The mysterious body
Of Jesus, son of Alpha.

In the translation we have substituted the name Jesus for the name Christ of the original, as being the clear meaning of the poet. He is alluding to the bread and wine of the sacrament, and says in effect, if the bread and wine in the sacrament are the body and blood of Jesus, then it was of them the body was made originally, and is perpetually renewed. It will be seen in page 10 that in the West the 'three Drops" were symbolised by the juice of apples, and all cereals by bread, both made sacred by consecration, and still in Welsh called "Elements" ("Elfenau"). Each allotment of wine or apple juice, and bread, consecrated for symbolical use, represented all juices and all cereals from which all carnal beings derive the life-giving forces. This was the original meaning of the feasts of Dionysus, otherwise Bacchus (the Sun). Jesus inaugurated his public ministry by a like consecration at a marriage, and each marriage was regarded as a religious act emblematical of the marriage on March 25th of Taliesun and Gwen, or Crairwy. A difficulty was experienced in the manipulation of the figures, because Taliesun and Gwen, or Venus, were brother and sister. The point is dealt with in pages 68, 90, 91. A marriage is now said to be emblematical of the mysterious union of Christ and his Church, which is the Font alone, for the Nave, the symbol of the Sacred Arkite Boat of the Queen of Heaven, is the emblem of Jesus' own second mother, his father being Christ—Messiah—the Logos. The Bride of the Solar Ram is unquestionably the Font-Uterus. The bouquet of flowers carried by a Bride at her wedding is an emblem of her as her husband's Fruitful Garden.

MAB SANT, OR, SAINT SON.

The name Mabyn Sant, of which Mab in the name is an abbreviated form, signifies St. Son in English. Mab Sant was the name given by the Monks to a popular revelry associated with each parish church in Wales.

It has been conjectured by even Cambrian scholars that the name Mab Sant alludes to the Patron Saint of a church. But why the Welsh name for a Baby Boy should be applied to a Patron Saint of a church is a thing no one seems to have been able to understand. As a rule the ancient Canonised Saints selected as Patrons of Churches were, at the periods of their Canonisation, dead. Each Mab Sant festival in Wales was extremely popular down to the early years of the nineteenth century. He is always the Same One, associated with all Churches. In the middle of the eighteenth century, the Welsh Religious Reformers, under the influence of the English Puritans of England, attacked the amusements of the Welsh nation, and the annual merrymaking of the masses of the people, called Mab Sant, became particular objects at which the eloquent orators hurled their most fiery darts. No doubt excesses had been introduced into the festivals, but instead of eradicating the evil and preserving what was of public benefit in the venerable "Mab Sant," the said reformers tore up by the roots both the wheat and the tares. So successful were they that the family harp of a thousand years was driven out of Welsh homes as an accursed and an unclean thing. There is some reason to believe that one of the causes for the furious attacks upon the ancient festival was the fact that each was associated with some church building or another. The earlier clergymen of the church, acting under the influence of the earlier austere Puritans of England, had come to sincerely believe that dances were ungodly pastimes, and that ale was a Satanic drink. Those clergymen denounced the Mab Sant with honest sincerity. The Mab Sant was really a survival of the earlier religion of Britain, in which the whole people congregated together to express their delight at the coming of the sun of the new year, and their gratitude to Hu Gadarn (the Word) for the new sun, whom they personified under various titles, Taliesun, Arthur, the Crowned Baby Boy (Mabyn). Vide the Iolo MSS., p. 265 to p. 285. The verses to the "Crowned Baby Boy" are of extraordinary interest as containing a mixture of ideas relating to the Druidic Ark, or Ceubwl (Canoe). Take for example:—

> The Crowned Baby Boy, so says Bardism,
>> Will strengthen Britain from the rising sea,
> When a Fleet will come to Caer Ceri,
>> Then woe to the Saxons with their rabble.

Caer Ceri is now Barry Port, Glamorganshire. The numerous other verses are more interesting, as ancient lore, than the Orphic Hymns, as showing the early confusion in the minds of the Ancient Britons on religious subjects owing to the resemblance of Christianity and Druidism to each other in the story of the Nativity and the Birth of Arthur, at the Winter Solstice, from the Ark of Cariadwen on the South Eastern Sea. Moses and Jesus are represented as having had two births: one from his natural mother, for whom Miriam stands, and the Ark of Bulrushes; and the second from the Virgin Mary, and the Boat of John the Baptist, or the Sanctifier. Joshua iii. 5. See the Ceremony of Sanctifying, p. 182, 88, Genesis.

We have in the above free translation of one of the verses an illustration of the expectation of Arthur's return, which prevailed among the native Britons during so many centuries, down to the time of the fraud perpetrated by Henry II. and the Roman monks, and especially those of Glastonbury. Then it was lyingly reported that the grave, coffin, and remains of Arthur were discovered at Glastonbury Abbey. Even Giraldus Cambrensis was in the modern phrase "taken in" by the shaven crown cheats who acted, no doubt, by the instigation of the said King.

It is perfectly certain the early Christians in Britain experienced the utmost perplexity owing to the remarkable coincidences between the new religion from Jerusalem and the venerable religion of Ancient Britain. One of the earliest efforts of the St. Augustine Church after the sixth century, when it made common cause with the Saxons of Kent, was to treat the native bardic mythological per-

sonifications of the Britons, as real personages of flesh and blood.
But they were too cautious to canonise Arthur under that name,
although alleged to have gone all over the world in
search of the Holy Dish of the Last Supper, "brought
by St. Joseph of Arimathea to Lloegr" (England), but
they named Arthur, St. George, and attributed the exploits of
Arthur to him, and represented Arthur as fighting the twelve battles
(Sun passing through the Twelve signs of the Zodiac) against the
Saxons, and finally killed by them at Camlan. The Druids gave,
among many other titles, to the Sun the names A-dda (Good Wings),
A-ddov (Amiable Wings), and A-wen (Holy Wings). Those are
attribute titles given to the Divine tenant of the body of the Sun,
as twofold, set forth symbolically by a Wren or a Dove. The monks
said A-dda was the Semitic Adam. Iva, a name signifying the
Equinoctial line upon which the Druidic Gwyddon or High Priest
stood, when at prayer, with his face towards the East. The name
in full is Ivan, or the I place, or station. The Druids called it also
I-Wen (Holy I). The monks said Iva was the Semitic Eve. They,
however, associated the close of each church edifice with the same
symbol and called also Iwen, and planting in each close the ever
green Taxus Baccata, called it Iwen, and told the Saxons its name
was Yew. One of the Druidic titles of the Sun in Spring was
Dovydd or Ovydd D, the D being in the bardic alphabet shaped like
the Celtic harp, and the name D-Ovydd ("Dafydd," or David) signifies in the first instance, the Youthful Harper. The monks seem to
have concluded this must have been the Shepherd King David. But
the other title, Dewin (Prophet) is the name always given in the
Welsh language to St. David, and they agreed he should be the
Patron Saint of Wales.

The bards were a musical brotherhood, and were in the habit of
striking their harps at the advent of the sun as the solar harper that
gave the keynote to the winged tribes of the woodlands, after the
songless winter-time. They further agreed Dovydd was "uncle to
King Arthur." But they were unable to divest themselves of the
idea Dovydd was associated with David, the Shepherd King, and
they wrote down, "Dovydd was descended from Eurddolen, son of the
sister of the Virgin Mary," and, therefore, apparently called David

in honour of David, his ancestor. That the compiler was not a Welshman is evidenced by the fact that Eurddolen, which is a Welsh feminine name, and therefore would not be given to "the son of a sister" of anyone. It is very significant that the Church has never ventured to call St. David neither Dovydd nor Davydd in Wales. The English form of the name, David, is in the form Davydd among the Britons of Wales. The Welsh Church name of St. David is Dewi Sant, or St. Dewin, that is to say, St. Prophet, but to disguise it. The terminal "in" has been lopped off. Another Druidic name of the Sun is Duw-Vrig, or the Branch of Deus. The Vrig (Top Branch), is in the singular number, (mutated form, Brig). One is inclined to think it is poetically intended to be understood as Branching Rays of the Sun. Out of this we have "Dyvrig," rendered in Latin St. Dubricius, "the first Bishop of Llandav." Then we have St. Mabon as the name of the Patron Saint of Llan-Vabon. Mabon is apparently a corrupt form of Mabyn "Sant," the same as St. Son, "the Crowned Baby Son" of Bardism. Probably the Norman-French monks pronounced the name Dubricius, Du-Briki-us.

THE BOOK OF DANIEL.—A ROMANCE.

BASED ON BABYLONIAN HISTORY AND CHALDEAN PHILOSOPHY.

THE CHALDEAN TRIAD.

Every effort has been made by scholars to reconcile the Book bearing the name of Daniel with the historical records of Babylon by Herodotus, Berosus, who was a priest of Babylon, and the Canons of Ptolemy. But the result has been a dismal failure. We in these ages will submit views from a Druidic standpoint, which will throw a new light on the question, and indicating that the work, a very interesting one, is a romance, in which we find history and the Chaldean, or Druidic, ideal respecting divine things, personified. It will occur to the most superficial observer that there is a very striking agreement between the order of the basis of the Christian religon, namely, Jesus, James, Peter, John, and Daniel, Shadrach, Mesach, Abednego. Further, the angel Gabriel, who was so much in evidence in the incarnations of John the Baptist and Jesus, is the divine instructor of Daniel, in obedience to the Voice (Logos). Dan. viii. 16. And this is explicitly stated as follows :—"And while I was speaking, and praying, and confessing my sin and the sin of my people Israel, and presenting my supplication before the Lord my God, for the HOLY MOUNTAIN of my God : yea, while I was speaking, in prayer, the Man Gabriel, whom I had seen in the vision of the beginning, being caused to fly swiftly, touched me about the time of the Evening Oblation. And he instructed me and talketh with me and said, 'O Daniel, I am now come forth to give thee skill and understanding.' " ix. 20, etc. We in the foregoing learn three interesting things. (1) That Gabriel, as his name implies, conveyed the instructions of the Voice of God, the King; (2) that Gabriel had wings (Mercury ?); (3) that he appeared as a Man. Thus Gabriel is an intermediary between the Messiah (the Voice) and Daniel. In the work of the incarnations of John and Jesus, Gabriel transmitted "the Power of the Highest" to Elizabeth and Mary, but at Bethabara (Bethania of the Jordan, John ii. 28, Greek), the Voice Himself descended in the semblance of a Dove. That was in Britain, Chaldea, and Egypt, the emblem of the Logos in his twofold nature as Elohim, p. 65.

The foregoing positions are exactly Druidic. In the first place we have Hu Gadarn and Awen, corresponding with the Voice, which is in the miraculous preservation of the Three Lads in the furnace, said to be "like the Son of God." In the second place, we have Taliesun (the Sun)) corresponding with Daniel. In the third place, we have Panydd, Alawn, and Gwron, corresponding with the Three Lads.

We submit, the foregoing need nothing added to prove the Chaldean and Druidic origin of the ground upon which the Book of Daniel is based, and with it the entire groundwork of the entire Bible. It is exceedingly curious, as well as interesting, that the great representative Council of Britain, the House of Commons, has preserved down to the present day the ancient arrangement of the early Druidic Theocracy of Britain, preserved doubtless since the remote period when they and their brethren, the learned Chaldeans, inhabited the countries north of Babylon from the Caspian Sea, north of Persia, to the Danube in the west. The House of Commons arrangement alluded to is as follows :—The Broad "Arrow" representing the Crown of Wales, the Speaker, and the Three Clerks, in line at right angles before him.

We will now briefly illustrate the confusion which has been introduced into the annals of Babylon, as has been the case every-where where religious controversies have spent their force. Berosus, a priest of Babylon, and therefore one to whom the best sources of information were available, states, about 300 B.C., the Babylonian kingly succession was as follows :—Nebuchadonossor, Evil-Merodach, Neriglissar (brother-in-law of Evil-Merodach), Laborosoarchod, and Nabonnedus, a citizen of Babylon, and in no way related to Nebuchodonossor (Nebuchadenezzar). He states it was in the reign of Nabonnedus Babylon was taken by Cyrus, king of Persia. That Nabonnedus withdrew from Babylon to Borsippus, where he surrendered to Cyrus, that Cyrus gave him Carmian to dwell in, and that he dwelt there in peace, and there ended his days. According to Berosus, from the death of Nebuchadnezzar to the surrender of Nebonnedus to Cyrus, were twenty-four years less three months. The date of the surrender to Cyrus is given as 538 B.C.

Now Herodotus, who flourished in 431 B.C., says the name of the king of Baylon when Cyrus took it was Labynitus, and that he bore the same name as his father before him. (Herodotus, Clio, 188. Ibid, 191). Here we have the last king of Babylon, named Nabonnedus and Labynitus. Herodotus states the last named was the king who surrendered to Cyrus. Herodotus does not tell us what became of Labynitus after Cyrus took Babylon, but in one thing his narrative corresponds with what is said in the Book of Daniel as to the proceedings in Babylon on that dreadful night : "It was a day of festivity among them, and while the citizens were engaged in dance and merriment, Babylon was first taken," at midnight. Now the city was thus taken by Cyrus. It was afterwards

subject to Persia.   But in 516 B.C. the Babylonians rose in rebellion
against Persia.   Cyrus was now dead, and the Persian king now
was Darius.   He marched to Babylon at the head of his army, and
beseiged it.   The seige lasted one year and seven months, when
Babylon was taken as the result of a self-sacrificing strata-
gem by General Zopyrus, of the army of Darius.   Be it now
observed, in Daniel v. 30, 31, it is stated that it was
Darius the Mede, who took Babylon.   Dean H. Prideaux has
endeavoured to get over this by stating this was King Cyaxares,
uncle of Cyrus. "Old and New Testaments Connected with History."
Part I. p. 122.   History states it was Cyrus who took it, and
describes his march from Sardis to Babylon with that in view.   It
is known that the celebrated Queen Nitocris of Babylon was daughter of King Cyaxares, and that she was married to Nebuchadnezzar
and survived him; but was dead in 516 B.C., when Darius retook
the city.   Clio, 187.

We have said enough to show the confusion which has arisen
as the result doubtless of good men endeavouring to reconcile the
statements of the Book of Daniel with real history.   In the foregoing we find the writer of the Daniel Romance confounding the two
sieges of Babylon with each other, and actually putting that of
Darius before that of Cyrus.   The seige of Cyrus, confounded with
that of Darius twenty years later, the royal banquet and the midnight race of the soldiers of Cyrus, some from above and others
from below Babylon, through the archway of the Euphrates, diverted
by Cyrus, seem to be the historical basis of the romance, and the
Chaldean religious personifications the other basis of it.

The statement of Herodotus that Labynitus, the last Babylonian native king, was a son of Nitocris, widow of Nebuchadnezzar,
seems to solve the problem.   She married a second time Rab-Mag,
who seems to have borne also a priestly name, the father of
Labynitus, who was, doubtless, a distinguished citizen.   After
the death of Laborosarchod, who had caused infinite trouble,
Queen Nitrocis, who must have had immense influence owing
to her transcendent talents, had enough sway to induce the
Babylonians to invest her son, Labynitus, by her second husband,

with the Purple, and to assist herself in the Government which he no doubt had already been accustomed to do during the preceding troubles after the death of Evil Merodach, her son by Nebuchadnezzar.

That Labynitus, on ascending the throne, assumed the name Nabonnedus, probably a name in Chaldean of royal import, like the prefix in the name Nebu or Nebo, in the name Nebuchadnezzar. Nebo means Navel, and was ,held as most holy, as being the channel of divine nutriment from one to another. As to the station in life of Nabonnedus before he was made king of Babylon, the following is the statement of Berosus:— After the death of Laborosoarchod, who was tormented to death, Berosus, states "the conspirators got together, and put, by common consent, the Crown on the head of Nabonnedus, a man of Babylon," an intimation clearly conveying he was not king of Babylon by descent, yet a royal Mede by his mother, Queen Nitocris, the beloved of Babylon. Apion, Book I., section 20. Herodotus obtained his facts personally at Babylon about a century after the surrender of it to Cyrus. It is stated in p. 322, in Ragozin's "Media," that a cylinder bears record that Beltshazzar was the son of Nabonnedus: (1889).

The Book of Daniel is in the Hebrew Bible, partly in Chaldean and partly in Hebrew. This fact proves it was originally written by a scholar well versed in both languages. This gives room to suppose it was written by a Jew either during the Babylonian Captivity or after the return of the Jews from Babylon to Judea, as the effect of the edict of Cyrus—not Darius, be it observed. The Jew who rewrote the Old Testament, which had been destroyed by fire in the destruction of Solomon's Temple and Jerusalem itself, was Ezra, or Esdras, as he is sometimes called. He was in high position in Babylon, judging by the attitude Cyrus assumed towards him in dealing with the Jews, whom Cyrus found in Babylon. A man occupying that position must have been educated in the highest learning of the Chaldean priests of Babylon, and must have been the connecting link between the conquered and the Babylonian conquerors. It is well known that in restoring the Old Testament to the Jewish nation, Ezra wrote the new edition in Chaldean Characters, abandoning the old Hebrew alphabet, now called the Samaritan. The original Hebrew Bible is still in the Chaldean alphabet. We desire to think well of Ezra. His splendid patriotism makes him in the eyes of history one of the noblest characters who have adorned the annals of mankind. It is said "he was a swift scribe." Ezra vii. 6. This expression is a reference to him made after his death by a later scribe. That the particulars were written in or after the death of Cyrus and Darius is proved by mentioning the name of Artaxerxes in chapter xv., 92 years after the first year of Cyrus in Babylon.

In chapter viii. Ezra is made to speak in the first person, and the Captives are referred to as returning, some in the reign of Cyrus, some in that of Darius, and others, finally, in the reign of Artaxerxes in the time of Nehemiah. It is stated Ezra lived till he was 120 years old, and was buried at Jerusalem. (Josephus xi. 5. 5). Others that he returned to Babylon, and died there. The story of Bel and the Dragon, which is the same as St. George and the Dragon, and Arthur and the Dragon, was formerly a part of the book of Daniel, The story in 2 Esdras xiv., attributed to Ezra, otherwise Esdras, as to how he recalled to memory the contents of the burnt O.T. is clearly a romance. He is said to have been given to him a liquid to drink, and that it fired, and he, Ezra, held his mouth open, and the ancient lost literature of Israel, now poured forth from his open jaws. Naptha was often a useful thing in the hands of ancient priests. It is very likely the Book of Daniel was written by Ezra in his extreme old age, when he put Darius for Cyrus in his romance by mistake.

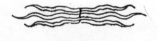

BABYLON.

The only part of the Book of Daniel which is correct history is that referring to Nebuchadnezzar, and his son, Evil-Merodach. (2 Kings, xxv., xxvii; Jeremiah lii. 31). Then the kings Neriglissar, Laborosoarchod, are skipped over, and then we come to Nabonnedus of Berosus's account, who, we submit, is the same as Labynitus, of

Herodotus. Now the name of Queen Nitocris is deliberately omitted by Ezra, because, in the name of Daniel, she, as the Goddess Beltis-Shazzar, consort of Bel-Shazzar, or King Baal, is introduced into the romance. The novelist could not without detection introduce her as bearing the names Nitocris and Beltis. But her name as Beltis-Shazzar is given to Daniel, and it is she who advised the King Bel-Shazzar to send for her protege, Daniel-Beltis-Shazzar, the wise man of her first husband, Nebuchadnezzar, said in the narrative to be the father of Belshazzar, the last king of the Babylonian succession, who historically was Nabonnedus-Labynitus, who lived under Cyrus in retirement at Carmia.

We now come to the introduction into the romance of the Chaldean Word of God as associated with Beltis-Shazzar (Daniel) instead of with Baal or Bel of the Chaldeans. Bel, or Baal, is, like Taliesun, the sun. But in Daniel Bel is dissociated from him, and is given as associated with the Hebrew Daniel instead. Thus the Chaldean and Hebrews words written on the wall, the condemnation of Bel represented as Nabonnedus-Labynitus, and slain at a banquet in the time of Darius, which banquet was in the time of Cyrus, during which, at midnight, Cyrus took Babylon in 538 B.C., whereas Darius did not enter Babylon till 516 B.C., then to put down a rebellion there against him after the death of Cyrus. Further, it is perfectly well known to scholars that Shad-Rach, Me-Shach, Abed-Nego, were the Chaldean names of their Divine Triad, and the fact that those names are fastened on three Hebrew lads by the Hebrew scribe, clearly reveals that the scribe's intention was to invent a fable whose main purpose was to indicate that the Word (Messiah) was a Jew and not Druido-Chaldean; that he hated Bel or Baal, of Babylon, and preferred four Jews—Daniel, Hananiah, Mishael, Azariah—though given the titular names of Beltis-Shazzar, Shad-Rach, Me-Sach, Abed-Nego, in the Druidic religion the three names of the sun on June 25th, March 25th, December 25th. He himself was still one sun. At the end of the Solar year, December 25, anciently the Orientals represented the Word as escaping from the wrecked body of the Sun Baal into and through Hell into Paradise, to be there re-clothed with a new body. Then returning

as the Infant Baal, ascending on high, leading captive captivity.
That is to say, as many as had, of good souls descended into the
shades during the previous year. The Sun as three under the
titular names, Shadrach, Mesach, Abednego, are represented descending into a "fiery furnace," but accompanied by a fourth, called "the
Son of God." In Druidism he was supposed to dwell in the sun's
Head. This part of the Druido Chaldean Solar drama is placed in
the reign of Nebuchadnezzar. Dan. iii. 25.

The Druids, in connection with the Rocking-Stone, symbol of
the Argo, or Sacred Boat, the tangible representation of the presence
of the Queen of Heaven, had a Crypt-Grave beneath the Nave
(Latin for Boat), representing the hold. That Crypt-Grave is a dun-
geon full of lions, in Daniel vi. 17 : "And a STONE was brought and
laid upon the mouth of the den ; and the King Sealed it with his own
signet, and the signet of his lords." On the morrow early, Nebu-
chadnezzer went to the Crypt-"Den," and in reply to the King of
Babylon, Daniel answered from below, "O King, live forever. God
has sent his Angel"—be it observed the words are not "an angel,"
but a particular one—"and hath shut the lions' mouths, that they
have not hurt me : forasmuch before Him innocence was found
in me." He was the Angel-Messiah, who says, "I am an Angel
of the Lord, come up from Gilgalto Bochim, and said, I made you go
up out of Egypt, and have brought you unto the land which I swear
unto your fathers." (Judges ii. 1 ; Heb. viii. 9). The same ancient
custom of sealing, as in the instance of Daniel, was observed in the
securing of the Crypt Grave under a Stone, in the instance of the
interment of the Messiah. "So they went, and made the sepulchre
sure, sealing the Stone, and setting a watch." Matthew xxvii. 66.
In Druidism the same ceremony is alluded to as follows :—

> "Mi a ryddav Elphin
> O vol y Twr Meinin."—"Archæology," Vol. I., p. 34.
> "I will liberate Alpha
> From the Tower Stone's hollow."

As we explain elsewhere, the later Druids borrowed the Greek
designation "Alpha," and called Hu Gadarn and his Soul, Awen—

the two being the Elohim of Israel—Elphin is a corrupt form of the name Alpha, the first letter of the Greek Alphabet, Jesus speaking of himself in the character of the Angel Messiah, or The Christ, said he was Alpha—the Beginning.   Rev. iii. 14.

ANOTHER ASPECT OF THE SAME CHARACTERS.

In the foregoing we see it intimated that Nebuchadnezzar was no stranger to the Son of God, for he is said to have admitted that the fourth person in the fiery furnace was like Him.   In the second place, Daniel himself intimates that he, who has closed the mouths of his savage companions, was the Angel Messiah, the same as the Son of God, called Christ by Greek philosophy, and Hu Gadarn by the Druids, and also Llev-Velus, or Sweet Utterance.   Sometimes he is called Llavar, or Speech.   The same Divine characters are thus next introduced.   "And it came to pass that when I, even I, Daniel, had seen the vision, and sought for the meaning, then, behold there stood before me the appearance of a Man.   And I heard the voice of a Man between the banks of Ulai, which called and said, Gabriel, make this Man to understand the vision."

"So he came near where I stood : and when he came, I was afraid and fell on my face ; but he said unto me, Understand, O Son of Man : for at the time of the end shall be the vision."   (Dan. viii. 15, 16, 17).

Again, "Yes, while I was speaking in prayer, even the man Gabriel, whom I had seen in the vision at the beginning, being made to fly swiftly, touched me about the time of the evening oblation.   And he informed me and talked with me and said, O Daniel, I am now come forth to give you Skill and Understanding."   Ibid ix., 21, 22. Flying Gabriel is the Chaldean Mercury, and he is the sun personified on the celestial equator (March 25), and his "day" in the list of seven days of the week is Woden's Day, called Dydd Merchyr, or Dies Marcurius, in the language of Druidism.   We have here the Hebrew scribe introducing the Voice (the Logos-Messiah), as if influenced by the evening sacrifice of blood.   This impiety was what eventually destroyed the Jews as a nation. For it associates the Word of the Highest, as in Ex. iv. 24, with Typhon, representing him as the Highest. Genesis xxii.; Ex. xii. 3, 21, 22. Here the fact the Passover is killed to please the Destroyer is admitted. Abraham in the 12th chapter of Genesis could have made the like admission, for it would have been true. In Ex. viii. 26, we see the Ram was so holy in the eyes of the Egyptians when used to symbolise the Sun from Nisan 10 to 14, or, in our calender, from March 21 to 25, that Moses tells Pharaoh his people dared not do it in sight of the Egyptians, "in the Land" of Egypt. But the Ram-Lamb was an "abomination" to Typhon, the Destroyer, being the symbol of the Sun, therefore of the vehicle of the creating faculty which he transmitted from the Word inhabiting the luminary. Thus the Typhon-Saturn votaries, while rendering homage to the Voice, killed and ate the symbol of the sun itself, in token of their strange doctrine that the sun was an "abomination." Isaiah has the same notion. Chapter xiv. 12, etc. All this teaching of blood offerings has been the curse of nations.

THE HERESY OF MOSES AND EZRA.

The positions in their relative relationship to each other in the Book of Daniel stand thus:—

>Saturn-Typhon.
>The Logos, or Voice, conveyed by Gabriel, whose name
>signifies, The Voice (Gab) of God King.
>Daniel, the Sun.
>Shadrach—Mesach—Abednego.

In the following we have another aspect of the same characters on high, with Daniel omitted.

One on the north of the river: one in linen on the waters of the River: another on the south of the river. Daniel xii. 5,6,7.

The one on the river is Michael.   The Hebrew Seven are named as follows : —

      (1) Raphael.   June 25th.

      (2) Haniel.

      (3) Michael.

      (4) Gabriel.   March 25th.

      (5) Zaphkel.

      (6) Zadkiel.

      (7) Gamalel.   December 25th.

The above enumerated SEVEN ANGELS are imitated in the SEVEN ANGELS of the SEVEN CHURCHES of Asia Minor.   Rev. i. 12, etc.   Here the Voice of the Son of the Man, Jesus (the Sun) sends his seven angels, the personified emanations of the Word, and manifested during the sun's progress over the seven planetary spheres between June 25th and December 25th.

Now in Daniel xii. 1, Michael is said to be the great patron of the Hebrews.   He is third in the above list.   He is identical with Mars, Tyw of the Saxons, and the Scandinavian Tuisco, God of War. In the Mount Sinai scene it was on the third day, Tuesday, the trumpet was heard sounding on the mount.   Ex. xix. 16.   Therefore, being the Destroyer, it is said, The Lord is a Warrior; the Lord is his name.   Ex. xv. 3.   We see in the foregoing Michael is represented as the Angel Messenger of Typhon, but Gabriel is the Angel Messenger of the Voice, otherwise The Christ.

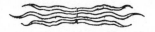

THE DUAL DEATHS AND RESURRECTIONS OF JESUS.

A problem which greatly puzzled the writer was the following :—The Baptism of Jesus and his ascension from the Boat of John the Baptist to the Canaan side of the Jordan at the very spot on the Jordan where the river had opened wide to enable the nation under Joshua and Eliazer, the high priest, to pass over with dry feet, the same thing as his entombment and resurrection from the grave under the great stone in the garden of Joseph of Arimathea, Jerusalem. The following words of St. Paul place beyond all question that Jesus's burial and resurrection implied exactly the same thing as his "Baptism" by St. John. Inasmuch that he was not buried in water, neither was he "Baptised" in water. The words of St. Paul are as follow : "Know ye not, that so many of us as were Baptized unto Christ (Jesus) were Baptized unto his death. Therefore we are buried with him by Baptism unto death : that like Christ was raised up from the dead by the glory of the Father, even so we also should walk in newness of life." Romans 6, 3. We find St. Paul describing the journey of the nation through the open passage of the Red Sea as a Baptism, and the descent of dew upon the nation from the miraculous Cloud, a symbol of the Holy Spirit apart from the Rod, emblem of Christ, in the hands of Moses, as a Baptism too. Here we have the same word employed to describe the lustration of the nation by the agency of holy dew, and their advent through the opening in the rent sea, into the Wilderness of Sinai. In the same sense were the nation Baptized unto Joshua, by passing through the opening in the river Jordan. The words of St. Paul are : "Moreover, brethren, I would not ye should be ignorant, how that all our Fathers were UNDER the Cloud, and that all passed through the sea, and were all Baptized unto Moses in the Cloud, and that all passed through the sea, and were all Baptized unto Moses in (by?) the Cloud and in the sea." 1 Corinthians x. 1, 2. In the Druidic system of religion, the Word as fertiliser of Nature's seed, operates on March 25th every year. Then on June 25th, when nature's herbaceous offspring has attained full maturity and growth, the A.Wen—called A.-Wen Hefin, or June—sanctified the work done. This A-Wen Hefin is an expression meaning the Holy Spirit of June, and June 25th was the Whitsun of Druidism, when the year was Crowned symbolically. It was the annual Pentecost of Britain. Now, owing to the adoption of the Jewish lunar year, the date is movable. Copying the venerable Druidic practice, an interval of time occurs between the symbolical generation of the nation from the Baris or shrine of the Queen of Heaven, emblemished by the opening in the Red Sea, and the dewy lustration from the Cloud. That did not take place until the Tabernacle was completed, and the priests ordained. Then the dew descended upon the Tabernacle, thus described by Josephus:—"The sky was clear, but there was a mist over the Tabernacle, only compassing it, but not with such a very deep and thick Cloud as is seen in the winter season, nor yet in so thin a one as men might be able to discern anything through it.   But from it (the Cloud) there dropped a Sweet Dew, and such as showed the Presence of God" (Holy Spirit) "to those that desired and believed it."   Antiquities, B. viii. c. 8, section 5.

We now come to the solution of the problem alluded to at the head of this chapter.   The Wilderness was the symbol of Tartarus or Sheol.   The Jordan, the dark River Styx of the Underworld. Canaan was the symbol of Paradise or Elysium of the same region.* Now the Jews were taught to regard the Wilderness of Sinai, the Jordan, and Canaan as sacred earthly counterparts of the subterranean regions mentioned, and Jesus commenced life by going down to Egypt, and coming thence.   Then he entered upon the wilderness part of the process, on the eve of his public ministry, and crossed the Jordan in the Boat of Baptism, because the Jordan no longer opened miraculously as it did for the nation in the Exodus; and he entered into the earthly Paradise, and began a "newness of life" . . as the Messiah.   In his death he underwent the realities of which the others were, in the eyes of the Jews, but sacred figures.

True to "the Mystery kept secret" (Romans xvi, 25), the Apostles at Jerusalem, on the Day of Pentecost (Whitsun Day), were crowned with a diadem having plumes, "Cloven tongues, like as of fire, and 'it' sat upon each of them."   This was another symbol of the baptism of the Holy Spirit, meaning the same thing as the descent of the Sweet Dew described by Josephus, as having descended on the Tabernacle.   We notice elsewhere the use made of "forty" in the Old and New Testaments.   Sometimes the forty are years, days, hours.   This was what St. Paul describes as "the Mystery of the Faith."   1 Timothy 3, 9.   Thus, too, Jesus is described "as spending Forty Days and Forty Nights in the Wilderness, to be tempted of the Devil," is intended, but concealed under a thin veil, to correspond with the Forty Years the nation wandered to and fro

---

* "Abraham's Bosom."   Luke xvi. 22.

in the Wilderness of Sinai. "And the Lord's anger was kindled against Israel, and he made them wander in the Wilderness Forty Years, until all the generation that had done evil in the sight of the Lord had been consumed." Numbers xxxii. 13, 14.* The next illustration of the Forty is Hours in stead of Years and Days. Jesus was, as regards his body, in the Crypt of the Great Stone Sepulchre forty hours, namely, from between the Ninth and Tenth Hours of Nisan 14th (March 25th), and the second hour (8 o'clock a.m.) on the 16th (March 27th), or Forty Hours, during which hours his Divinity was in both Hell and Paradise or Elysium, in the last-named with the Devil's captives. See pages 145 and 146.

We need not remind the reader that the sacred number forty, throughout the Old and New Testaments, is derived from the old Druidic notion that forty hours elapsed between sunset on December 25th, and Sunrise on the 27th, between the death of the Old Sun and the birth of the New One from the Sacred Baris of Cariadwen, Queen of Heaven.

---

* Jesus likewise was "driven into the wilderness, to be tempted of the devil." Mark i. 12, 13 ; Matt. x. 1 ; Luke iv. 1, 2.

SACRIFICING THE ELDEST SON.   HORRORS!

In the first pages of this work will be seen the ancient story of the conflict and perpetual enmity of Black Wings (Pluto, otherwise Saturn) against the Sun under his various titles or names, as Arthur, Taliesun, Adonis, Horus, Tammuz, Baal, etc.   Black Wings was supposed to be a bodyless spirit, hence A. Ddu, or Black Wings, wings being Druidic symbol of a spirit.   The other symbol of a spirit is a serpent.   The serpent came to be employed as a spirit symbol because it moves from one place to another without hands and feet, as a spirit is suppo ed to do.   Night was in Druidism the Kingdom of Darkness ; Day was the Kingdom of Light   The king of the former was Black Wings ; the king of the latter was the Sun (Son).   Till the Sun came there was no light, and Black Wings ruled supreme. Therefore, the Sun was regarded as an intruder into the Universe. He had much annoyed Black Wings, who is continually endeavouring to recover his lost supreme dominion.   The varying lengths of night and day, or darkness and light, were regarded as evidences of the conflict raging between the two rival forces in the air.   As soon as the Sun descended into his Great Bed (Gorwel) in the West, "o'er the shaded billows rushed the night" (Homer) and Black Wings resumed his reign.   But on the morrow the Sun re-appeared in the opposite direction, and again ruthlessly drove back Night before him "down the melancholy way" (Homer).   Winter was regarded as Black Wings' General, and he killed in all directions.   On the shortest day of the year, December 25th in the old calendar, Black Wings was supposed to kill the sun in the air while midway over the line of the Tropic of the He-Goat (p. 71).   But Black Wings could never catch the Winged Soul of the sun.   In the South-West, riding the billows, was the sacred Boat (Thebet-Argo) of the Queen of Heaven (Cariadwen—Isis I.—Minerva-Medusa), and into that the winged soul, Hu Gadarn, flew for protection (p. 17), which was always there rendered.   He was there re-invested with a new body, and after the lapse of 40 hours, re-appeared as a Crowned Babe, and therefore King Arthur, son of Uthr Ben, or Enormous Head.

The British Druids seemed to have held his childhood necessitated the protection of his mother, the Queen of Heaven, and they constructed the enormous Serpent of Avebury (Ab Rhi) with her head on the summit of a hill and facing that part of the horizon where the Young Sun appeared on the first morning of the Solar new year. There the Queen was called Kyn-Nydd, pronounced Kean-Neith. The brook near it retains the name as "Ken Net." Kyn Nydd signifies the First Turner of the Wheel. That is to say, the solar machinery.

The first verses of the first chapter of St. John's Gospel contains a complete admission of the Druidic doctrine that the Word (Logos), called Melodious Voice and Invincible Hu, by the ancient philosophers of the West, was the first begotten Son of the Almighty; that he created all things, and not His Father (v. 3); that the Word was a God like his Father, and that the Word is that "Light which lighteth every man as he cometh into the world" (v. 9). Greek. In the words "in him was life, and the life was light,' the "him" alludes to the Sun as the physical Head containing the Word, who is the Light. We next come to a being who is called Darkness, who is pursuing the Sun, to capture him and make him his prisoner. In the revised version the fifth verse is rendered, "And the Light shineth in darkness, and the Darkness apprehended (arrested) Him not." Observe here in the first place darkness is non-personal, but in the second, Darkness is an active personality, and is a Black King in pursuit of a King whose attribute is Light, the attribute of his antagonist is darkness.

On Calvary the Black King overcame for a while : "And it was now about the sixth hour"—hour of noon—and a darkness came over the whole land (earth) until the ninth hour (3 o'clock) : the Sun failing." Greek. St. Luke xxiii. 44, 45. Here Jesus and sun are one and the same, and the Dragon of Revelation xii. 1 overcomes him (p. 50).

As we say elsewhere, the Druids, like the Hindoos do still, believed the solar system was a vast revolving wheel, turned from East to West, by the Queen of Heaven. It appears they supposed its axle bar passed horizontally through the earth. In the History of Taliesun (Sun) he is made to say he sits on high in the chair of the Sun fixed in the solar wheel. The expression is "wheel of Baal" (Sun). It seems therefore the Druids supposed there was a chair for

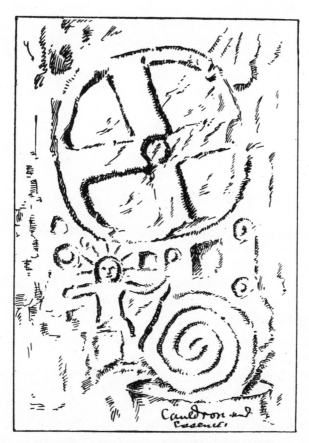

From a Stone in South Wall, Llangammarch Church, Breconshire.

Birth of Arthur-Taliesun in Paradise (Gwenydfa) from the Spirit Mother Cariadwen, Queen of Heaven, implied by the serpent hieroglyphic on the essence of her Cauldron, above the heavens as a Revolving Wheel (Rhod), with the Earth fixed in its centre.

The above is the Serpent Mother of the Brazen Serpent in the Wilderness.

Hoffi'r wyf dy lan breswylfa,
  Arglwydd lle'r addewaist fod ;
Nid oes drigfa debyg iddi
  Mewn un man o dan y RHOD.

Baal," and this conveys that the idea of the chair came to Druidism with the Phœnicians. The Druids have perpetuated the idea in "The Chair" of the Eisteddfod and at Oxford. The Druids regarded the sun as a Trinity; his soul as dual; essence of fatherhood in the concrete, and spirit (Elohim, or Gods), symbolised as a wren or dove; and the sun himself as the creation of the Seminal element in the Word of the HIGHEST. The spirit in the Word was the Father of each soul life. See St. John's viii. 19 and 29; Ibid 10, 30. He is here speaking of the Word as his Father, and he himself as the product of the Word, who is also "in him," since the descent of the Dove.

The Ancients found this triad their most perplexing dogma, and it is still a doctrine most difficult to comprehend. The Hebrews made it more difficult still by representing Saturn (Black Wings) as the Father of the Word, and repudiated the sun altogether, for that is the meaning of their sacrifices of the Bull, Ram, and the He-Goat, which were the Egyptian Zodiacal signs of the sun himself, and therefore of the sun's corporeal substance, in Spring and at the Winter Solstice.

Now, the principal symbol of the sun himself, apart from his tenanting the Elohim, was each eldest son in a family. The Word in the sun was the eldest-earliest-son of the Highest, and it was he who first disturbed the reign of Black Wings. Each son, as a fertiliser, was the direct agent on earth of the Christos, the Seminal principle in the Word of the Highest (Coelus). "We are his offspring" (see p. 8), states the Greek poet, and, as our Father, he is bitterly hated by Black Wings, otherwise Saturn, Typhon, or Anarchy, otherwise the Destroying Angel.

It was supposed by the worshippers of the Destroyer, that the sacrifice of an eldest son, as the agent of the son on earth, was very pleasing to their God. Be it observed, the eldest daughter is not required, because she is inert, and a non-producer, without the male. We have here probably the reason why women were held in a low condition among divers nations in the East. But they, as non-producers of themselves would be favourites with devil worshippers. **Lev. xii.**

In Mythology Saturn is represented as the Son of Coelus, Celu of the Druids. Saturday is the day of the Sun in the month of Dec. (25) in the Seventh Planetary sphere, and being at the end of the solar year, he was said to be old, and is the third in the triad of Egypt of the Royal Shepherds. Old Saturn was said to have cut off the genitals of his Father Coelus. This means that he had stolen the Logos, or the Word of Coelus, and appropriated it to himself. It is clear the Hebrews substituted Saturn for Coelus, and represented him as terribly antagonistic to the Word, represented most impiously, as his Son, instead of being the Son-Word-Name of Coelus.

The earliest attempt we find in the Scriptures to associate Saturn, the God of circumcision, with the Word is in Exodus iv. 24 : "And it came to pass by the way in the inn, that the Lord met him, and sought to kill him, because Moses had neglected to place the Saturnine mark on the privy part of one of his sons." Be it noticed the Voice (Word) of the Brilliancy in the Bush had entered into the Rod of Moses, and had converted it into a Serpent, the Egyptian emblem of a spirit-wisdom, because a serpent, like a spirit, can go from one place to another without pedal organs, and the Divine Rod—the Christos—was in the hands of Moses at the inn while on his way to Egypt, in obedience to the Divine Voice in the Brilliancy in the Bush. It was the Rod (Christ) which saved the life of Moses !

In Egypt, the young Ram was the symbol of the Spring sun, when the luminary is the instrument of the fertilising emanation of the Word in the sun, which word is called Father Iu, Amen, or Jupiter Amen, called also Amen Ra or Christos (Heb. ii. 26). In the instance of Abraham, Saturn demanded Isaac, the patriarch's miraculous son (Deut. xxxii. 18), begotten by the Rock (Gen. ixl. 24), and the Pillar was the emblem, like the Rod, of Christ. Abraham was given his choice : either the Son or the young Ram he had to immolate to appease the appetite of the awful God whom Abraham worshipped. Genesis xv. 17.

It is represented that between four and five centuries later, a Destroying angel came, who is clearly Typhon, another name for Saturn or Set (Seth). The God who sought to slay Moses at the inn, demanded the slaying of Isaac, demanded one or the other—the eldest son or the young Ram of the Passover; demanded also the sacrifice of the incarnate son of the Christ on Calvary, namely Jesus of Nazareth, the Lamb of God, containing the Logos of Cœlus, instead of whom is substituted the "murderer from the beginning" (John viii. 44). Jesus in this verse is alluding to a supernatural being who was "in the beginning" and was then at heart a murderer, and had murdered each sun's corpus at the Winter solstice ever since. He further ordered the murder at each Passover of the eldest son of each Hebrew family or his young Ram substitute.

Isaiah with glee describes him going up to Jerusalem with his garments dyed with the blood of the God of Edom and Bozrah alluded to in Revelation xi. 8, as the locality "where their Lord also was crucified." This is translated honestly in the present revised edition.

To revert to the subject of the eldest son in the religion of the Hebrews. We said already that the reason why the life of the eldest son was demanded by the terrible God whom the Hebrews worshipped in conjunction with the creating Word of Cœlus, whom earlier the Jews dethroned and placed horrible Saturn in his stead, was because the eldest male son "that opened the womb" of his mother was the earthly agent of the Seminal principle of the Word on earth. In other words, that he is the officer of Christ.

It is perfectly well known to every scholar throughout the world, that the most solemn of oaths was that taken on the membrum virile. It was regarded as swearing by the Divine fertilising secretion. In our translation of the Old Testament, it is called the "hand under the thigh." Gen. xxiv. 2; viil, 29. Some commentators, knowing the expression referred to the Phallus, have inferred it refers to the sectione circumcisionis. That sign is a mutilation of the organ in honour of the Destroyer, like killing the eldest son of each family, and to carry the devotion to Satan still farther, "some made themselves eunichs" (Matt. xix. 12). In Leviticus xii. will be found the apologetical sacrifice mentioned as demanded by the God of the Hebrews for propagation, and thereby carrying on the work of generation, commanded by Elohim (Christ and the Holy Spirit) in Gen. i. 22 28; vii. 17; ix. 7; xxxv. 2. In Gen. i. 26, man is made as body and soul after the image of Elohim, who is Essence, and therefore Father (Christos and Oil), and Holy Spirit (Father of Souls). Thus we see that between Saturn and the Creating Word as two principles, a furious antagonism existed on the part of Saturn, who had been represented as the Most High God, and Father of the Word.

THE MALE ASS IN HEBREW WORSHIP.

Finally we adduce an irrefragable proof that the reason of enmity of Saturn towards each eldest son was that the last named was a fertiliser of the feminine ova. In Egypt, and, indeed, in all ancient countries, the male Ass was a very pronounced symbol of male virility. Some of the nations had bedposts ornamented with the heads of male asses. In Ex. xiii. 13, we read as follows: "And every firstling of an Ass thou shalt redeem with a young Ram; and if thou wilt not redeem it, then thou shalt break his neck; and all the firstborn of Man among thy children shalt thou redeem"(with a Ram likewise). Thus clearly, the First Born Male Child, and the First Male Ass of his Mother, were equal in value as two sacrifices to the God of the Hebrews. Jesus was an Eldest Son: Christ-Messiah, as the Amen, or the Word, was the Only Begotten Son of the Highest, and He was the Beginning of Creation. Rev. iii. 14. The Colt of an Ass which, with his Dam, accompanied Jesus into Jerusalem on Nisan 10th, the day the Paschal Ram, was to be captured according to the ordinance of Moses, was of the same value as Jesus Himself as a sacrifice in the ransom of mankind. Christ-Messiah bore the same relationship to Jesus which the "Angel" of Genesis xxi. 1 and 2, bore to Isaac, whose essence was every Jew and Jewess. Christ-Messiah was that "Angel," therefore, it is said by St. John, "He came to his own (things—Greek), and they that were his own received him not." St. John's Gospel i. 11. The allusion is to the Divine origin of the Hebrews as set forth in Deut. xxxii. 18; Gen. xlix. 24; Isaiah li. 1, 2; Gen. xxii. 1, 2, etc. This is what is meant by the words: "And it came to pass, when men began to multiply on the face of the earth, and daughters were born unto them,

that the sons of Elohim (Gods) —the Hebrews—saw the daughters
of men that they were fair; and they took them wives of all which
they chose." Gen. iv. 1 and 2. Cupid and the Love-Spirit, Eros
and Psyche are other names of Elohim, considered as Essence and
Soul, or Body and Soul, united in one person.

It is taught that the God of the Hebrews was so delighted with
the offering to him in sacrifice of the life of an eldest son that on a
foreign king doing so he would turn and rend the Jews themselves,
who had been victorious against that King till then.
They gave a Ram instead. And when the King of Moab
saw that the battle was too sore for him, he took with
him 700 men that drew the sword, to break through, even unto the
King of Edom; but they could not. As a last resort, the King of
Moab, much to be pitied, saw, or believed he did, a way that would
turn the God of the Hebrews against even his own "chosen people."
Then he took his eldest son, that was to have reigned after him,, and
offered him for a burnt offering upon the wall. And there was a
great indignation against Israel; and they departed to their own
land." 2 Kings iii. 26, 27. The system rouses the ire of every
reader. He is the same horrid Divinity who is represented as commanding Abraham as follows: "And he said: Take now thy son,
thine only son Isaac, whom thou lovest, and get thee to the land of
Moriah, and offer him there for a burnt offering, upon one of the
mountains which I will tell you of." Gen. xxii. 2. It will be noticed, the eldest son had to be burnt. Therefore, the substitute
young Ram was always roasted in each Hebrew family. Jesus ought
to have been dealt with in the same manner. But the nearest approach to the roasting in his case was the terrible heat of Gethsemane. The "swet" is evidently intended to represent the drippings
of the roasted young Ram of the Passover.

The true meaning of the following is, that the God of the Hebrews would not allow Jericho to be rebuilt, until he received the sat-
isfaction of seeing the foundation of the new city laid in the body of
an eldest son, who had been offered as a burnt offering to him. In
the preceding verses it is said Ahab and Jezebel had adopted the
worship of Baal, as the Phœnicians did, and Baal was the personified
sun, Lucifer giver of light, and Son of the Morning (Is. xiv. 12).

But in the midst of the defection of Ahab from the national worship of Israel, Hiel, the Bethelite, built Jericho, he laid the foundation thereof in Abiram, his firstborn, and set up the gates thereof in his youngest son. 1 Kings xvi. 34; Joshua, vi. 26. Observe the name, Bethelite. Jerusalem had gone after Baal, Ahab, and Jezebel. In this dilemma the earlier tabernacle had produced a true worshipper of him who demanded the eldest son as a burnt offering to himself, and Hiel of Bethel did this, and more, for he added his youngest son Segub; and Hiel's fidelity is contrasted with the backsliding of Ahab.

In Bell's Pantheon, under the article "SATURN," we read that Tiberius Cæsar crucified the Priests of Saturn for offering infants at his altar. And that at Carthage infants were sacrificed to Saturn. "After the Carthaginians," states the same author, "were defeated by Agathocles, they, in order to appease the anger of Saturn, whom they thought they had neglected, and who they supposed had in consequence caused their defeat, sacrificed 200 of the sons of their nobility; and 300 more, liable to be discovered, voluntarily surrendered for the purpose."

"This cruel custom among these people (Carthaginians) was the subject of an embassy to them from the Romans, who, though they much esteemed and honoured this God, yet could not approve a practice so horrid, and therefore endeavoured to prevent its continuance." Saturn's statue was of brass, with hands extended, which no sooner received the person sacrificed, than he dropped him into a fiery furnace.

Sanchoniathon, the Phœnician writer, who flourished before the Trojan war, B.C. 1184 or B.C. 1127, has written what he thought was "history," when what he narrates is simply the allegories of the ancients, relating to the solar myths of the Druids, otherwise Mabynogion. The white leaders of mankind having migrated to the West, and there, especially in Britain, found peace from the wars of the East, the East only retained a confused knowledge of the original creed, based on the movements of the heavenly bodies, speculations respecting the causes for the changes or varying relation of the sun and the earth to each other; the varying lengths of day and night; the ever changes in the seasons, things plain enough to us at the present day. The descent of the sun in the west and his return on the morrow in the east, were things that greatly perplexed the ancients. Sanchoniathon wrote as follows touching the subject of the Eldest Son:—

"It was the custom among the ancients, in times of a great calamity, in order to prevent the ruin of all, for the rulers of the city or nation to sacrifice to the Avenging Deities, the most beloved of their Children as the price of their redemption. They who were devoted for this purpose, were offered mystically. For Kronos (Saturn), whom the Phœnicians call Israel, and who, after his death, was made a God, and stationed in the planet that bears his name, when he was King, had an only son by a nymph of that country. An only son in the language of that country is called IEOUD (JEW). And when great danger from war beset that country (Palestine), he adorned the altar, and invested this son with the emblem of royalty (a Crown) and sacrificed him." Cory's Fragments, p. 21, preserved by Eusebius, the Christian secretary to the Emperor Constantine the Great.

It is hardly necessary to remind the reader that the sun travelling on each December 25th in the track of that star caused the name Saturn to be given to the star. The original name in Ancient Egypt, etc., of the sun in that track appears to be Sydyk, or the Righteous One. He is Ner in Druidism, and when Saturn was in Britain adopted as the name of the seventh day, the Druids joined Ner to Gwen (Venus), and called Friday Gwen-Ner, or Venus and Nereus. He is represented by the Greeks as familiar with the Sacred Apples of the Druids of Britain. (Lampriere).

In Ex. xiii, we find two acts of devotion recorded. In the first place, we have the Destroying Angel devoutly acknowledged, by offering to him each firstborn of man and beast bought by him by accepting in Egypt for each, a young Ram of the beasts, the male ass alone was to be redeemed. And he is associated with the Sea, because it was held he rested nightly in the Sacred Argo or Ark, upon its waves. Each firstborn beast to be slain and made dead like the unleavened bread. But each firstborn son is to be redeemed (v. 13). In Numbers iii. we find how the children are to be spared the sacrificing knife. In the second place, the Angel of the Covenant (Christ, the Word) is acknowledged, by his name as the deliverer being inscribed on the hand and between the eyes (Phylactery) inscribed with the letter Shin as the sign of Amen Ra, the Dove emblem. In Numbers iii, 40, we find the first-born counted for the altar, if not redeemed. They numbered 22,273, and it was now discovered this Lord who had sought to kill Moses at the inn, had decided to immolate a whole tribe instead of 22,273 young Rams, Moses and Aaron now counted the tribe of Levi, and found they only numbered 22,000. Here they were 273 short to represent the total number of the first-born (Ex. xiii. 13). After consulting the Lord, Moses announced to the nation that the Lord would accept five Shekels (15s) for each of the 273, for each of whom there was no Levite substitute. The 30s given by Judas to the High priest correspond with the price of the eldest son and the Colt of Ex. xiii. 13. Now, were the 22,000 Levites to be sacrificed and eaten by their brethren, the sons of Aaron? In chapter viii. we find the 22,000 scraped and washed as meat, yet alive. But after all had been made ready for the horrible slaughter and the feast afterwards, the Lord makes the 22,000 Levites a gift to Aaron and his sons. Numbers viii. 9, etc. The reason why Rams were not now demanded as substitutes was, that Rams or Lambs of the Passover had been already accepted for them in Egypt.

Finally we have the testimony of Justin Martyr in his Apology, p. 67. It is intimated in the following words, that the Gentile philosophers of the second century held that Jesus was offered in sacrifice to the God Saturn. The following words are Justin Martyr's allusions to the said allegations : "For why did we not publicly confess even these things to be good and prove them to be divine philosophy, saying that when we kill a Man, we celebrate the Mysteries of Saturn, and that when we take our fill of blood (as is said of us), we intimate what you do to (in the worship of) the idol you honour, on which is sprinkled the blood not only of animals, but of Men.' In p. 18 the same early Christian Father alluding to the similarity of some cardinal doctrines of the Christian religion and Paganism, states sapiently as follows : "Before He" (Christ) "was born among men . . . . Evil Spirits, by the instrumentality of Poets, spoke in Anticipation of these Things, ... as events already accomplished."

Tertullian, in his De Carno Christi, states the similarity of Christianity to Paganism was due to God having been engaged before hand in rehearsing Christianity. Nonsense could not go beyond this idea. Still we must not forget the doctrine of antetypes or foreshadowings. But that is supposed to have been limited to the Jews.

THE ORDER OF THE CAMP IN THE WILDERNESS.

The Camp of the Hebrews in the Wilderness is planned with a view to the four Cardinal Points. To the East from the centre, Judah; to the South, Reuben; to the West, Joseph represented by his two sons, Ephraim and Manasseh; to the North, Dan. In the centre was the tribe of Levi. In Genesis ixl. we read that Reuben was Jacob's eldest son, but in the order laid down by Moses we find Judah placed first (Numbers ii), and is the sixth son of Jacob. To Judah is given the position by birth belonging to Reuben. At the time these ancient writings were compiled, Egyptian learning, chiefly religious, was the leading learning of the Eastern world. Till sometime prior to the expulsion of the Royal Shepherds by the roused natives, the sacred bull Apis (Taurus of the Zodiac) had been the Sign of March 25th. Now Apis had been set aside, and the young Ram had been adopted as the Zodiacal sign of March 25th.

This fact alone is a conclusive proof the Egyptians did not worship either the Bull or the Ram, and that they merely used them as Spring Sign successively. Reuben was discarded in imitation of discarded Apis. Judah, therefore, is stationed in the camp in the direction of the sky, where the sun was then rising in the sign of the Ram, due East on March 25. But Judah is called a Lion's whelp. This is direct opposite to the character of a young Ram. The Lion here is the Lamb's foe, and here we see the station of the Lamb given to his direct opposite. This is the Typhonic plan in all the Old Testament. The Hebrews slew the Egyptian Lamb as a burnt offering to "the Lion's whelp," the Old Lion being Saturn. (Isaiah lxv. 25; Ibid ii. 6, 7, 8). The anthithesis, be it observed, of a Young Ram, in his station in the "east toward the rising of the Sun." All the Kings of the nation except Saul, were of Judah. Jesus of Nazareth was from Judah, the Lion's whelp, and yet he is called "the Lamb of God," who has always been slain since the beginning of the Jewish "world," evidently since the starting of the Exodus from Egypt. We here see that the Lamb of the Passover represented the "enmity," represented by the Kingship of the Jews (Eph. ii. 15), who was slain as such.

It will be remembered that each family of ten in number brought a lamb of its own on March 25th, to be slain at the altar of the Temple. As representing the "Enmity" of Saturn each Paschal Lamb was slain! 1 Samuel xiii. 7.

As the result of withdrawing Levi from the Circle of the tribes in four divisions, a void was left, and to fill up the gap, Joseph was divided into two tribes, viz., Ephraim and Manasseh. We thus know by the position of those two half tribes, namely, due west, that the tribe of Levi originally occupied that direction, and there-fore, the direction of the setting sun from the station of Judah, due East. The point is that of the Sun at the time of his setting when Jesus died on the cross on March 25th, that is to say, Nisan or Abib 14. The Lamb was captured on the tenth of the month. Why the tenth, like the tenth of Tishri, date of the Atonement, is ex-plained, was due to the 21st (13th) being correct, and the 14th (25) incorrect astronomically.

In our observations on the letters I.A.O. to the effect that each is to be understood as a sign, and the three collectively constitute the sign of the Christ as Father, the Holy Spirit, and the O, the Sun's Orb as a Head, and the three collectively, constitute the sign of the Trinity in unity, we point out that Iao is the root of the name Jehovah. Dr. Inman states that the name Jehovah in Gen. ii. 4, can be rendered Yeoh (I.A.O.) is Iah. Here the O sign is omitted as constituting without the O the sign of the Mind, or Word of Coelus (Kelu) apart from the Orb of the Sun who is created by the Chrism in the constitution of the Word itself. IA is in O (the Sun), there-fore IA is IAO, and, to give Dr Inman's spelling, YEOH is JAH.

Dr. Inman states further, that the name in 2 Kings xi. 2, signi-fies, JAH is seven-fold. These are the seven attributes of the Word

in the sun, when during the year travelling through the seven planetary spheres. They are said to be in Christ. Rev. iii. 1.

We point out elsewhere that the Jew with the letter Shin on
the forepart of his Phylactery on his forehead—with his O-like head,
and the Mind (the Elohim) within his head—symbolises the Sun's
Orb.

Let the reader refer to the illustration on page 96, and he will
see the monogram I.A.O. as Father, Holy Ghost, and Son (Sun). It
is to the three signs King David refers in the words:—

> I will say of the Lord, He is my refuge and my fortress :
> My God, in Him will I trust :
> He shall cover me with His FEATHERS,
> And under His WINGS shalt thou trust :
> His Truth shall be thy shield and buckler.
>
> Psalm ixc. 4.

Ruth the Moabite, is told she had come "under the Wings of
the God of Israel to trust." The Mercy Seat was covered with
wings. Ex. xxv. 20. But the most direct reference to the wings of
the Word is in Malachi iv. 2, where we read: "But unto you that
fear MY NAME (IAO) shall the Sun of Righteousness arise, with
healing in his Wings," the latter being the emblem of the Holy
Ghost as the Wings of the Dove (A-Wen). It will be observed
the function attributed to the wings is healing, and refers
to the healing being applied to soul and not to bodies, one
of the functions of the Holy Spirit, the other being creating new
souls, to inhabit those bodies created by the agents of the Seminal
principle of the same Word or Elohim.

Now, Isaac is represented as the son of $\vee$ (IA, or Jah) by
aged Sarah, for that is the meaning of "and the Messenger did unto
Sarah as he had spoken, and Sarah (as the result of what he did
unto her) conceived, and bore to Abraham a son in his old age.
Here Abraham is made the Foster Father of Isaac.

The Stone-Pillar was in Egypt the symbol of the Fatherhood in
the Word, and in Deut. xxxii. 18, and Isa. li. 1 and 2, the Divine
Father of Isaac is clearly indicated. The whole story is that of Hu
Gadarn, or to employ the Greek name, Christ, is the Father of the

Sun's body, the first of the creatures created by him, and the Only Son begotten directly by Himself. He is the "Child" of Isaiah ii. 6. Sarah is made to play the role of Cariadwen, and Sarah's Delphos is substituted for the Ark of Druidism. Observe Isaiah compares it to inert vacuity, as Kybele is represented by the Greeks. Now, Isaac is a Son of vacuity, as Kybele is represented by the Greeks. Sarah is a "Pit." (Isaiah li. 1). Now, Isaac is placed in the character of the Sun on earth, and Saturn-Typhon demands him as a sacrifice to himself. Abraham takes him to the Mount in obedience to the command of Saturn, but at the last moment Saturn accepts the Egyptian emblem of the Spring sun which succeeded the Bull Apis in Egypt, p. 65.

Each Jew represents Isaac, and each Lamb of the Passover symbolises the Ram slain by Abraham as a substitute for Isaac, and consequently as a substitute for each eldest son who represented each succeeding family of the nation. Jesus was an eldest son. His Father was, as in the case of Isaac, the Seminal Christ (Jupiter, Cupid, Eros, etc). in the two-fold nature of the Word. But, in accordance with the change which had been introduced in the East, placing the young Goddess Semele as the mother of the annual Sun as the Solar Boy—the name Bacchus being given to the Sun himself instead of to his nocturnal warmth—Young Mary, aged 14, is begotten with child by the Power of the Highest, the Word Power is here instead of Messenger (Angel) in the instance of the fruitful visitor to Sarah.* But the ancients knew what they were about, and in the instance of Jesus, he is given a second birth from the Ark of Cariadwen, Queen of Heaven, on the Jordan, where the nation was born again, the second time into the earthly Paradise.

St. John admits point plank that Christ the Word was the Father of the Hebrews, for he says he came to his own, and his own received him not. He was, too, like the word in the Sun, the father of his own body, and reversing the proceedings in the instance of Isaac, rejected the Ram sign of the Sun, gave himself in sacrifice.

Referring to the entire nation as if it were Isaac himself, it is

---

* Hebrews i. 3.

said : "When Israel was a Child I loved him, and called my Son out
of Egypt." Hosea ii, 1. The Voice (Logos) which had spoken unto
Moses from the blazing bush instructed Moses to say to Pharaoh :
"Thus saith the Lord : Israel is My Son : even my first born." This
conclusively identifies him with the Sun, the first born of every
creature. Ex. iv, 22, 23 ; Col. i. 17. The purpose of Jesus being
taken down an infant to Egypt was to convey he and the nation
were identical. Matt. ii. 15. The Hebrews themselves are actually
called "The Sons of Elohim," rendered God instead of Gods (Christ
and the Holy Spirit) in Genesis vi. 2.

JUDAS AND THE THIRTY PIECES OF SILVER.

We have seen that the writers of the four gospels have carefully followed the forecasts of the Old Testament in their narratives
of the life and death of Jesus. He as the Christ is the only son begotten by the Father, the Almighty (Celu—Coelus—Agnosto. Theo)
himself. The Hebrews place Saturn of the Scythe for Him!
Jesus is the Carnal offspring of the Word (Christ) by the Virgin
Mary, while the Holy Spirit is the Father of his human soul.
By the descent of the Dove—an Egyptian Symbol—p. 65—both
Christ and the Holy Spirit, called the Spirit of Truth (St. John xiv,
17 ; Ibid xv, 26 ; xvi. 13 ; 1 John iv. 6) entered into his physical
body as the Druids held the Wren, symbolising Hu Gadarn and
Awen descended into the sun when on new year's morning he newly
created a Mabyn a Coronog Vaban (Crowned Babe) ascended from
the Boat of the Queen of Heaven, which Boat resembled the Crescent moon in Shape, and sometimes was symbolised by a Great Fish
called in consequence Delphos, the Greek for Womb, the Boat being
the birthplace of the Sun, was called the Womb of the Queen of
Heaven. p. 50. In the illustration in p. 50 Nature (Semele) is
shown, in accordance with the corrupt Druidism of Egypt, as on
Deck of the Boat as the mother of the Royal Babe Sun. Now, Jesus
is, as Judah (Ieod), identified as both Lion and Lamb for reasons
given in another page. As the High Priesthood, apart from the

High Priest, who carried the High Priesthood as an emblem by the White Kirtle he wore, and by the He Goat he sacrificed, and the two combined symbolising the oldest God of Egypt, namely, Pan, Barabbas, a murderer, symbolised the other He Goat—called Scape Goat—was sent away to Azozel or Satan, and Jesus was "made Sin." Here Saturn-Worship swaggers as holiness, and holiness is called Sin! Ezra must have discovered in Babylon that the He-Goat of the Day of Atonement was a Sacrifice to Satan, and rather than upset matters, he allied the Second He-Goat with the other.

Now, there appears to be an esoteric meaning underlying the story of the high priests, the thirty pieces of silver, and Judas. In Ex. xiii. 13, we find it implied the eldest son in each family, and each firstling of an ass that was male, were of the same identical value, (Num. iii, 47), namely, "five Shekels a piece by the poll." A Shekel is 3s., and five of them 15s. Now both the eldest son and the Colt symbolised the same object, namely, the Seminal principle in the Elohim (Logos) or Eros and Psyche, or, in other words, the Word as creating Father and Soul. In Zec. xi. 13, the Elohim—the Word—speaks himself, and refers to the two five shekels, or 30 pieces of silver. Judas is he to whom the High Priests, under the law, paid the ransom of two 15s., and anciently Moses and Aaron handed over that sum to the service of the Tabernacle. In Matthew xxvi. 15, the high priests hand over the money to Typhon-Judas the price of Elohim in Zec. xi. 12 and 13. The Price under the law was for redemption, when there was no substitute, as in Nu. iii. 45, 47. But the high priests Sacrificed Jesus, the eldest son—what became of the colt is not mentioned—and Typhon-Judas, being too honest to take both the sacrifice and the thirty pieces, goes back, carefully observe, and throws the money down on the floor of the sanctuary. He was better than his priests!

SATURN-ISRAEL, JUDAS ISCARIOT, AND ST. PAUL.

Judas Iscariot is here deliberately intended to represent in his own person the incarnation of Saturn Israel. These subtle attacks on the character of the sacrifices under the ceremonial law, could not be well understood by the learned Jews, especially by all the sons of Aaron, Levites, and Scribes. But it is perfectly clear that the earliest Christians most correctly illustrated the true nature of those sacrifices of the sacred animals of Egypt. But the obvious intentions of the Jewish reformers was frustrated by Saul of Tarsus, by proclaiming and teaching, that the cruel death of Jesus was the fulfilment, or type, of all the old antetypical sacrifies of the Hebrews. M. Renan states, the other apostles called Saul-Paul, Nicolas or Satan, in the sense we now call Satan, Old Nick. St. Paul's History, cx. p. 158. In Revelation ii. 6, 15, we appear to have the followers of Paul called Nicolaintes, whom St. John states, "he hates," as being, it appears, of "Satan's Synagogue." Ibid iii. 9. Peter intimates he himself does not half understand Paul's writings, and therefore his sermons. 2 Peter iii. 15. But Paul was mistaken honestly. It is evident by his speech on Mar's Hill that he believed the God to whom the Jews offered rivers of blood, was the Agnosto Theo of Athens. Acts xvii. 23 But he whom the Athenians called An Unknown God, was Coelus of the Druids of Britain and France, where it seems the greatest Greek, Pythagoras, who, states Archbishop Potter, taught that blood sacrifices were sinful, learnt the lesson. Nowhere else, but of the Druids, could Pythagoras have learnt, in that epoch, that sublime lesson; for all other nations, except perhaps Persians, offered blood sacrifice to the Gods, celestial as well as infernal. In the Mort D'Arthur, B. xx. c. 4, Mordred is King Arthur's Judas. See bottom of page 208, touching Judas's station according to the rule of Moses.

Observe St. Matthew's error touching these words, mistaking Potter's Pot for Potter's "Field." The LXX. B.C. 300 translate the words, Furnace---and describe it as a Furnace in the House of the Lord, apparently associated with the national mint, for the thirty pieces of silver are ordered to be dropped into the melting pot of the Mint. Zec. xi. 12; xi. 14. In verse 11 it is clearly stated the Staff (Rod) of Beauty, called by the LXX. beautiful Staff, was a symbol of Christ-Messiah (Logos) of God. The reader will recollect what we state as to the meaning associated with the Rod of Moses, etc.

THE ROYAL TRIAD OF THE HEBREWS.

In all the ancient cults of the nations, deriving their ideas from Druido Chaldeans, a Triad was a fundamental emblem. Therefore, when the Hebrews came to found a monarchy as an acces- sory to the ancient Theocracy, they proceeded to describe a Triad. King David had Seven brothers. A Triad had to be made out of those seven. But in the old Druidic cult, the seventh died, and the next succeeding him had to be a Mabyn, or Baby Son, called Ba-Bel, or Baby-Baal, in Chaldea, Infant Jove elsewhere. But in Israel the Seventh was Saturn-Typhon, the Destroyer, and it would have been as absurd to represent him as succeeded by a son of his— it will be remembered that in parts of the East, the Old Sun of one year was supposed to be the father of the next—as it would have been to represent Abel as married, and having a son.

We detect a trace of the difficulty Ezra experienced here. In the Zodiacal plan, the Sun was described as old in the Ninth sign, viz., that of the He-Goat (Pan-Noah), corresponding with December 25th. Having humanised the twelve signs, as twelve sons of Jacob-Israel, the third of a Triad, Jacob's first born was the eldest, whereas in the Druidic plan, the last Sun of the Solar year personified was the Old Man, and he in the East the father of next Baby Son or Infant Jove. Now in Gen. xil. 27, Ezra represents Benjamin as "Raving as a Wolf: in the Morning he shall devour the prey, and at Night he shall divide the spoil." Here is the character of Abel given to Benjamin. This is the "Wolf" of Isaiah ii. 6. In old astronomy, March 24th-25th marked the end of one zodia- cal year, and the beginning of the next. In this Junction of old and New, the Sun as Old Baal was, after the lapse of forty hours, succeeded by Babel, or Infant Baal, and no doubt after, in accordance with the astronomical law, called the Precession of the Equinoxes, Old Jove was succeeded by an Infant Jove; or the Sun as an Old Ram succeeded by a Young Lamb. This is hinted at in the Words, Our Old Man was crucified with him, but he re-appeared as an Infant Jove (Lamb) from the Crypt-Grave of the Garden. Now, it appears that Ezra intended to represent the Old Ram as a Wolf (Benjamin), devouring the Paschal Lamb. King Saul was of the tribe of Wolf-Benjamin, and therefore, in Hebrew parlance, the son of Wolf Benjamin. This was too absurd, and Ezra proceeded to compile a pedigree more in accordance with Druido Chaldean usage. But he found it necessary to start at the old basis, instead of at the succession, as he did with Benjamin and Saul.

Here is what Ezra did :—

> Samuel-Saturn : same as Typhon-Pluto.
> Jesse and His Wife.
> King David.

(Made a Christos by the Oil from the Horn of Samuel as Jacob made the Stone Pillar at Bethel. The Sun Symbol is omitted, but the God Pan is represented by the Kid).

> Eliab—Abinadeb—Shammah. (1. Sam. xvii. 13).

Here David or Dovid, is introduced as the Spring Sun, as Judah is described in Numbers ii. 3 : "And on the EAST side, toward the Rising of the Sun, shall they of the Standard of the Camp of Judah pitch throughout their armies." In Spring, the Sun, called here on March 25th, Dovydd in Welsh, was supposed to be amorous. Who is ignorant of the legend that the sun is dancing on Easter Sunday? David was amorous to a degree, and a dancer. David, like the sun, gave bread and wine to the "camp." 1 Samuel xvi. 20.

Jesus, the Lamb of God, the Infant Jove, was Son of David. Here the Physical Body of the Sun is Sacrificed ; and that is implied by the darkness from the hour of noon till nearly 4 o'clock ; sunset time in Britain on December 25th.

STONE HENGE—THE ANCIENT PALLADIUM OF BRITAIN.

The Druidic temple, called Stone Henge by English people, is by far the best known Druidic relic in Britain. The English name is a compound Saxon one, and signifying Stone that hangs ; not by any means a poetical appellation. The temple was known to the Ancient Britons under several names, each of which is a monument to their poetical fancy. The best known name is Cor y Cawr, or

Core of the Giant, meaning the sun in the character of the Infant Hercules, otherwise Infant Jove. Another name is Caer Cariadawg, or Love's Enclosure, and the terminal Awg is an intensitive, meaning full of. We find it in Drain-awg, full of Prickles, a Hedgehog. But the most striking name of Stone-Henge is Lloer-Gaer. This name abbreviated is Lloegr: the name by which England, where Stone-Hedge is situate, is known in Wales, and wherever the ancient British language is spoken. Lloer Gaer signifies the Lunar Enclosure. In Welsh place names it is the rule that the adjective precedes the noun; in almost every other instance the adjective follows the noun. In Welsh the Moon is familiarly known under three names: Llauad (from Lleu, Light), Lloer (Lly and Oer; the Cold One that extends out), and Llun (Image). No doubt the Latin name of the Moon, viz., Luna, is derived from this name, but in Welsh, the name is given only to the Crescent Moon, as being the Image of the Sacred Baris or Arkite Shrine of the Queen of Heaven. In old Welsh, the name Dinas is used in the sense of Strong hold, being a name compounded of Din (Hill) and Aes (A Shield), and both united meaning A Fort. Now Archdeacon Williams, Cardigan, one of the most learned men of his time, states in his Gomer, "Notices continually occur in the older Bards of a mystic Dinas, situated upon and among the waters to which" (in reference to which) "worshippers went in procession on great festivals with sacred songs and hymns." Further, "we know from other sources that the great temple on Salisbury Plain (Stone-Henge) was supposed to be surrounded by a boundless sea." Geology teaches us that in extremely distant times Salisbury Plain was at one time a vast lake. This may be the explanation as to how the enormous stones of Stone-Henge were conveyed to the place, from (it is conjectured by the quality of the stones) the sea. The temple remains on the highest elevation of the Eastern and Southern side of the plain, after the water had gone.

The temple of Stone-Henge is the great Britannic emblem of the sacred Baris or Ark-Navis, otherwise Argo, of Cariadwen, Queen of Heaven. It will be seen in the illustrations in pages 71 and 50 that on each prow of the sacred Baris, is a round ancient shield. Those indicate symbolically the fortress or Dinas character of the sanctuary of the Infant Hercules, otherwise Infant Arthur, otherwise Taliesun Merddyn, Morien, or Morgan, in the Ark and under the immediate protection of the said Spirit, monarchs of the universe. In Druidism she bears the title of Gwr-ach, which is like the Greek title Pallas, given to Minerva-Medusa. Thus Stone-Henge was an image of the Palladium of Britain.

> Could angry Pallas, with revengeful spleen,
> The Grecian navy burn, and drown the men?
> She, for the fault of one offending foe,
> The bolts of Jove himself presumed to throw;
> With whirlwinds from below she tossed the ship,
> And bare exposed the bottom of the deep.
>
> Virgil's "Aeneis," I. 60.

THE BOAR OR "BORE."
The Twrch Trwyth or Bawdd. (See page 195),

Argos boasted it had the Palladium. Of course it had, for the Argo or the Sacred Navis, now the Christian Church building is its successor. The Greeks (states Mysteries of the Cabiri), having read Hippa (a Mare) in mistake of Hipha (a Galley, or Ship), represented the sun as a horse, Pegasius, the colt of the Mare. This also gave origin to the fable about the wooden horse of Troy.

"The sides were planked with pines." Virgil's Aennis, 2, 20.

Scholars are familiar with the story of Hecataeas, the Milesian, 600 B.C., who states that in the great ocean stream opposite France (Gaul) is an island, not less in size than Sicilly, stretching towards

the north.   The inhabitants are called Hyperboreans, because their
abode is more remote from us than the wind we call Boreas.   It 's
said that the soil is very rich, and fruitful, and that the climate is
so favourable that there are two crops every year.

Their fables say that Latona (Lleuad?) was born in this island ;
and on that account they worship Apollo (Taliesun) before other
divinities, and celebrate his praise in daily hymns.

They confer the highest honour on their Bards as being
his priests.

There is in this island a magnificent temple to this God, circular
in form (Avebury), and adorned with many splendid offerings.

And there is a city also (Bath) sacred to Apollo, inhabited
principally by harpers who, in his temple, sing sacred verses to the
God, accompanied by the harp in honour of his deeds.

The language of the Hyperboreans is peculiar, and they are
singularly well affected towards the Greeks, and have been so from
the remotest times, especially those of Delos (Sacred Island), and
Athens (sacred to Pallas, otherwise Athene).   It is even stated that
some Greeks have travelled thither and presented offerings at their
temple, inscribed with Greek Characters.   They also say that Abaris
went thence in ancient days to Greece, to renew their ancient
friendship with the Delians.

It is related the Moon appears but a short way from this
island.   Woodward's Wales, p. 49.   It will be observed Hecataeas
is relating what he has heard.   The Moon is Stone-Henge seen side-
ways, as an emblem of it, as explained above.   Bath was Caer Bathon
of the Britons, Water of the Sun by the Romans, Acmen Castra or
Camp of the Oakmen (Druids) by the Saxons.

At Stone-Henge the Sacred Arkite shrine is represented as
moored underneath the earth, the columnar supports of which are
symbolised by the enormous tripod, or, rather, three upright stones,
which formerly stood like the legs of an ancient British stool, or Cae
Tair.   Lying on their summit was the Cromle-ach, or vast stone
lying horizontally upon them.   The Sacred Ark beneath symbolises
the sacred Argo in the work of steaming up the Divine Rhin y Pum-

wydd as a feminine essence to be fertilised by the rays of Hae Gadarn passing through the Sun (Taliesun).

At Sunrise on June 21—anciently 25th—the sun, as designed by the arrangements of the venerable structure, is represented crowning the earth with radiant glory, for then there is a flashing into the sanctuary of sunshine on White Sun-day, or the old British Pentecost. Many go there the night before, to be ready to witness at sunrise on the morrow the startling phenomenon. The Crowning of the Earth is shown in p. 100, only that there it is done by the old sun as Pan, whose apotheosis in Syria was on June 25th instead of December 25th. As explained elsewhere, this was the result of Egyptian confusion, due to the Royal Shepherds monopolising December 25th for Typhon-Saturn, with the consequence of placing old Osiris on June 25th—longest day instead of the shortest one. Then, the Syrians placed Pan and Tammuz in that position, the priests following the example of those of Egypt. The birth of John the Baptist is dated June 25th, as the erroneous birthtime of Infant Pan, the old Pan, his father, represented as occurring forty hours before. But as Tammuz, the old Sun on June 25th was best known in Syria. Ez, viii. 14.

An emblem of the Sacred Ark of the Queen of Heaven was symbolised on most lakes and sea coasts of this country, and the Arms of Dunwich, East Anglia, show it to this day. In the "Myvyrian Archæology" are verses to the Arkite shrine, symbol used on the Western coast of Wales. It begins as follows :—

"I'll suplicate my Goddess who yields abundance :
Thou ownest heaven and earth, gently ye ocean of God—
It is the hour of the nativity of my brilliant Rhi—
An hour when the sea will perform a mighty deed,
And the heads of Bards will (in consequence) be higher than
    their Methaglyn Vials :
It comes from the green, the Border of Pict-land (Ireland in
    the west),
A peaceful enclosure it is on the broad lake :
A defended circle without ramparts—the sea is around it :
All Britain salutes thee !

There are eight stanzas in all, of the above nature, in extremely ancient Welsh. We have endeavoured to translate the sentiments rather than the verbatim et literatim, as specimens of the entire composition. See Adonia (Bell's Pantheon).

Both Stone-Henge and Avebury are situated in Wiltshire, and both to the north of Salisbury. They are about twenty miles apart from each other. The country about each is thickly studded with tumuli, or Wheel-Mounds (Beth-Rodau) or graves, which indicate the former religious character of both temples, around which the pious forefathers of Britain sleep underneath daisy bed coverlets, and in the midst of a country whose air is madrigal with the songs of skylarks ascending to greet the Goddess of the dawn, called Gwawr by the Ancient Britons. This central spot of Britain must have been, owing to the two national temples there, the great place of assemblages of Britons. As we see above, pilgrims came here from the sacred island of Delos—

"Where Delos rose and Phœbus sprung,"

What, then, must have been the nature of the attractions to the Britons themselves? British local place names are often monuments of other days, and here we have the axiom verified. In Ancient British a festival is called Gwyl, from Gwy (Dew), and Le (Place), a name given in reference to acts of lustration performed priests.

> Old Corynaeus compassed thrice the crew,
> And dipped an Olive branch in Holy Dew,
> Which thrice he sprinkled round: and thrice aloud
> Invoked the dead, and then dismissed the crowd."
>
> Aeneis, B. VI. S. 325.

WILTON, WILTS.

The Wil in the name Wilton, or, Wil—Town, after which name the County is named Wilt Shire, is clearly derived from the Cambro British Gwyl. Baxter conjectures, states Lewis' Typography, that Wilton is the site of the Ancient British Caer Guilon. The U had formerly, like the modern W in Kymraeg, the sound of the long O as in wood and good. Therefore, Caer Gwyl-on would be the modern way of spelling the name. But now comes the most startling confirmation.

THE ARMS OF WILTON.

This is the Sacred Ark of which Stone Henge is another symbol. A Chapel-Royal (Nave) is shown within the sacred Oval, Baris or Arkite Shrine. Over the roof is the figure of the Winged Sun, as a

Arms.

Winged Child (Taliesun or Arthur, Royal Boy), son of Uthr Ben (Head), the old Sun of the end of the preceding year. See p. 2. (Specimen verse). At the lower end of the Baris is the figure of a dead person ascending from the Crypt or hold, of the Nave or Baris.

The river of Wilton is called Willy, obviously a corruption of Gwyl-le : Festal Place. Thus we have the Druidic import of Stone-Henge preserved in the arms of the town, after which Wiltshire derived its name. At each end of the Chapel-royal, inside the Baris—on its deck—is a spire, like Boaz and Jachin near the great stone on Mount Zion. (1 Kings vii. 21). They were symbols of the testes of Coelus, cut off by Saturn.

In dealing with the religious teachings of the ancients one must always bear in mind we are in the presence of the remote past, when letters had not yet been even thought of, and when objects and their surroundings were selected and set apart to be symbols of ideas. For example, a serpent was selected to symbolise a spirit because like a spirit, it is limbless, and yet moves from place to place. A golden serpent, or one of brass, symbolised a good spirit. A red ser-pent, or fiery, a bad or destroying spirit. This system of symbols is still preserved in what we call heraldry. Wings and one or more feathers, were also favourite symbols. Among the Druids stones arranged in circles, Maenhir, Cromleach, Dolmaen, and as trailing serpents, were chief emblems. Bees and other winged insects were used because of their respective duties in the system of Nature. The egg was a favourite symbol, because when unfertilised, it con-tained inert matter in solution. When fertilised it illustrates the great mystery, Nature and the Sun's rays, in combination.

Avebury symbolised the whole round flat bottomed earth, sur-rounded by the sea. The Cromleach and its circles Nature inert : the great Obelisk and its circles, the masculine power transmitted from the sun, fertilising Nature.

Stone-Henge, as a sacred Hipha, Arech, Navis, Argo, Nave, Llong, Voel, Bolgroen, Rocking Stone, and Ceubawl (scooped Pole), the Cybele of the Greeks, symbolised the imagined vehicle of the Spirit Queen of Heaven, employed by her as her translocator and repertory between the world of Spirit and the present material earth. In that sense Stone-Henge was the Mother of Nature and the Sun. Her spirit is shown under the figure of a serpent incuba-tor, round an egg. She is the same serpent as that which was the Guardian of the Acropolis at Athens, Athena being one of her titles,

Herodotus, Urania, S. LI. As Medusa, she, as a Crescent, roams
the Sea. P. 17. She is called also Gorgon, which name seems to
be the same as the Welsh Coran and Corcan.

The hazy tradition that the stones with which Stone-Henge
was constructed came from Ireland, is no doubt due to the fact that,
in Druidic times, many a sacred Coracle, symbolising the same Argo
of Cariadwen as Stone-Henge did, plyed between Britain, to the
East from Ireland, and the Werdd Don, or Green Wave, as the Britons still name Ireland. The return journey of the coracle was to
be understood as passing back underneath the earth, through the
Shades, called in Welsh Byd Hud a Lledrith. It was to illustrate how
the Infant Hercules was conveyed in the Sacred-Boat of the Queen of
Heaven, to the South East, to rise there into the sky on the morning of the Solar new year, and defended in his attempt by the Queen
Spirit, Kyn-Nyth, a title of the said Majesty, and as feminine Divine
Wisdom, symbolised by the vast Stone Serpent of Avebury,
whose name is preserved in the name "Ken Net" brook, a tributary
of the Thames at Avebury. Any reader who might wish to obtain
more information touching the customs relating to the Coracle or
Arkite shrine and the Infant Sun, should consult Bell's Pantheon
under the name Adonia.

In the Arms of Wilton, we have pictured the Infant Sun ascend-
ing from Stone-Henge symbolically, as the symbol of the "Peaceful"
Bulwark, prepared by Cariadwen, Queen of Heaven, for the Sun's
accommodation, on the Ocean. As a substance the Sun (Taliesun,
Tegid, etc.), is the joint Son of the essence of her Galley and the
Seminal element of the Word of the Highest; and now the Christos
(Iu-Pater) is Himself, as body and Soul (Holy Spirit) in Him. The
Christ is Father, the Soul is Spirit, the Sun is Son. The Poet
Athanaeus, quoted by Bryant (Analysis, Vol. 2, p. 405) refers to
the Ark of the Queen of the Heaven as follows:—

> 'Twas in a golden shrine
> That Helios (Taliesun) passed:
> Helios, Hyperion's Son:
> O'er Floods and Oceans wafted far away.

To Erebus the sad realms of night :

His Aged Parent (Queen of Heaven) there he found,

And the kind comfort of his better days. (See p.17).

Then the poet describes Delphi, the Shrine, and the Gods, Apollo and Holy Spirit (Elohim), ascending from the Cave of Delphi, fringed with laurel, as the hirsute appendages of the Delphos of the "new birth" of Apollo (Sun) and tenants— here a Cave is substituted for the Arkite Boat or Baris—the poet says as follows :

"Then to the Sacred Grove he sped —

The sacred Grove of Laurel"—emblem of Victory over death. Here Apollo (Sun) is a Trinity in Unity.

There, as was believed, the Word of the Highest entered the Vulva of the Pythian Priestess, seated in a hollow golden vessel on a Tripod, and spoke to the priests from her inside. Archbishop Potter's "Greece," vol. I. pp. 325-6-7. In page 325 the British origin is admitted.

In the story of the Nativity of Jesus, we have the Cave, we have the Virgin, and we have the demi-Baby God in the "Manger," having been delivered there. In reference to The Delphi Cave Tripod, Young Priestess—always on the occasions nude, representing Nature or Venus—Archbishop Potter states : "Some say that under the Tripod, sometimes a Serpent appeared and herself gave answers." This Serpent was the Spirit of the Cave, otherwise the Arkite Shrine, of which Stone-Henge was the principal emblem in the world. She was the Same Spirit that drove Jesus from her boat on the Jordan to the ordeal with Satan, half brother of the sun, according to mythology.

The late learned Principal Edwards, Bala, Obit, March, 1900, drew my attention to the following from the pen of Father Tertullian (A.D. 193-220): "But you do not receive this" (Christianity) states this early Christian Father, "as you did not receive Christ in that early period, when he was studying how to address, free, and judge mankind, in the guise of the flesh, when he was not yet born, because not about to die." "Thus even God was always studying how to live with men on earth : no other than the Word (Sermo), who was to be in the flesh. He was then learning to prepare the faith for us, that we might more easily believe that the Son of God had descended into the world, by learning that something of the same kind had before taken place." De Carno Christi, C. Vi., and Praxeas, C. XVI.

SHORT REMINDERS, OR CWTACYFARWYDD.

It will be borne in mind, the Ancient Britons, like the Ancient Egyptians, had no popular system of literature, such as most civilised nations have at the present day. They had letters which they carved on bars of wood, and the letters bore the name, Coel-Bren-y-Beirdd, which is in English, Faith of the Bards. The Druids were all Bards, but were in three orders:

Druids, Bards, Ovates.

The Druids, as the most sacred, and therefore highest, wore white, the colour of Light, and, therefore, of Purity and Holiness. The Bards wore Blue, the colour of the sky, and, therefore, of the environment of the Sun.

The Ovates wore Green, the colour of Emerald earth. Green and White were the Royal National Colours of the Ancient Britons, and the Leek, being in both colours, became their national badge. We learn inferentially, the army of the Britons wore green and white as the colours of the uniform, for a bard describes a Briton King at the head of his marching forces as follows:—

> Gwyr tal yn ei ganlyn,
> Mil myrdd, mewn gwyrdd a gwyn.
>
> Tall men followed him.
> A numberless host, in green and white.

HESUS.

See page 50

*From a bas relief found
under the Choir of the Church of
Notre Dame, at Paris in 1711*

Montfaucon Ant: Tom 2.Pl.age.

ESUS, HESUS, HESOUS JESUS. IESU.

The above figure is supposed to be that of the Druidic Hesus referred to
by Lucan in his poem. It cannot be intended for Jesus of Nazareth.

MABYNOGION.

This was the name all who adopted Druidism or Bardism as a religion, called themselves, in the sense Christians call themselves, Crist'nogion. Mabyn is to this day the Welsh for Baby Boy. The Mabyn here is the Infant Sun of the Solar new year. He is Infant Arthur, called also Taliesun, Gwyn ap Nydd (Neith) the dd having in Welsh the sound of th in though. Neith, as in Egypt, is a title of the Queen of Heaven, called Cariadwen, etc., in Britain, Isis I. in Egypt; Kybele, Minerva, Medusa, etc., by other nations. Neith signifies Turner of the Wheel of the Solar System, as explained in the text. The old philosophers supposed the earth to stand immovable out of the Ocean, but that the firmanent revolved around it. Psalm xxiv.

DRUIDS.—In Welsh this is Dyriwyddon, or Wrenites. The Wren was in Western Europe, a sacred symbol of Elohim, or Word of God, in the same sense as the Dove was in Egypt, Syria, etc. See back of the Sun-Bull in p. 65, Leviticus xii. 8. To this day the Welsh call the Wren Dyriw, or Thy Kindred. Thus the Mabynogion claimed relationship with the Word of God. p. 156. This is the same as the meaning of the Greek poet Aratus, quoted by St. Paul in the open air temple, therefore a Druidic one, on Mar's Hill, Athens, before the Areopagites, or Judges of the National Council, which ages before had condemned Socrates to death. The immortal words are :—

"For we are His offspring."
Cum Sole et Luna semper Aratus erit.—Ovid.

By the way, the words in the original, translated, The Unknown God, are, An Unknown God, clearly a God in the Pantheon of some other nation (Coelus?). The literal meaning of the Great name of the Almighty in old British is Celu (Keli) after which the Celts are so named, is, One Hiding Himself. In reference to the Word in the Sun, as The Generator, we read as follows:—Some altars were designed upon which neither fire nor blood could lawfully be placed, but only cakes, fruits of the earth, and inanimate things. Near the Temple of Horn, at the Island of Delos, which was sacred to Apollo (the Sun) Generator, Pythagoras, who thought it unlawful (impious) to put animals to death (in sacrifice) used to make oblations. Arch. Potter's Antiquities of Greece, Vol. I. p. 230.

The Unicorn is a heraldic design by which was meant the same thing as the Altar of Horn, at Delos. Psalm xxii. 21. The Jews are by Isaiah described as the Children of Elohim, as those of the Unicorn. xxxi. 7; Ps. xcii. 10.

CLER.—This is the Welsh for all Flies. The Druids regarded flies in general, especially Bees, as agents of the sun in conveying sap from the active to the passive seeds in the system of nature. Beelzebub, correctly spelt, Baal-Zebub, means Baal of Fly, Zebub being Hebrew for Fly. Thus the Hebrews call the Sun (Baal) a demon, in the same way that Isaiah alludes to the sun derisively as Lucifer or Light Fire, Son of the Morning.

SERPENTS.—The Druids bore this name, because a serpent being limbless, was used by them as a symbol of a spirit either good or evil.

AWEN.—This name is the Ancient British appellation of the Holy Ghost. It is compounded of A and 'Wen, or Holy V—the old style of inscribing it—being the sign of a pair of wings: A spirit symbol, like the wings of the sacred Dove and the Wren. The Holy Spirit being masculine, it is certain the ancients called the sign, Awyn. (Vide Archdeacon Williams' " Gomer," p. 14).

IESU.—The different ways this sacred name is spelt in very ancient Welsh writings, indicate the perplexity of the Early British Christians in reference to it. We learn in the writings of the Romans of pre-Christian times, that Druids worshipped Hesus. Lucan I. v. 445. This is, too, the Latin form of the Saviour's name. It is akin to the Greek form of his name. Another form of the name is Hesperus. He is said to be "brother of Japetus" or Japheth. He had a garden, noted for its Golden Apples (p. 10), three daughters, like those of Arthur's Court-Circle, a Great Serpent which never slept. This is the Kynnyth serpent of Avebury, Wilts, symbol of the Queen-Spirit of Heaven. The Garden is Britain, and

Britain as the emblem of the whole earth, was, in its turn, symbolised by each Druidic Circle, Mound, Din, and Circular Mountain
dedicated to Divine worship, for "he shall plant the Tabernacles of
his palace between the seas, in the glorious holy mountain." Daniel
xi. 45. The figures, like those of Psalm xxiv., are borrowed from
Druidism. Here is another: "And this Stone, which I have set up
as a Pillar, shall be God's House." Genesis xxviii. 22; Ibid 49, 24;
Judges xvi. 31.

Now, the Christianised Druids, concluding Christianity was,
after all, their own religion, come after them from the east, called
Jesus, Taliesun, but dropped the first name in the compound, and
called him Iesun. Afterwards the terminal n was dropped, and it
now bears the form Iesu.

THE END.

THE ROCKING-STONE, PONTYPRIDD.

Heaven's Queen it animates,
Creation's morn it passed the Gates;
Nevydd Nav walks its holy deck,
Oh, keep it from Vandalian wreck!
It spoke to Druids in ancient days
Of souls' voyage to Paradise.

PERORATION.

NOTE ON STONEHENGE.—THE SHECHINAH OF DRUIDISM.

An Oval figure, of which the illustration in page 276 is an imitation, is in the interior of the gigantic circle of stone pillars at Stonehenge.   In works on Stonehenge the said Oval symbol is described as an Ellipse, because it resembles in shape the orbit of the planets.   It is, however, shaped like an egg, and was symbolised by the mundane egg which the Archdruid wore suspended on his breast.   Its contents symbolised the essence which is fertilised by the rays of the sun, called Cariadwen Taliesun; the earth itself was the solidified result.   The Oval figure was the symbol of the sacred Boat of Cariadwen, Queen of Heaven.   See page 17.   Between the sides of the Boat shrine and the inner side of the lofty granite circle around about it, was a circular corridor which was exactly 300 feet in circular length.   This could conveniently hold 100 white robed Druids kneeling around engaged in prayer, all with their faces towards the Boat shrine in the centre of the area.   The Cromleach, consisting of three gigantic lofty upright columns, and having on their summits a horizontal slab, 16 feet long, four feet broad, and ten inches thick, was astride both the corridor and the sacred Boat symbol, and thus the Boat—the Argo of Britain—was symbolised as passing into a cove inside the outer great circle.   It is exactly opposite to where the sun rises over the horizon at 4 hours, 15 minutes, on the morning of June 25—the day anciently supposed to be the longest one of the year.   On the down opposite is an immense upright stone called "the Pointer," because it indicates the point on the horizon where the sun darts up from the underworld on the morning of the longest day, when "the true Tabernacle" of that year has been finished. The grand entrance in its relation to the inside of the temple has been so arranged that the sun appears as if on the top of the Pointer, and pouring his brilliancy into the centre of the sacred Boat (Navis).

We behold the 100 Druids on their knees at 4 o'clock a.m. on June 25th, waiting for the rising sun to appear, and when he arrives, suddenly flashing his beams liked a winged cherub into this most venerable Holy of Holies. A vast Rocking Stone importing the same thing as this Boat Shrine, was, and is still, on the site of the Holy of Holies at Jerusalem. By the side of the corridor is still standing the Maen Said or Pillar of Stone, emblem of the creating "Power of the Highest," and the groove channel under its lowest side, for the flow of the Chrism from its point, is still perfect. But the flashes of June 25th symbolised the descent of the Awen, or Holy Wings, the ruidic name for the Holy Ghost—the Comforter. In the Cimmerian language of Druidism he is called Awen Hefin, or the Wings of June. Possibly the custom in the early church, notably at Canterbury around the shrine of Thomas a Beckett, and at Westminster Abbey around the shrine of Edward the Confessor, was borrowed from the custom described as in vogue around the Oval Nave of Stonehenge. Dean Penrhyn Stanley states the crescent (Llun—Image) showing a side view of the Sacred Boat of Stonehenge, is in the Chancel of Canterbury Cathedral. The arrival of the Awen was greeted with the words "Holy, Holy, Holy," by the kneeling multitude on the downs outside, and the sound of praise was like the murmuring of the ocean.

> " Ond daeth lluoedd estron dan arfau;
> A chlwyfwyd yr addfwyn a chledd."

It appears that the sacred Ark, or Boat, was facing the sun when rising, and in it were powerful glass reflectors, doubtless leaning against the inside curve of the sacred Ark. In the Chair of Taliesun (Myvyrian Archæology, p. 38, vol. I.) the Sacred Boat is called Glass Coracle (Corwg Gwydrin). Poet Southey in his Madoc, materials for which he undoubtedly took from Iolo Morganwg, supposes the mystic coracle was entirely of Glass, and wrote as follows :—

> In his crystal
> Whither sailed Merlin with his band of bards,
> Old Merlin, master of the mystic lore;
> Belike his crystal ark, instinct with life,
> Obedient to the mighty Mistress reach'd
> The land of the departed; there better
> They in the clime of immortality;
> Themselves immortal, drink the gales of bliss,
> Which o'er Flathynys breathe eternal spring,
> Blending whatever odour make the gale
> Of evening sweet, whatever melody
> Charms the woodland traveller."—Southey's Madoc, XI.

It seems in this fresh light on the interesting subject, that Caer Wydrin (Glass Town Burgh, now Glasstonbury) derived its name from the local Ark with glass reflectors like those at Stonehenge, reflecting back the rays with dazzling brilliancy. It is worthy of note that the subject of the poem in p. 38 deals with the aspect of the earth in the month of June, etc.

> Camp yn mhob noethfaes,
> Pan yw Dien Gwylith;
> A gweled Gwenyn,
> A gludant ac ystoriant.

> A camp in every open place,
> When Diana distils dew;
> And the wheat cutting,
>   And the busy bees
> Carrying and laying in store.

STONEHENGE, THE SHIELD OF ACHILLES.

It will be observed that the massive outward circular framework of Stonehenge describes the shape of an ancient Kimmerian Britannic shield. In the remote epoch which witnessed the rearing of this Cor-y-Cawr, or Church of the Giant, every religious idea was

communicated by a hieroglyphic, called **Arwydd, or On Wood,**
because wooden staves were the Druidic Books, and being wood,
and unlike the enduring polished marbles of Egypt and baked brick
tablets of Niniveh and Babylon, the Druidic books of Britain perished. Stonehenge circle, as a shield, symbolised the shielding might
of Hu Gadarn, the Invincible Elohim of Druidism, consisting of
masculine essence and soul.   The Lunette shaped gold breastplate
of the Archdruid, called Moren, has two shields, one against each
of the points of that symbol of the crescent shaped Boat. See p.
149.   In pages 80 and 483 of Iolo MSS. there is mention of Japheth,
eldest son of Noah, making an enormous target or shield, with a
Llun in it—Llun is still the name of the crescent moon in Welsh,
and is called because it is the Image of the Sacred Boat of Stone-
henge, etc.   Then it is stated that Japheth's motive in constructing it was "to signify that he and his brothers—Triads, p. 210—
possessed the whole world." **Here we find it hinted at that Noah's**
Thebet or Ark is identical with the sacred Arkite Boat of Druidism,
and that the outer circle of Stonehenge, like the celebrated shield of
Achilles, symbolises the whole round earth with the Ocean encircling it, like the trench does round about Stonehenge.   Homer
describes the shield of Achilles as being under the Great Bear, therefore it indicates Stonehenge as near as an ancient Greek could do so.
The Noahic associations seem to have been introduced into the Welsh
narrative by a Christianised Druid in very early times, for the
Welsh of the narrative is extremely archaic.   In the Ark of Noah,
the body of the dove represented the Christ and its wings, the Holy
Ghost.   The raven, as in Egypt, symbolised Pluto, and the third
brother of Japheth is described as a clown: another way of describing the third character in each of the triads in page 210.

Describing the Shield of Achilles, as the image of the round
earth, as the ancients supposed its shape to be, Homer writes thus ·

> " There shone the mirrored Master Mind,
> There earth, there sky, there ocean, he designed ;
> The unwearied Sun, the moon completely round,
> The starry lights that the ethereal convex crowned :
> The Pleiads, Hyads, with the Northern Team,

> And Great Orion's more refulgent beam :
> To which, around the Axle of the Sky,
> The Bear, revolving, reveals his golden eye,
> And shines exalted on the Ethereal Plain,
> Nor bathes his blazing forehead in the Main."

This was because the land of Britain was under it.

Vulcan having constructed the shield with numerous artistic designs, emblems of the round earth below, and the firmament above, completes his task as follows : —

> "The Broad Shield complete, the Artist Crowned,
> With his last hand, and poured the Ocean round."

Iliad XVIII (last pages).

The "Golden Eye" of Ursah Major is the Polar Star.

THE HOLY OIL OF THE STONEHENGE COLUMN.

The Holy Oil, or Chrism, was called by the Phœnicians Ambrosia, and is still called in India Amrita. It is said to be the food of angels, and those partaking of it acquire immortality. It is said to be the oil with which Jupiter annointed his locks to make them imperishable. In fact, it is the "meter" for the Rock of Horeb. It is the Holy Oil which Jacob poured on the column at Bethel, and Samuel poured on the head of David, afterwards called (in the second Psalm) the Annointed, or Christus, because he had received the Chrism. In simple language, it is the nourishing essence in all solids and liquids. The bodies die because they are incapacitated from partaking of this ambrosial essence. That the Phœnicians had become dominant at Stonehenge is evident by the fact that, judging by the name of the adjacent town, Ambrosiabury (now Amesbury), is a Tyrian name of the Chrism. Its Kimmerian, or Welsh, name is Rh'n, which is the root of the Welsh name for virtue, viz., Rhinwedd. We have several place-names in Wales indicating the same Phœnician influence, viz., Bala, Derfel, and Talchan. The latter means, in Phœnician, King's Son. Even Britain itself is called in old Welsh writings the Island of Baal—y Fel-ynys. We have the name, further, as a termination to the name Llyw-Elyn—King Cyn-felyn (Belinus, who established Billinsgate Market, in London). The Ambrosia is represented to-day by the wine of the Sacrament of the East, but in Britain it was represented by the juice of the apple. (See page 8).

In the Scandinavian legends, the Ambrosia or Amrita is the essence of the Apples guarded by Idum, and the Gods derived perpetual vigour by eating the said Apples. They are the Apples that we describe in p. 10, and their mystic meaning in p. 8. As we state elsewhere, the Apples were used in Western Europe in the same sacred symbolical sense as the Grapes were in the East, and in those parts of Europe which derived their religious ideas and symbols from the East. As stated elsewhere, Bacchus is in Druidism, Gwy-ion Bach, the personified fertilising heat of the sun, while Apollo is the sun's light personified primarily under the name Taliesun. But the Greeks, who represent both Bacchus and Apollo as the sun, nevertheless represent them as two brothers.

In the Kimmerian, or Welsh tongue, the Ambrosia is called unguent, as Gwer, from which is derived in that language the name "Gwres," heat. In Greek mythology a vintage feast in honour of Bacchus was called Ambrosia. Here we find the wine alluded to as Ambrosia, the food of angels. In Homer's "Odyssey" (Book V.) we have the Ambrosia alluded to as also made into cakes, like the Manna of the Exodus was made into. The God Hermes, otherwise Mercury, is described as conveyed by the great navigators, the Phœnicians, to an island ten days' sail from Greece, where a Goddess dwelt in a "Cave" (the Cove of Stonehenge). The Druids were called Gods.

> "The bold Phœnicians there, whose haughty line
> Is mixed with Gods, half human, half divine."

The Goddess of the Cave is described as a spinner, which is one of the titles of Cariadwen, Nymph of the Caev, for Homer states :

> "She with work and song the time divides,
> And through the loom the golden shuttle guides."

Having arrived at the cave, Hermes found it surrounded as follows : —

"Without the grot a various Sylvan scene
Appeared around, and groves of living green."

Then the Goddess provided divine food for Hermes, which is described as follows : —

"The Nymph the table spread :
Ambrosial cakes and Nectar rosy-red :
Hermes the hospitable rite partook,
Divine refection !"—Odyssey, Book V.

Here we have the Manna and the "water" from the Rock of Horeb, the latter being the "Nectar rosy-red." The Rock was Christ. Deut. xxxii. 18.

A confusing peculiarity of the Jewish religion is, that both "the Destroying Angel" (Saturn) and "the Angel of the Covenant," who is the Creator Elohim, or Christ, and his Soul are, though in conflict with each other, worshipped in it. Thus the Ram and He Goat, are plain as symbols of the "Houses" of the Sun on March 25th and December 25th respectively, and the flesh of the former is eaten and that of the latter burnt, that the Destroying Angel may be pacified ; two pints of wine is drank as representing Ambrosia and the blood of the Lamb. Num. xv. 5-6. But in verse 5 the two pints of oil is the Ambrosia, while the wine represents the blood of the Lamb. Thus we find the worship of Saturn implied by "the blood of Grapes," and the worship of the creating word, who creates with oil, implied by the oil mixed with flour as directed in verse 5.

We are distinctly told that the "fruit" of the "Tree in the middle of the Garden" of Eden was the food of Gods. Gen. iii. 6. The essence of that fruit was, symbolically, the Druidic Rhin, the Phœnician Ambrosia, and the Hindoo Amrita. The Serpent was Christ and Elohim, and told the truth. The Lord God was Saturn, and told the reverse, he being Saturn. The story represents the old conflict between Saturn and Jupiter, represented to have ended on Calvary.

THE HINDOO AMRITA.—CREATION BEGUN.

It is stated in our translations of Hindoo mythology that the Amrita, the Ambrosia of the Phœnicians and Greeks, and the Rhin of Druidism, was first obtained as the result of the Gods Churning the Ocean. By the Ocean is to be understood the contents of the sacred contents of the Thebet or Ark-Coracle of the Queen of Heaven, symbolised by the sacred Corwg Gwydrin of Stonehenge, and in other holy temples, and also by the Ark of Noah, where the Amrita generated all corporeal bodies by the fertilising action of the Gods, those Gods being named by Moses Elohim (Gods). Those in Greek mythology are Eros, otherwise Cupid, and Psyche, or the Logos, constituted of Sperm, and Soul, or Christos, and the Holy Ghost. By "Churning" is to be understood the act of generation by the co-operation of the two Divine principles, masculine and feminine, as instruments of the two essences referred to. Moses states the same ideas as follows, "And the Earth was without form (contents of the sacred Thebet, the Egg shaped Ark-Coracle), and void: and darkness was on the face of the deep (the Ocean upon which the said Arkite coracle rode from the other world), and the Spirit of God (the dual Word—Elohim—symbolised by the Dove) moved (spawned) on the surface of the deep." That is to say, conjointly the two elements—that in the Argo or Arkite coracle, and that from the Cock Dove—produced the Amrita, which, fertilised Chrism or oil, then entered upon the work of creation. Genesis i. 2. In the creation the Sun was made into a Tabernacle for the Elohim, or Christ the Word and Holy Spirit.

THE VESICA PISCIS, OR VISCERA PISCIS.

The oval shaped illustration on page 276, and on the title page of this volume, is technically called Vesica Piscis, or Bladder of the Fish. From immemorable times it has been regarded as a Christian Church symbol of great sanctity. But no one seems to understand why Bladder of a Fish was adopted as a sacred ecclesiastical symbol. It is well known to scholars that one of the titles given to Jesus Christ in the Greek Testament is Ichthys, or Fish, and naturally enough, people have seen some connection between the Vesica Piscis and the title Ichthys or Fish. The ecclesiastical Cope is a symbol of the body of a Fish, and, therefore, is armless or sleeveless. The Mitre, when looked at from the side, is seen to be a symbol of the Head of a Fish. Thus a Bishop, wearing mitre and cope, symbolises a complete Ichthys. Further, the cowl or hood worn by the Protestant Clergyman over his surplice, is the symbol of a Fish, and its tail is seen when the cowl is down between the shoulders. St. Paul, writing to the Romans (c. xiii. 14), evidently borrows the figure of the symbolical Fish-uniform of the High Priest of ancient Roman paganism when writing to the Christian converts at Rome, "But put ye on the Lord Jesus Christ." Afterwards the Symbolical Fish uniform was transferred from the figure of the Pagan Pontiff to that of the Christian prelate.

In the ancient religious philosophy of Paganism, before it was confused by the Greek fabulists, they were consistent in their symbolical figures, and when symbolising the sun by his priest as a Fish, would symbolise the sun's mother as a Fish also. In pages 2, 127, 165, a Delphos (Matrix), otherwise Dolphin, is given as being the Sun's mother. But the absurdity of symbolising the Sun as a Fish, appears to have been too much for the credulity of Egyptians, Phœnicians, etc., therefore, the young Sun is in each of the two first illustrations mentioned above, as a Man-Child, called Mabyn by the Druids. In the Arms of Brighton he is a Star : in those of Portsmouth he is a Star rising from a Boat. Here we have the two figures for the mother of the Sun, which divided the ancient nations. The Druids employed three symbols to denote her : (1) a Serpent, (2) an Egg, and (3) her Son (Sun), a cock, while her spiritual incubating power was symbolised by a hen, called in Druidic mythology, y Iar Cariadwen, or the Hen Cariadwen, mother of Taliesun ; (3) sacred Ark under several appellations. The figure of a Serpent as symbolical of feminine divine wisdom—see serpents about the brows of Cariadwen, introduction page—appears to have been one of the symbols cherished to the end of Druidism as a creed. Moses represents the Christ under his plural name, Elohim, as a brazen serpent slain to satisfy the red dragons of Inferno. It will be seen that the Dolphin Fish and the Sacred Ark (p. 50) symbolised the same thing, namely, the Argo or Ark of the Queen of Heaven. Thus we see clearly that instead of Vesica Piscis the name was originally Viscera Piscis, or Belly of the Fish, or Dolphin.

In the Rev. Dr. Isaac K. Funk's "Standard Dictionary" is given an illustration of a "Vesica" Piscis from a MS. of the 13th century, showing the Blessed Virgin Mary lying on her back in it, and standing at intervals, around its edge, seven doves. These represent or symbolise the same thing as did the Seven Churches of Asia Minor, viz., the Seven emanations of the Queen of Heaven, or the Navis Church on earth. They symbolise, too, the Seven daughters of Atlas or Adlais (Echo) of the Logos-Voice. They entered the Soul of Mary Magdalene into the tabernacle vacated by the seven evil spirits, as the echoes of the emanations of the Voice of Christ, the Word.

The Seven Spirits of God are the notes of the Song of the Lamb (Rev. iii.). The Seven Churches Echo them back. In the same sense Moses's Song is echoed back by Miriam. Exodus xv. 1 to 21. Miriam and her maidens' voices and timbrels symbolised the joyous music of the Church as representing the Sweet Music of the Whole Earth.

As is often pointed out in this volume, the Druids and other nations deriving their notions from them, believed there was a new sun every year, the old one dying tragically at sunset on Dec. 25th, and his new successor born from the sacred Boat, or Galley, of the Queen of Heaven, on the morning of the 27th, or in 40 hours after the death of his predecessors, or the morning of the third day after the death of old Sol. Each young sun became thus old and perished tragically, and was succeeded by his young successor (P. 71), and in each tragedy the Word—sometimes represented as a winged child, and at other times as a dove (17) fled to the sacred Boat for safety from the fury of the murderer of his body.

It is evident the idea of the lapse of 40 hours between the death and re-appearance of each succeeding one, originated within the Arctic Circle and that part of it where the sun disappears altogether, and remains invisible from sunset on December 25th till sunrise on the 27th.

Scholars trace the Kimmerians (Ancient Britons) coming down in the direction of the Caspian Sea from Southern Russia. They are the Gimirrai of the brick cylinders of Nineveh, and under that name they are the Magicians and Astrologers of Babylon. (Vide Thompson's Magicians and Astrologers of Babylon, Index).

Another startling fact is, that the Hebrew or Chaldean name of the Tabernacle of Aaron is Maes Gwyn ; literally, White Environ- ment, but signifying Holy Place. The Throne of Heaven is called White Throne, and is described as circular in shape. Rev. iv. 3 and 4.

Now, in the fore~ jing is pointed out that the Sacred Boat or Ship, and the Fish (Viscera Piscis) are often confounded one with the other. Joshua's first name was Hoshea (Deut. xxxii. 44). "Hoshea, Son of Nun," that is, Son of Fish, but the Septuagint, or the LXX., translate the same verse, "Joshua, son of Nave," or Boat, thus indi- cating the LXX. knew that Nun (Fish) and Nave (Boat) signified the same thing symbolically, namely, the sacred Ark of the Queen of Heaven, which the open Gulf in the Jordan, with the Ark of the Covenant held up, as it were, on its deck, symbolised. Joshua iii. 15, 17. In Numbers xiii. 17, the LXX. call Joshua, Ause (Ausem), son of Nave. No mention is made of Joshua's natural mother, but we know by the rule of the Druids, which Moses followed as his map, Miriam was Hosea-Joshua's natural mother, and that Nun- Nave was his second mother, from whom he was "born again" from the gulf of the Jordan into the Rest and newness of life in the earthly Paradise. The same plan is observed in the history of the Joshua-Jesus of Christianity. He is son of Miriam (Mary) according to the flesh, but is the Son of Nave-Spirit, where Joshua, followed by the nation, was born again. Moses died as the old Sun, he was succeeded by Joshua as the young sun, his successor. Even the "three days'" or 40 hours of Druidism, are observed between the assumption by Joshua of Moses's authority, and putting his authori- ty into execution. Joshua i. 11. Observe Jonah or Dove (p. 17) in the Fish-Boat during part of one day, a whole day, and the beginning of a third day, and that the same thing precisely is in the account of the sojourn of the body of Jesus in the stone sepulchre and his Divinity in Paradise, there preaching to the captives of Satan.

In the history of Noah's Deluge, we have the same figure, only that three years are given instead of three days.

Further, we may call attention to the fact that in consequence of some transcriber mistaking Hipha (Boat) for Hippa, the old Sun is represented as an aged entire, and his successor as a winged colt, called Pegasus. That seems to have been the last stroke to the destruction of the ancient Druidic religion among the nations outside Britain.

THE ELDEST SON AND MALE COLT OF AN ASS.

"Rod of Beauty (in the original, Delightful) and Rod Bands."

Zachariah xi. 7.

"And I took unto me two Staves : the one I called Beauty, and the other I called Bands."

The foregoing is a striking illustration of the Oriental style of allegory and mystery practised in religious teachings. In verse 11 it is clearly intimated that the Rod Beauty, like the Rod of Moses, signified Christ-Messiah, or the Word of the Lord, the first Lord of Psalm cx. But who is the Rod Bands? The name Bands, or Bonds, affords a clue to the mystery : it is the Colt of an Ass, and Bands implies the servitude of the quadruped. The incarnate Christ bearing the name Jesus, is the Rod of Beauty, and the Colt Male is the Rod Bands.

> "Behold thy King cometh to thee :
> He is just, and having salvation ; lowly, and riding upon
> an Ass,
> And upon a Colt, the foal of an Ass."—Zachariah ix. 9.

It is an ambiguous expression, for it is left doubtful whether it was the mother ass or the colt he was riding, or each alternately. "And the disciples went, and did as Jesus commanded them, and brought the Ass and the Colt, and put on THEM their clothes

(Saddle-Cloths?), and they sat Him thereon. Matt. xxi. 5. St. John states it was on the colt He rode to His sacrifice. C. xii. 15. St. John presents before us thus the picture of the Rod Beauty and Rod Bands, joined or tied, as it were, together. St. Mark makes a statement of still greater importance: he agrees with John that it was on the Colt the King-Messiah rode, but adds "it was a colt tied, whereon never man sat." Mark xi. 2. Now, according to the law laid down in Ex. xiii. 13, it was unlawful to use the first male colt of an ass before it had been bought of the God of the Hebrews with a young Ram, therefore, this unused Colt was the Lord's. See v. 3. St. Luke agrees with this. C. xix. 30, etc.

The Two Olive Trees with a gold pipe from each pouring forth holy oil (Chrism, or oil called Ointment) was of the same symbolical character as that with which David was Christened by Samuel; Jacob Christened the Stone Christos at Bethel; in short, it is the oil of the Rod. Zach. iv. 12.

"We speak the Wisdom of God in a Mystery: even the Hidden Wisdom.—1 Corinthians ii. 7.

————

HISTORY OF THE GOD SATURN.

See Rev. J. Lempriere, D.D.'s "Classical Dicitonary."

In this volume, we have often alluded to the God Saturn, and pointed out he is Satan under that name. His other names are Black Wings (Addu), Pluto, Typhon; in short, the last named in each of the triads given in p. 210, except those of Britain given in that page; and in page 217, except in the Christian Triads, in the formation of which we find a laudable effort to remove the devil from the third position, and substitute in his station a character more in accord with "the Order of Melchisedek.' It is necessary to remind the reader that the God Coelus, mentioned below, is the Duw Celu of the Druids, which is pronounced Keli: that he is Agnosto Theo, an Unknown God of the Athenians, and that the name Celu, an active verb, signifies One Who is Hiding Himself from mankind, and that the Celts are so named after His name among the Druids. To make things clear, we shall, for the sake of brevity, interpolate in brackets observations on Lampriere's text.

"Saturn, son of Coelus, or Uranus, by Terra, called also Titea. The said Uranus is Aran : a He Goat. This identifies Uranus with the God Pan,* who is the sun personified in the Zodiacal sign of the He Goat, the Ninth sign of the Zodiac, and corresponding with December 25th, Old Style. The alleged identity is, therefore, a mistake. Terra is the Latin for the Earth, and Titea is the earth's essence. To this day Welsh women call the paps of the breast "Titee." This is illustrated in p. 34, where the Goddess Venus is giving "Titee" to the Infant Sun. The sap itself came from the Queen of Heaven, who, being a Spirit, is invisible. P. 50. (Here Saturn is substituted for the Infant Sun). "Saturn was naturally artful, and by means of his mother he revenged himself on his father (Coelus), whose cruelty to his children had provoked the anger of Titea. (Here we appear to have an allusion to the anger of Nature, as a nourisher of all living things, at the rule of Celu, to the effect that all must die in their turn)." The Mother armed her Son (Sa: ... n) with a Scythe, which was fabricated with the Metals drawn from her own bowels—and Saturn made his father a eunuch. And there are some eunuchs, which have made themselves eunuchs, for the Kingdom of Ouranos's sake. Matt. xix. 12. Origen, in his zeal, had himself made an eunuch because of these words.—Neander.

But no eunuch was allowed to enter the temple, because the Name there, represented by the Winged Unicorn, or Shechinah, symbolised Elohim or Christ-Messiah and the Holy Spirit, as creators of bodies and Souls. But notwithstanding, Isaiah represents another God saying of eunuchs, "Thus the Lord says of the Eunuchs, who keep my Sabbath (Saturn's Day) and take hold of my covenant, even unto them will I give in mine house and within my walls a place and a name better than of Sons and daughters." Is. lxvi. 4-5. (Deut. xxiii. 1). Saturn for ever disqualified Coelus from

---

* The Old Sun is the Zodiacal sign of the He Goat on December 25th. Thus the Almighty Coelus is confounded with him.

begetting children because those whom he had had he treated with unkindness and confined in the Infernal Regions. But after the mutilation of Coelus (the Most High of Druidism), the sons of Coelus were set at liberty, and Saturn obtained his father's kingdom by the consent of his brother (Satan) on the condition he (Saturn) did not bring up any male children. (The two brothers Saturn and Azozel, received on each Day of Atonement a symbolical God Pan each. Lev. xvi. 7).

"Pursuant to this agreement, Saturn always devoured his sons as soon as born, till his wife, Rhea, unwilling to see her children perish, concealed from Saturn his sons Jupiter, Neptune, and Pluto, and gave him, instead of his children, large stones, which he immediately swallowed, without perceiving the deceit. Then Satan (Titan is the name given by mistake) was sometime after informed that Saturn concealed his male children, therefore he made war against him, dethroned and imprisoned him, with Rhea and Iu-Pater (Jupiter), who was no sooner grown up than he flew to deliver his father Saturn, and to replace him on his throne. Saturn, unmindful of his Son's kindness, conspired against Jupiter (when he had heard he raised cabals against him) ; but Jupiter banished him from his throne, and Saturn fled for safety into Italy, which received the name Latium (Lateo—to be hid), as being the place of Saturn's concealment.

Then follow other silly stories of the most ridiculous character. Here we see an attempt to give to Satan the character of the One Hiding Himself as the name Kelu, or Coelus, signifies. Roman slaves were allowed holidays in honour of the escape of Saturn from his son Jupiter, and his broken fetters were exhibited symbolically everywhere. The festival in his honour was held at the Winter Solstice, or December 25th O.S. The festival, which lasted three days, was called Saturnalia. We hear no more of Coelus, except among the Druids of Britain and Gaul. In the foregoing we behold Coelus, or Almighty God, dethroned by his son Saturn, and he by his son Who is called Father Iu.

He is the man who is in the heavens : he is THE Man

whom the Son on earth is his son (the article "the" is in the Greek version, and in Welsh, but out of the English version).

The foregoing is the origin of the deadly feud between the Gods, Father, and the Son. According to others Jupiter only was symbolised by a Stone Pillar.* We know that to be correct, for it was the symbol of the Linga, called also Phallus, Priapus, Maypole, etc. Jupiter being the principle of Fatherhood in the constitution of the Logos, the Stone-Pillar can only be his emblem. Moses calls the Christ—the Shepherd—Stone of Israel; and St. Paul identifies it with the pre-incarnate Christ in the words, "the Rock was Christ." Gen. ixl. 24; 1 Cor. x. 4.

---

* One of these symbols of Christ is to be seen at Stonehenge, holding up from falling the vast leaning stone north side of it. It has carved along its lower side a semicircular groove, for the streaming holy oil poured on the point.

THE ARK OF THE COVENANT AND HER QUEEN MOTHER.

The reader will have seen that the ancients employed natural objects to symbolise their ideal spiritual personifications. It is clear to everybody that the Ark of the Covenant is one of those personifications. She is called "the Virgin of Israel." Referring to the Ark of Israel in Babylon, Jeremiah writes, "Turn again, O Virgin of Israel, turn again to these Thy cities: how long wilt Thou go about, O Thou backsliding Daughter?" C. xxxi. 21, 22. In these pages we have shown that a Boat-Shrine and the Dolphin Fish were two of the symbols adopted by the ancients to symbolise the Spirit Queen of Heaven, in the same sense as the Nave and Font symbolise the same two personifications in the Christian Church. The gulf in the Red Sea was another symbol of the Queen Mother and Miriam was then the symbol of the Ark. In the Gulf of Jordan, the Ark itself was the symbol of the "Daughter." A prominent feature of the Hebrew narrative is, a varety of symbols used to denote the Spirit Queen of Heaven.

Now we find the Hebrew Tabernacle in the Wilderness enveloped in the Skin of a fish called in the Hebrew version by the Arabic name Tachash. This has been incorrectly translated "Badger's Skin." Ex. 26, 14. This is Arabic for both the Seal and Dolphin. Thus the Ark of the Covenant, which symbolised Nature, otherwise Gwen, Venus-Semele, was in the Wilderness wrapped in the Sealskin.mantle of her mother, Isis, Queen of Heaven. That the covering of Seal-Delphos Skin bore immediate relation to the Ark of the Covenant, we find confirmed by the following:—"And when the camp setteth forward, Raron shall come, and his sons, and they shall take down the covering vail, and cover the Ark of Testimony with it; and shall put thereon the covering of Tachash Skins, and shall spread over it a cloth wholly of Blue." Numbers iv. 5, 6. Elsewhere it is said the purple, symbol of Royalty, that of the Messiah—the Christ—covered the Tachash Skins, during a march.

We can now understand why the Virgin and Child are shown as lying down in the Oval-shaped belly of the opened Fish. In the Temple, at least after the return from Babylon, the great stone which is still in the Mosque of Omar on the site of the ancient Holy of Holies, was the symbol of the Queen of Heaven's shrine or Coracle, instead of the Seal-Delphos symbol of her instrument when roaming the seas between the seen and unseen worlds. Probably in the later temple a small box rode the stone as in memory of the original Ark. Josephus sapiently tells us that the Romans found "nothing" in the Holy of Holies. The Romans, too, must have regarded the said sacred stone of the Gimirrai, as "stone, and nothing more." See p. 50.

To Miriam is given the role of Semele, otherwise Isis 2, the Gwen (Venus) of Druidism, in the placing of the infant Moses in the Thebet, called by translators, Ark of Bulrushes, nearly one hundred and twenty years before the arrival of the exodus from Egypt on the eastern bank of the Jordan, when Miriam died at Kadesh, in the Wilderness of Sin, in the first month of the fortieth year after the departure from Egypt. At that time we are told Moses was eighty years old. Miriam was then at least ninety or ninety-two. At the time of her death she was about one hundred and thirty two years old, for Moses died aged one hundred and twenty, within the same year. Numbers xx. 1; Deut. xxxiv. 7. In Numbers xiii. 16, we learn the following: Joshua was of the tribe of Ephraim, that he was one of the twelve representatives of the nation sent by Moses as spies into Palestine, and that it was on that occasion Moses gave him his new name of Joshua, instead of Oshea. The various ways the former name he bore is spelt, indicate the consciousness of Hebrew scribes of the problematical nature of his history. Josephus states that Hur married Miriam. But Calmet states others assert Hur was a son of Moses. It will be noticed particularly that no mother, except Nun-Nave, is given to Joshua in the Scriptures. No father of Joshua is mentioned at all. But in the system of Oriental mythology, where the Old Sun is represented as the father of the next Young Sun, old Moses stands for the father of young Joshua.

THE CIRCULAR TEMPLES OF THE DRUIDS.

It is well known that each sanctuary of Druid'sm was circular in form, and bordered by twelve stones raised as pillars. Such ancient circles, in more or less state of repair, are found, states Payne Knight, "from the shores of the Baltic to the river Ganges in India." This indicates the former universality of the Druidic mode of public worship. Another significant fact is, that the world has no others than ancient Cambro British names to designate the structures associated with those sacred circles. Col. Condar in his survey of Palestine, Heth and Moab, could find no other than Kimmric apellations for the numerous stone structures, apart from buildings, he came across in the wilds of those interesting countries. Usually those sacred circles were on High Places, hence the Psalmist states:

"The Mountains shall bring Peace to the People,
And the little hills, by righteousness."—Ps. lxxii. 3.
"I will lift up mine eye unto the Hill,
From whence cometh my help:
My help cometh from the Lord."—Psalm xxi. 1.

To the present day the Bards of Wales open their proceedings in their circle of stones in the open air, by proclaiming Peace (Hedd-wch). The following sublime words of Isaiah, speaking apparently of the Archdruid of the Gimirrai :

"How beautiful upon the Mountains are the feet of him
Who bringeth good tidings—that proclaimeth PEACE."

Why mountains, unless in allusion to one upon mounds and mountains who, while stationed thereon, vociferated Peace to all madding nations? Where else on earth to-day is Peace persistently cried in national gatherings, except among the Druids of Wales? These descendants of the Druids of Asia Minor and Britain still stand on high and cry Peace to all nations as the White robed ancestors did from the summit of Mount Ararat before Abraham received bread and wine from the sacred hands of the Archdruid Melchisedek, Priest and King of Salem, a home of Peace.

The circle of twelve stones encircling the Maes Gwyn—still the Cambro British name of the Tabernacle among the Jews—symbolise the twelve signs of the Zodiac circling the dome of the sky. Thus we see that the Druids pictured themselves while in their circle, high up in the heavens, with the circle of the Zodiac round about them. In accordance with the erroneous ancient astronomical ideas of all nations of antiquity, they supposed the sun, whom they personified under many titles, travelled through the twelve signs during the twelve months of the year. To this day the dome of the sky is called Buarth Arthur, or the Tauprine Enclosure of Arthur (Sun). The Polar Star was the centre of the circle. The constellation Ursa Major was called Aradr Arthur or Arthur's Plough, because being shaped like a Plough and apparently passing all around the Polar Star during each twenty-four hours. The stars were poetically called Arthur's Cows, because of the Taurine character being given to the Sun on March 25th from above 6000 years ago till 4000 years ago, when the Ram (Aries) symbolical character, was given to it, and 2000 years ago Ram was abandoned and Fish (Icthys) was adopted as the symbol of the sun. For the reason for those changes see any Encyclopædia for the solar law called Precession of the Equinoxes. Time itself is called Amser in Welsh, a name literally meaning Reference to Stars. Gen. i. 14.

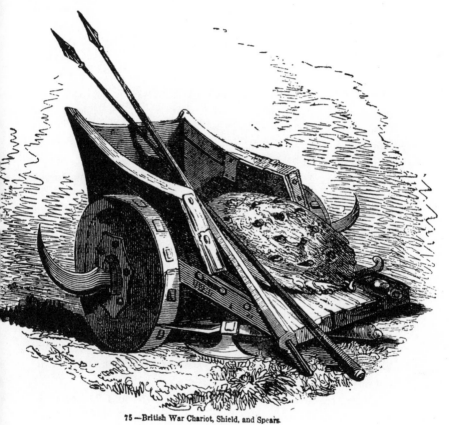

75—British War Chariot, Shield, and Spears.

THE TABERNACLE OF DOVID, WHICH HAD FALLEN.

In conclusion, we invite the reader to place himself in imagination in the audience of the twelve apostles, and St. Paul at Jerusalem, described in Acts xv. The Lord Jesus was Priest and King after the same order as that of which Melchisedek also was Priest and King. Melchisedek was not a son of Abraham, and he was therefore a Gentile, and his orders likewise were universal, and not exclusively Abrahimic, as was the priesthood of Aaron, the kingship of the Gentiles being added very reluctantly by the Jewish theocracy. The Jewish order of Aaron and the royal order of the Gentiles, as represented both by Melchisedek and Jesus, had come into severe conflict at Antioch, the chief city of Syria. Melchisedek had blessed Abraham, and through him all of the sons of Isaac. The God Pan had blessed Jacob at Penuel, and had invested him thereby with his priesthood, which was the national priesthood, which was symbolically immolated by the officer of Saturn-Israel, Aaron, every Day of Atonement on the altar at Jerusalem. Pan, in the person of John, the son of Zacharias and Elizabeth, had become incarnate for the special purpose of transferring his priesthood from Levi and the family of Aaron to the tribe of Judah, thus uniting the priesthood and monarchy. John conveyed it to Judah, and thus the two make one new man in the person of the Lord Jesus, and thereby join together representatively Jew and Gentile in one person, who himself was the incarnate word — the Christ Elohim.* The supremacy of Saturn-Israel is maintained by both Ram and Hind, substituted in Ps. xxii. for the he goat and blood besprinkled white kirtle, by being sacrificed conjointly in the person of the Lord Jesus.

Now, the great question the twelve apostles and Paul had met to consider in the memorable council reported by St. Luke, dictated probably to him by Paul, was the following : Were the Christian believers to undergo the rite of circumcision? It was a crucial question. The God whom the Jews had hitherto worshipped in conjunction with the Elohim of the burning bush, had sought to slay Moses because he had neglected circumcision, and Moses's life was

---

*Ephesians ii. 14.

saved by the interposition of the Rod representing the Christ Elohim. Ex. iv. 24. The Council of the apostles, under the leadership of James, the brother of Jesus, agreed that Jesus had abolished circumcision. Thus it is clear that circumcision was not in "the order of Melchisedek." It was the mark of the adherents of "The Destroying Angel," who had played such havoc in Egypt. Let the reader refer to page 216 and the chapter on Judas, etc. Jesus had said, "Before Abraham was, I am." He was before Abraham was, in two senses. He, as the Amen, the Christ Elohim, was before the world was created. He was before Abraham was, by his priesthood and kingship "after the order of Melchisedek." That order had long disappeared from the Eastern world, but flourished still in Britain and Gaul. It was still, however, known to the learned in Palestine, and doubtless in Egypt also, under the name "Tabernacle of Dòvid," which perplexed theologians have supposed was that of King David. David never had a tabernacle in a religious sense, and at the time the apostolic council was held, both the temple and Jerusalem were standing. The council agreed that the following refers prophetically to Christianity :—"In that day I will raise up the Tabernacle of Dovid (Dovyth) that is fallen, and will rebuild the ruins of it, and will set up the parts thereof that have been broken down, and will build it up as in the Ancient Days, that the remnant of men and all the Gentiles, upon whom my Name is called, may earnestly seek Me, saith the Lord, who does these things." Translation of the LXX. Acts xv. 16, 17. Amos ix. 11, 12. Amos is unquestionably referring to Bethel, Gilgal, and the numerous other fallen sanctuaries, still dotting the eastern side of Jordan, structures similar to our own fallen Stonehenge, Avebury, etc.

Thus we see that, according to the Apostolic decision, Christianity is Druidism revived under a Greek name.

> Gwyneb daear gyssegrasant
> O wlad i wlad;
> A rhyw demlau syn godasant
> O wlad i wlad;
> Syndod pawb yw eu Cromle'chau,
> Gorchest Cewri yw eu Cylchau;
> I chwyfio'n gewyll rho'nt y creigiau,
> Byth mewn parhad."

THE END.